Puritan Christianity in America

Puritan Christianity in America

Religion and Life
in Seventeenth-Century Massachusetts

Allen Carden

 **BAKER BOOK HOUSE**
Grand Rapids, Michigan 49516

Copyright 1990 by
Baker Book House Company

Printed in the United States of America

Library of Congress Cataloging-in-Publication Data

Carden, Allen.
    Puritan Christianity in America : religion and life in seventeenth-
century Massachusetts / Allen Carden.
        p.   cm.
    Includes bibliographical references.
    ISBN 0-8010-2543-5
    1. Puritans—Massachusetts—History—17th century. 2. Congregational
churches—Massachusetts—History—17th century. 3. Massachusetts—
Church history—17th century. 4. Massachusetts—Religious life and
customs.   I. Title.
    BX7148.M4C37   1990
    285'.9'0974409032—dc20   89-48606
                                                              CIP

for
Denice
Annette
Anita

Contents

Acknowledgments

The preparation of this volume has been both a labor of love and an ordeal by fire. Those who helped make completion of the project possible include my wife, Denice, who often encouraged me to persevere when it was tempting to do other things. Daughters Annette and Anita are to be commended for letting their father dominate the home computer while sometimes ignoring their desire for attention. Peg Fosmark of Biola University who now knows more about the Puritans than she ever intended to know, has assisted faithfully in the typing of revisions. My colleagues at Biola University and Spring Arbor College are hereby thanked for contributing to scholarly environments in which this sort of effort is encouraged. Among my colleagues, special thanks is due to Mark Sargent of Biola University whose encouragement and suggestions on style and substance have been of significant help.

Introduction

Use the word "Puritan" or "Puritanical" today and many modern minds are flooded with images of dour, austere, repressive, colorless people who perceived life as something to be endured rather than enjoyed. Partial responsibility for this stereotyping rests with the Puritans themselves; there were a few in their midst who were, by modern standards, sanctimonious almost beyond belief. However, many current ideas about the Puritans are based on lack of information or misunderstanding of who these people were, what they believed, and how they lived. Many of the ideas and values today designated as "Puritanical" were prevalent in the Victorian era of the last century and would have been quite foreign to the Puritans of the seventeenth and early eighteenth centuries.

Lack of understanding about Puritanism in America is not due, however, to a dearth of scholarship in this field. American Puritanism has fascinated and frustrated generations of historians, and the amount of research undertaken on this topic is staggering. Equally staggering is the myriad of often contradictory conclusions reached regarding the nature of Puritanism. Puritan scholar Perry Miller maintains that Puritanism was "an organized synthesis of concepts which are fundamental to our culture" and that the first three generations of New Englanders "paid almost unbroken allegiance to a unified body of thought."[1] On the other hand historian Darrett B. Rutman tells us that "there was no Puritan way . . . merely actions, reactions, interactions."[2] There is lack of agreement among students of Puritanism concerning even a precise definition of the term "Puritan." To clarify what is meant by "Puritanism" in this book, we shall define it as primarily a reformist religious movement comprised

1. Perry Miller, *The New England Mind: The Seventeenth Century*, 2d ed. (Cambridge, 1954), pp. vii–viii.
2. Darrett B. Rutman, *Winthrop's Boston* (Chapel Hill, N.C., 1965), p. 274.

11

of individuals who took issue with the Church of England in matters of polity, style, and to a lesser extent doctrine, and who desired to discard "Romish" practices, to exercise congregational autonomy and authority, and to build their society on the Bible as the final authority. Their views were held with a fervor generally unmatched by their Anglican contemporaries. The American Puritans did not, however, formally or technically separate themselves from the Church of England, but instead desired to purify it, even if from afar in their own way in the New World. This definition thus excludes, perhaps arbitrarily, the Separatists of Plymouth, Anglicans content with the status quo, Quakers, Baptists, and other nonconforming sects. It is also important to acknowledge that while Puritanism was at its core a religious movement, it affected many facets of society, politics, and culture in both England and America.

Although the Puritans have been the focus of hundreds of journal articles and monographs within the past century, historians have often minimized or misunderstood the spiritual dimension of the Puritan experience. Most recent studies have betrayed a limited perspective, dealing with a particular town, individual, family, or issue. It is hoped that this volume will provide a concise yet thorough synthesis of the Puritans' own ideas and recent scholarship in order to provide the reader with an overall perspective encompassing the multifaceted experiences of Puritan Christianity in America.

The study of New England Puritanism owes much to the late Perry Miller. Considered by many to be the dean of American Puritan scholars, Miller established a model of Puritanism that attempted to make the Puritans intellectually respectable to twentieth-century minds.[3] His work, broad in scope, has greatly influenced the direction of research in the last four decades. Miller believed that a "New England mind" existed in the seventeenth century—that American Puritanism was a coherent, unified ideology. Miller emphasized the rational, logical, and intellectual aspects of the Puritan experience and saw as central to their thinking the covenant relationship between God and man.

It must be acknowledged that Miller made great contributions to our understanding of the Puritans, yet his work was not without significant flaws and omissions. Recent scholars have questioned Miller's interpretation of the high degree of unity and coherence which he claimed existed in Puritan New England. In contrast to Miller's views of intellectual and theological orthodoxy in

---

3. An excellent critique of Miller's work can be found in George M. Marsden, "Perry Miller's Rehabilitation of the Puritans: A Critique," *Church History* 39 (Mar. 1970): 91–105.

seventeenth-century New England, other historians in the past quarter-century have been pursuing evidence of heterodoxy, especially in the realm of social experience. Perhaps more serious is the fact that in delineating the "New England mind" Miller underemphasized the principal source of Puritan thought—the Bible. Instead of acknowledging the central role of Scripture, he largely ascribed Puritan ideas to an array of philosophers, churchmen, and logicians. Miller also paid scant attention to the role of Christ in the Puritan thought and, by emphasizing the rationalistic aspects of Puritanism, Miller left little room for the role of faith in the Puritan religious experience. In attempting to secularize the Puritans, Miller has distorted somewhat our understanding of them; this is a situation which calls for correction.

The Puritans have left a rich and varied legacy to American civilization. Much of their contribution has been positive; some of it has been detrimental. The imprint of Puritanism remains, sometimes in a form divorced from its original religious context, in the way many Americans think and act today.[4] Evangelical Christians in America have been especially influenced by the Puritans, and yet are often unaware of the historical connections between the Puritan era and their own. The Puritans who lived in New England three centuries ago can teach modern Americans much about how to live; they can also serve to warn of serious pitfalls. Our own lives are likely to be enriched as we better understand ourselves through their experiences.

An attempt has been made in this volume to quote from original Puritan sources where appropriate in order to give the reader first-hand exposure to the Puritans' ideas in their own richly expressive language. To capture faithfully the flavor of the Puritans' own writings, quotations have retained original spelling and punctuation, except in cases where considerable confusion might be caused to the modern reader.

4. For an excellent treatment of this subject, see Sacvan Bercovitch, *The Puritan Origins of the American Self* (New Haven, 1975).

Chronology
of Selected Events

1603 Queen Elizabeth I dies and is succeeded by her cousin James VI of Scotland, who becomes James I of England and Ireland.

1607 Jamestown, Virginia, is founded as the first English settlement on mainland America. Separatists from Scrooby, England, leave for Leyden, Holland (members of this group who later come to America become known as Pilgrims).

1608 Quebec is founded as a French colony by Samuel de Champlain.

1611 King James authorizes a new English translation of the Bible (the Authorized or King James Version).

1616 John Smith of Virginia publishes *A Description of New England*, the first accurate description of the region available to Englishmen.

1619 The Virginia House of Burgesses meets as the earliest representative colonial assembly in America.

1620 The Pilgrims sail for America from Plymouth, England, on board the *Mayflower* and establish Plymouth Colony in New England.

1623 The Dutch formally organize New Netherlands (later New York) as a colonial province and settle it the following year.

1625 King James I dies and is succeeded by Charles I.

1626 Roger Conant settles Naumkeag (later renamed Salem), Massachusetts.

1629 The Massachusetts Bay Company is chartered by the royal government in London.

1630 A Puritan migration of one thousand settlers arrives in New England under the auspices of the Massachusetts Bay Company.

Boston is established under the leadership of the first governor of the colony of Massachusetts Bay, John Winthrop. The "Great Migration" is underway for the following decade, during which some 18,000 Englishmen will arrive in the colony.

1632 The colony of Maryland, designed as a haven for Catholics, is granted a charter by Charles I.

1635 Connecticut is colonized by English settlers from Massachusetts.

1636 Harvard College is founded at Cambridge, Massachusetts. Roger Williams establishes Providence in Rhode Island after being banished from Massachusetts for dissenting from the religious and political establishment of the Bay Colony.

1638 Anne Hutchinson is banished from Massachusetts as an "antinomian" and settles in Rhode Island.

1639 The first printing press in North America is established at Cambridge, Massachusetts, by Stephen and Matthew Day.

1642 The English Civil War begins (lasts until 1646).

1647 The Old Deluder Satan Act is passed by the General Court in Massachusetts, mandating that every town of fifty families appoint a schoolmaster, and every town of one hundred families establish a grammar school.

1649 With Puritans firmly in control of the English government, Charles I is beheaded and England is declared a Commonwealth.

1652 Maine becomes a part of the Massachusetts Bay Colony.

1653 English Puritan leader Oliver Cromwell becomes Lord Protector of England, Scotland, and Ireland.

1660 The Stuart monarchy is restored to England with the return of Charles II.

1661 John Eliot completes his translation of the Bible into the Algonquian language.

1662 A synod of New England ministers accepts the concept of extending church membership to individuals who have not undergone conversion experiences (the "Halfway Covenant").

1664 The British seize New Netherlands from the Dutch and rename the region New York.

1675 Metacom's War (King Philip's War) begins (ends in 1678). This proves to be the bloodiest conflict of the colonial period, pitting expansion-minded white settlers against New England Indians.

1679 New Hampshire is recognized as a separate province from Massachusetts.

1682 William Penn establishes Pennsylvania as a haven for Quakers.

1684 The charter of Massachusetts Bay is revoked and the colony comes under direct royal control.

1685 Charles II dies and is succeeded by his brother, James II.

1686 James II establishes the Dominion of New England to streamline colonial administration. Sir Edmond Andros is sent to America as Governor-General.

1688 The Glorious Revolution in England forces James II to abdicate. William and Mary take the throne.

1689 After receiving word of the Glorious Revolution in England, New Englanders arrest Governor Andros and undo the Dominion of New England.

1691 A new charter is given to Massachusetts, which includes a royal governor and a representative assembly. Plymouth Colony is absorbed by Massachusetts. Religious freedom is guaranteed to all Protestant Christians in Massachusetts.

1692 Witchcraft trials in Salem Village result in the execution of nineteen persons.

1

Background
The Puritan Movement in England

Puritanism originated in England, under conditions that were peculiarly English, although it was also nourished by Continental reformers. Yet one would be mistaken to think of English Puritanism as a movement totally new and unrelated to the past. It had roots going back to the Catholic Middle Ages and, as the Puritans themselves would argue, to the New Testament church itself. Yet, it is to sixteenth-century England that we must turn to understand how the Puritan movement gained a meaningful, recognizable form.

The English Reformation

It is one of history's ironies that the Englishman on whom the Roman Catholic Church had bestowed the title "defender of the faith" was later to become the prime mover in leading England away from the authority of Rome. Henry VIII, an armchair theologian of sorts, ushered in the English Reformation more for personal and political reasons than for religious ones. Seemingly unable to sire a male heir to the English throne by his Spanish wife Catherine, and piqued by the papacy's refusal to annul his marriage to her, Henry manipulated Parliament into breaking away from the ecclesiastical authority of Rome. Relations between the English monarchy and the papacy had been strained before, but now through Henry's prodding, the Reformation Parliament in 1534 established the Church of England and recognized the king as the supreme earthly head of the English

Church. While this had much to do with authority, it had little to do with doctrine or the genuine reform of ecclesiastical abuses.

Yet there was in England at this time a growing number of sincere Christians who advocated significant religious changes and who pointed out that the new English Church was barely distinguishable from the Church of Rome. These reformers looked back to the activities of John Wycliffe and his evangelistic followers of the late fourteenth century for precedent and inspiration in their quest for a purer, more biblical faith. Henry found it advantageous to make an occasional concession to them, yet some in their ranks felt unsafe in England. In fact, some of the strongest voices for greater Protestant reforms came from Englishmen such as William Tyndale and John Hooper, who found it prudent to live on the Continent and contribute to the cause by bombarding their homeland with printed religious treatises.

When Henry VIII died in 1547, having had six wives and a long-awaited son, the reformation in England had progressed so little that a return to the Roman fold could probably have been carried out with little difficulty. Henry's heir, a sickly child who took the throne as Edward VI, was by necessity under the influence of others. When it came to England's religious orientation Thomas Cranmer, Archbishop of Canterbury, formed royal policy. Cranmer desired to lead England into closer fellowship with Continental Protestantism and succeeded in introducing Protestant ideas that would have cost him his head in Henry's day. During Edward's brief reign the clergy were permitted to marry, images were removed from the churches, the Book of Common Prayer was published and revised, and a Protestant doctrinal statement known as the Forty-Two Articles was drawn up.

It seemed as though England was clearly in Protestant hands, but not all Englishmen were of one mind in matters of the faith. Staunch Catholics chafed under the Edwardian reforms, even as more radical Protestants bemoaned the slowness of progress toward a perfect church. And then there were a large number of clergy and people who were neither strongly Catholic nor Protestant, somewhat confused by the changes engulfing them, but willing to follow the official line in matters of religion, whatever it might be, if for no other reason than that of expediency.

Changes under Mary and Elizabeth

The death of young Edward in 1553 brought his half-sister Mary, a devout Catholic, to the English throne. Mary was determined to restore her domain to the true faith of Rome, a task made more difficult, but not impossible, by the changes made during Edward's reign. She encountered stiff resistance in some quarters and conferred martyr-dom on enough Protestants, including Thomas Cranmer, to become known as "Bloody Mary." A few hundred others fled into exile on the Continent where English Protestant communities developed in Frankfurt, Zurich, Basel, Strasbourg, and Geneva. It was in Calvin's Geneva, where John Knox settled, that seeds which later bloomed into Puritanism were perhaps most effectively planted and nurtured.

English Protestants breathed a sigh of relief when the reign of Mary came to an end with her death in 1558. Since Mary had no offspring, the throne passed to her half-sister Elizabeth, daughter of Henry and his second wife, Anne Boleyn. Since it was Henry's desire to marry Anne that had sparked the English Reformation in the first place, and the Roman Catholic Church never recognized Henry's divorce from Catherine of Aragon, it followed that by necessity Elizabeth was a Protestant. For her to adhere to Catholicism would be to deny her own legitimacy and in essence cause her to disavow her claim to the throne. As it was, a Catholic claimant to the English throne did exist in Mary, Queen of Scots, granddaughter of Mary Tudor.

Elizabeth, a shrewd, practical, and highly intelligent woman, real-ized that the only viable option to pursue was a middle-of-the-road re-ligious position within a Protestant framework if she intended to re-main in power. Elizabeth did not wish to offend her Catholic subjects to the point of having them clamor for Mary, Queen of Scots. On the other hand, she could not afford to totally alienate the reformers who supported her. The result was a religious compromise known vari-ously as the *via media* or Elizabethan Settlement, which probably satisfied no one except those thoroughly indifferent to matters of reli-gion. England was Protestant enough to earn Elizabeth papal excom-munication in 1570, and yet was too reminiscent of Rome to win the hearts of devout reformers.

The Emergence of Puritanism

The Elizabethan Settlement was not seen as the final solution to England's religious dilemma, and zealous Protestants, especially the Marian exiles returning from the Continent, expended considerable ef-fort to purge the English Church of relics of Rome—certain cere-monies, vestments, terminology, and the like—while placing greater emphasis on biblical preaching. The term "Puritan" was initially used derisively of those zealously wishing to purify the Church of England. Elizabeth's pleas that her subjects unite religiously and accept the established church position on matters nonessential to the faith fell largely on deaf ears. In 1565 Archbishop Parker's enforcement of regu-lations requiring uniformity of clerical vestments met with strong resistance and resulted in a pamphlet war. By this time we can clearly see active "Puritans" in the English experience.

It is difficult to apply the term "Puritan" too rigidly, however. As Wallace Notestein has observed, "it is hard to draw a sharp line between Puritanism and the naturally religious impulses of the sober-minded English of the time."[1] Yet during Elizabeth's reign a distinct, although not static, dissenting viewpoint did emerge which we can reasonably call "Puritan." Concerned initially with purifying the Church of England from "Romish" contamination, Puritans in time developed strong opinions on social, economic, and political matters as well and came to have a profound influence in Parliament.

When Matthew Parker died in 1575, Queen Elizabeth named Edmund Grindal Archbishop of Canterbury. Puritans saw Grindal as a friend and believed that the long-awaited hour for significant church reform was at hand. In spite of Elizabeth's distaste for Puritanism and her repeated instructions to a reform-minded Parliament not to meddle in religious matters, Grindal was able to initiate some reforms that pleased progressive Puritan spirits. The preaching function of the clergy was encouraged, the Geneva Bible (whose strongly Calvinistic annotations had been disliked by Parker) was printed in England, and overt papists were removed from positions of influence. Grindal was also enthusiastic about raising the educational level of the ministry. An informal system of continuing education, known as "prophesyings," was begun involving regional groups of clergy sitting under the instruction of the more learned of their brethren. Elizabeth saw these gatherings as a potential threat to conservative church order, however, and demanded in 1576 that prophesyings cease. Grindal would not comply with the royal request and was suspended from office. Grindal's removal was a shocking blow to Puritan hopes, and a growing number of dissenters began to see value in a church free of bishops.

By this time there could be seen within the overall Puritan movement several different attitudes toward how the church should be governed. The Presbyterian wing wished to do away with episcopacy and replace bishops with elected representatives to larger bodies and ultimately to a central governing body (Calvin's plan). Power flowed in such a system not from the top down, but from the church membership up. Those inclined toward Presbyterianism were generally in no mood to dismiss the Anglican Church as thoroughly reprobate but instead hoped to work for improvements within the system. The Presbyterians enjoyed some success in the 1580s, but deaths in the

1. Wallace Notestein, *The English People on the Eve of Colonization* (New York, 1962), p. 149.

ranks of their leadership and increased government enforcement of conformity severely weakened the movement by 1592.

Congregationalism was another version of church government in which power flowed from the members of the congregation without interference from an external hierarchy—each congregation was autonomous. This was to become the prevailing practice in Puritan New England. The most puristic of the dissenters found this system preferable to any other but also found it unlikely to work in the existing Anglican Church. These dissenters, known as Brownists or Separatists, gave up on the Church of England, separated themselves from it, and often worshiped in secret. It was such a group, better known today as the Pilgrims, that founded Plymouth in New England in 1620. There were yet other Puritans, perhaps the majority, who continued to view the Church of England as their church and who were willing to tolerate even bishops, so long as the ministry consisted of godly and learned men plainly preaching the true gospel of Christ from the Word of God. It was this emphasis on clear, biblical, evangelical preaching and genuine piety that produced a common bond among Puritans, regardless of their differences over church polity. Puritanism was concerned primarily with man's depravity and God's plan of salvation, and as a spiritual rather than a social movement it gained adherents from all classes in England. Some were attracted by the movement's vehement anti-Catholicism, others by the Puritans' scathing critique of the morals of court life and ethical standards in general throughout the land. For those hungering for the plain and intelligent preaching of the Word of God, Puritanism provided hearty nourishment. In later years English Puritanism carried with it broad social and political implications, but during Elizabeth's reign it was primarily a movement rooted in the spiritual realm.

The 1590s saw the spread of Puritanism to an ever-widening lay audience, as the Puritan-dominated universities at Oxford and especially Cambridge produced scores of Puritan preachers who often found influential lecturing positions apart from the established church and hence were largely immune from government harassment. Religious lectures were very popular in many quarters and reflected a public hunger for the preaching of the Word by qualified theologians. Most of these lecturers were Puritans, including many former clergy who had been dismissed from their pulpits by the government. These lecturers, hired largely by a growing middle class, helped foster the idea that the minister should be hired by the people and also had a significant effect on stimulating interest in personal Bible study. Little was done to curb these lecturers during Elizabeth's reign, although there was concern that lecturers might undermine the authority of the established church.

James, Charles, and Puritan Frustration

Elizabeth's long reign came to an end upon her death in 1603. The new monarch, James I, had been brought up on Calvinist doctrines in Scotland, and Puritan hopes were high for ecclesiastical reform. Very early in his reign, Puritans took the initiative and presented the new English king with the Millenary Petition (supposedly containing a thousand signatures) asking for religious reforms. Unfortunately for the Puritans, James had found his Calvinist upbringing distasteful, and believed Presbyterianism to be counterproductive to royal power. The king called a conference at Hampton Court to discuss church matters in early 1604 and, while he showed sympathy with some Puritan concerns, James made it clear that conformity was expected of English pastors. The relief the Puritans expected did not materialize; in fact their position deteriorated. In 1604 it was required that lecturers be licensed by a bishop and subscribe to essential Church of England views, including the Thirty-Nine Articles. This was not consistently enforced, however. James I is best remembered for his support of a new English translation of the Bible, the so-called Authorized Version of 1611. This new version did not meet with early acceptance and most Puritans for the next three generations preferred the Geneva Bible.

When Charles I took the throne in 1625 the English Church took a decided turn toward the high-church Arminian views of William Laud who was named Bishop of London and later Archbishop of Canterbury. Puritans with anti-Catholic zeal were also troubled by the declining anti-Catholic stance of the English government. Cheered by England's defeat of Catholic Spain's armada in 1588, Puritans now bemoaned the refusal of the Stuart monarchy to aid the Protestant cause in the Thirty Years' War on the Continent, a war which many believed would influence permanently the religious face of Europe. When Charles I married a French Catholic princess, he seemed to confirm what many Puritans were thinking—that England was back on the road to Catholicism. Some Puritans now lost all hope of England ever possessing a church or society that would please God. As religious nonconformists were harassed, some of them saw their best hope in leaving England altogether, as the Pilgrims had done when they fled to Holland in 1608 and from there to the wilds of America in 1620.

2

The Puritan Vision and the American Promise

As many Puritans in the 1620s saw it, England faced impending disaster. Things were not as they should be, in spite of decades of Protestant domination in that land. It was clear to these reformers that the English Church and government had not done nearly enough to purify the religious life of the nation. Surely God grew impatient with a people who had the truth but were doing so little with it. Puritans became concerned not only with their own personal sins, but also with the sins of the nation at large, and the feeling grew that the government was too indulgent of evil in its various forms. References to Sodom and Gomorrah appeared in Puritan sermons as a warning of what would befall England if God were to give the land what it deserved. When natural or man-made disasters befell Englishmen, the Puritans looked beyond the ostensible causes to find spiritual lessons and warnings of greater judgments to come.

Threats to the Faith

England in the early seventeenth century was in many respects a pleasant land, but not without serious problems, especially from a Puritan viewpoint. A depression hit the textile industry in the 1620s, causing economic hardship throughout much of the nation. Within the Church of England, many churchmen were falling into what the Puritans came to view as the heresy of Arminianism, a belief that salvation is a matter of free will and to a degree dependent on good works and hence not permanently secure for all believers. Even Charles I seemed favorably inclined to this viewpoint, and many of the choicest positions within the church went to men of this persuasion. Other irritants which encouraged some persons of piety to join the Puritan ranks were the low quality of the clergy and the church's apparent lack of concern about the matter. Educational preparation and spiritual commitment were both lacking in many cases, and the wages paid by the church were insufficient to attract and hold many able clergymen. Yet at the same time, many in the church hierarchy lived lives of splendor, as did Archbishop Whitgift with his retinue of hundreds of servants.

By the 1620s, Puritanism had broadened its base and had a particularly strong following among the more educated of the middle class, including many lawyers, although Puritans could be found in all segments of English society. Especially helpful to the movement was the political and financial support of educated men who knew the law and who had substantial resources at their disposal. They made the eventual Puritan settlement of New England much smoother than would have otherwise been the case.

The Puritans saw in Parliament their last and greatest hope for returning England to true godliness. The House of Commons was under Puritan influence to the point of demanding ecclesiastical reforms that included the suppression of Arminianism. Unfortunately for the Puritans, Charles' answer to this was to dissolve Parliament in March of 1629 with the prospects of his recalling it into session rather dim.

Thus the Puritan hope for an effective redress of ecclesiastical and social wrongs crumbled at a crucial time when Protestantism on the Continent appeared to be in great danger. In France, the Protestants were in a desperate situation. A Huguenot rebellion in the city of La Rochelle against the Catholic king was suppressed by Cardinal Richelieu in 1629, resulting in the loss of the Huguenots' fortified cities and armies. Also on the Continent, the Thirty Years' War, essentially a German civil war between Catholics and Protestants, was raging. In the late 1620s German Protestantism was nearly inundated by Catholic forces pushing forward with their Counter-Reformation. The Edict of Restitution, announced by the emperor in 1629, declared that all church properties secularized since 1552 were to be restored to the Catholic Church. German Protestants despaired; it seemed as though the century-old Reformation was being undone before their eyes.

England's Dismal Prospects

These Protestant disasters on the Continent did not go unnoticed by English Puritans. Some saw in these events the impending total collapse of true religion in Europe, leaving England alone to carry the torch of Christian truth. And yet England's condition was so sinful, so precarious, that it was more likely that God would judge her than be able to use her for his purposes. John Winthrop, soon to play a dominant role in the settlement of New England, reflected the thinking of many Puritans of the day when he wrote to his wife of the "evill and declininge tymes" that were upon them and warned that they should

> looke for some heavy Scourge and Judgment to be comminge upon us: the Lord hath admonished, threatened, corrected, and astonished us, yet we grow worse and worse, so as his spirit will not allwayes strive with us, he must needs give waye to his furye at last; he hath smitten all the other Churches [Protestants on the Continent] before our eyes, and hath made them to drinke of the bitter cuppe of tribulation, even unto death; we sawe this, and humbled not ourselves, to turne from our evill wayes, but have provoked him more than all the nations rounde about us: therefore he is turninge the cuppe towards us also, and because we are the last, our portion must be, to drinke the very dreggs which remaine: my dear wife, I am veryly perswaded, God will bringe some heavye Affliction upon this lande, and that speedylye.[1]

This decidedly pessimistic outlook concerning the future of England left Puritans with a number of choices. They could remain in England and hope that they were wrong in their predictions of wrath to come, or they could work hard to bring about changes that would appease a displeased Deity. Another option that grew increasingly attractive as the storm clouds of God's fury appeared to be gathering was to leave England and carry to another, safer location all the best that English society and Christianity had to offer—in short, to establish a New England.

The American Option

The Puritans were not the first to choose the latter option. Within recent memory, a harassed group of Separatists from the village of Scrooby had left England for Amsterdam and Leyden in the Netherlands, where they could expect toleration of their religious views. These rural Englishmen found, to their dismay, that toleration in another country solved some problems but created a whole set of new ones. Their English way of life began to disintegrate as their children grew up more Dutch than English, and often drifted away from

1. Quoted in Edmund S. Morgan, *The Puritan Dilemma: The Story of John Winthrop* (Boston, 1958), pp. 29–30.

the church. As perturbed by events in England as these folks were, they were proud of their English heritage and desired to maintain it at almost any cost. The price paid was another removal, this time to the shores of North America. Receiving a grant from the Virginia Company and a promise from King James that they would not be persecuted, these Separatists, or Pilgrims as we now know them, set out for America on board the tiny *Mayflower* in September of 1620. Landing far to the north of their original destination, the Pilgrims made the best of it and, after scouting the coast, decided to settle on the shores of Plymouth Harbor. By 1629 the Pilgrims' starving days were over and the little colony gave evidence to their English brethren that Englishmen could survive, and perhaps even thrive, in the New World.

The Puritans, like their Separatist cousins, also desired to preserve a godly, united English society, although they were not willing to dismiss the Church of England as a totally corrupt church as the Pilgrims had done. A Puritan beachhead of sorts was established at Salem, a tiny community that resulted primarily from the failure of an earlier fishing village at Cape Ann. From the Salem settlement came a request for a grant which eventually led to the reorganization of the New England Company into the Massachusetts Bay Company. Why Charles I would give a group of religious nonconformists a charter with so many rights and privileges remains an enigma, but the Puritans who were granted the charter for the Massachusetts Bay Company were indeed pleased. One unusual feature of the charter was the fact that no place of meeting of the company officers and stockholders was prescribed. It was decided to take advantage of this situation and to have the governor and officers of the company physically resident in the New World to provide on-site leadership, not only for the company, but for the company's colony as well. On October 20, 1629, the officers of the Massachusetts Bay Company, known as the General Court, selected John Winthrop as their governor. Winthrop wrote his wife that it "hath pleased the Lorde to call me to a further trust in this business of the plantation, than either I expected or finde my selfe fitt for."[2] Winthrop soon found himself in charge of organizing a major Puritan migration to the shores of New England. He authored and circulated a document giving reasons why a Puritan plantation in New England was justified, stressing deteriorating social conditions in England and concluding that the enterprise "appears to be a worke of god, for the good of his church. . . ."[3] In March of 1630,

---

2. Quoted in ibid., p. 49.

3. John Winthrop, "Reasons to be Considered for Justifieing the . . . Plantation in New England" (1629), repr. in Jack P. Greene, ed., *A Documentary History of American Life*, vol. 1 of *Settlements to Society* (New York, 1966), p. 63.

Winthrop and nearly one thousand settlers left England in eleven vessels, bound for the Promised Land.

The Righteous Justification

Winthrop and his followers believed that it was God's work they were doing and that they had received a commission from the Lord himself for the establishment of a godly English society on the shores of Massachusetts Bay in New England. Yet they were also painfully aware that the majority of Puritan brethren who chose to remain in England might interpret their migration as desertion. As much as they disliked certain features of the Church of England, the Puritans who left for America took pains to clarify that they were still within the fold, that they had not deserted their church or their homeland. This was one of the major tensions faced by the Puritans—they had a desire for holiness while realizing the impossibility of perfection in a sinful world. At the same time they feared the pitfalls of extreme separation from that world.

Somewhere en route in the Atlantic, Winthrop again set forth the objectives and ideals of the proposed Puritan enterprise in America. On the *Arbella* he exhorted his fellow sojourners that they had

> entered into Covenant with Him [God] for this worke. Wee have taken out a commission. . . . Now if the Lord shall please to heare us, and bring us in peace to the place we desire, then hath hee ratified this covenant and sealed our Commission, and will expect a strict performance of the articles contained in it; but if wee shall neglect the observation of these articles which are the ends wee have propounded, and, dissembling with our God, shall fall to embrace this present world and prosecute our carnall intentions seeking greate things for ourselves and our posterity, the Lord will surely breake out in wrathe against us; be revenged of such a people and make us knowe the price of the breache of such a covenant.

Winthrop then set forth the ideal of a just society with a communal orientation as central to God's will for the enterprise. He also reminded the people that they would be a model for all of Christendom to observe and emulate:

> Now the onely way to avoyde this shipwracke, and to provide for our posterity, is to followe the counsell of Micah, to do justly, to love mercy, to walk humbly with our God. For this end, wee must be knitt together, in this worke, as one man. Wee must entertaine each other in brotherly affection. Wee must be willing to abridge ourselves of our superfluities, for the supply of other's necessities. Wee must uphold a familiar commerce together in all meekness, gentlenes,

patience and liberality. Wee must delight in eache other; make other's conditions our oune; rejoice together, mourne together, labour and suffer together, allwayes hauving before our eyes and our commission and community in the worke, as members of the same body. Soe shall wee keepe the unitie of the spirit in the bond of peace. The Lord will be our God, and delight to dwell among us, as his oune people, and will command a blessing upon us in all our wayes. . . . hee shall make us a prayse and glory that men shall say of succeeding plantations, "the Lord make it like that of New England." For wee must consider that wee shall be as a citty upon a hill. The eies of all people are uppon us. . . .[4]

These migrations to New England in the 1620s and 1630s were without precedent in the English experience. Other colonial ventures in Virginia, Newfoundland, and elsewhere had been undertaken by adventurers or the genuinely needy and were concerned with turning a handsome financial profit. But in the case of the Pilgrims and Puritans, responsible family men who had no need or craving for adventure willingly traveled with their families and their possessions to a wilderness environment largely for the sake of ideology. A commitment of this nature proved to be both the strongest foundation for launching a new commonwealth and the most precarious, for there was no guarantee that the next generation would share the vision of the founders. Hence the leadership's frequent admonitions to maintain the values of the original mission: to create a godly English society in America that would be a shining beacon to the rest of the world; to maintain an environment where society would be based solidly on the Word of God and brotherly affection; and to provide a setting where the Lord could be worshiped in spirit and in truth and families could be raised without exposure to the social ills and religious heresies of Old England. In short, New England was to be the last, best hope of mankind.

The Vision Tested

This vision was attractive enough to lure about 18,000 Englishmen, mostly Puritans, to New England between the years 1630 and 1640. Even more Englishmen, including a good number of Puritans, settled on various islands in the Caribbean Sea and also in Virginia and Maryland. It was in New England, however, that the Puritans made the greatest effort to duplicate the English village way of life within the constraints of a "holy commonwealth." Those who came with Winthrop and those who followed in the next decade were mostly

4. John Winthrop, "A Modell of Christian Charity" (1630), repr. in ibid., p. 68.

people of moderate means, along with a handful who enjoyed substantial wealth and another handful who were genuinely poor. The New England Puritans were very literate and an unusually large percentage of the men had been educated at a university. Not all of the settlers in early New England shared the religious commitments and zeal of the Puritan leadership, but most were at least sympathetic with Puritan ideas.

Winthrop brought the vanguard of his party into port at Salem in June of 1630. The bedraggled inhabitants of this tiny town and their crude Indian-style dwellings helped convince Winthrop that staying here would seriously damage the morale of his fellow travelers. It would be better to make a fresh start, and so the shores of Massachusetts Bay to the south were scouted. Winthrop chose the site of Charlestown for his headquarters, and set about to build a house while other settlers began to establish farms and towns in surrounding areas. Due to a shortage of spring water in Charlestown, Winthrop and several families decided in the fall of 1630 to move across the river to the hilly, spring-fed peninsula which the Indians called Shawmut. Here they founded the town of Boston, named after the English town in Lincolnshire, and soon this new town was the economic and political center of the Massachusetts Bay colony.

Although the first few months in New England brought unexpected hardships and many settlers sickened and died, Winthrop's confidence was unwavering. He wrote to his wife Margaret, who was remaining in England until the birth of another child, that "I thank God I like so well to be heer, as I doe not repent my comminge: and if I were to come againe, I would not have altered my course, though I had foreseene all these Afflictions: I never fared better in my life, never slept better, never had more content of minde."[5] Nearly two hundred died that first winter in a climate that was colder than anything they had known in England, and another two hundred returned to their homeland that spring. As it turned out, the first winter was the worst, and the colonists who endured fared much better in subsequent years. Despite tales of woe told by those returning to England or others simply writing to relatives and friends back home, New England grew as the activities of the English Church and the king kept a steady stream of Puritan refugees coming for a decade. The Puritan leadership was convinced that, mixed together with ample affliction, God was blessing his work. A New England in the wilderness of America was becoming a reality.

5. Quoted in Morgan, *Puritan Dilemma*, p. 62.

3

The Biblical Basis
of the Puritan Way

The intensity of the Puritans' beliefs and actions is adequately understood only when one realizes their devotion to the Bible as the Word of God. Their absolute belief in the Bible and the God of the Bible was the fundamental motivating force behind their worldview and the establishment of New England. While Old England still tugged at their hearts, God's Word was not being sufficiently honored in that land. Given the choice of the comforts of England where violations of God's laws were rampant or the wilderness of America where God's Word would receive its rightful place, thousands chose the latter.

It should come as no surprise that the principal source of Puritan ideology was the Bible itself. What is surprising is the way in which some historians, most notably the late Perry Miller, have ignored or minimized the Puritans' biblicism while attempting to unearth nonbiblical roots for Puritan concepts. Instead of accepting the Puritans' own statements about their reliance on Scripture, Miller turned to more humanistic sources. In his massive work *The New England Mind: The Seventeenth Century*, he makes passing comments about the Puritan acceptance of Scripture, but his emphasis is on "the four quarries from which the Puritan scholars carved out their

Much of the material in this chapter was previously published as "The Word of God in Puritan New England: Seventeenth-Century Perspectives on the Nature and Authority of the Bible," *Andrews University Seminary Studies* 18 (Spring 1980): 1–16.

ideas and doctrines"—European Protestantism, special interests and preoccupations of the seventeenth century, humanism, and medieval scholasticism.[1]

The Puritans obviously did not operate in a cultural vacuum; they could not help but be influenced by the intellectual and cultural climate of their day. Miller, however, apparently ignored the Puritans' own appraisal of the role of Scripture in their lives and thought, concluding that "they said in one moment that everything was to be gained by going to the Bible for the articles of belief" while "in the next they went also to other books, to systematic treatises on divinity, to methodized tomes on doctrine and ethics, to classical antiquity, to medieval scholasticism or to monumental restatements of it." Miller felt that under the influence of the logician Petrus Ramus, the Puritans held that "the Bible should be approached exactly as should the natural world, as a welter of raw material out of which the propositions of art were to be refined by the process of invention and disposition." In fact, it was Miller's contention that Puritan divines believed that "no man could understand Scripture who had not been schooled in rhetoric as well as in logic"—this despite the Puritan clergy's frequent assertions of the plainness of Scripture and the role of the Spirit of God in revealing biblical truths to the reader.

The Authority of Scripture

Despite twentieth-century attempts to secularize and rationalize Puritan theology to make the Puritans more acceptable in the modern age, the fact remains that the absolute authority they ascribed to the Bible and its consequent central place in their lives were clearly and consistently declared by the seventeenth-century clergy of New England. The authority of Scripture was such a certainty to Puritan minds that, even in stating their doctrine of biblical authority, men whom Miller described as eminently rational and logical did not hesitate to use the Scriptures themselves as the weightiest evidence to determine and to support their view of the nature of the Bible.[2] Indeed, to Puritan divines, the authority of the Bible was so important and so obvious that even to raise a question on the matter was to succumb to "strange temptations, hellish blasphemies."[3]

---

1. For the quotations in this and the following paragraph, plus other related concepts, see Miller, *New England Mind*, pp. 7, 92, 108, 190, 310, 341.

2. See Cotton Mather, *A Scriptural Catechism* (Boston, 1691), p. 1; Increase Mather, *Angelographia* (Boston, 1696), p. 44.

3. Thomas Shepard, *The Sound Believer* (Boston, 1736), p. 64. This work was written in the seventeenth century but not published until many years after Shepard's death.

The authority accorded to the Bible was a direct result of the Puritans' belief in its divine authority. According to Increase Mather, the Bible "ought to be received on that sole account of the Authority of the Speaker. Hence often in the Scripture, it is said, Hear the Word of the LORD, and Thus saith the LORD: Intimating that because of the Authority of the Speaker, men have infinite Reason to Hear and Fear, and to Believe and Obey."[4]

Pastor Nathaniel Gookin of Cambridge, Massachusetts, urged his New England flock to believe firmly that biblical injunctions were "the commands of the great God and his authority is stamped upon them."[5] Boston's Samuel Willard, while quoting the words of David in the Old Testament, was quick to point out that "they were not his own words, but such as the Spirit of God dictated to him, and spake by him, whereof he was only the Instrument of their being committed to record. They therefore came out of the Mouth of God. . . ."[6] Increase Mather on one occasion spoke of the Scriptures as "the word of Christ . . . because Hee is ye Author of it."[7]

The lofty and penetrating nature of the biblical message made its divine origin evident to Puritan eyes. Said Thomas Shepard, minister at Cambridge, "There is such a majesty stirring, and such secrets revealed in the Word, that if men will not be willfully blind, they cannot but cry out, 'The voyce of God, and not the voyce of man.'"[8] Assurance that the Scriptures were the Word of God could further be seen "from the majesty, glory, holiness, truth of a God which shines forth in them."[9] According to Increase Mather, only God could have authored the Bible because "there is such a Divine majesty to be seen in it, as is not in any other Book. . . . The Scripture is His Word, for it reaches ye very thoughts of ye Heart."[10] John Eliot, minister and missionary to the Indians from the church at Roxbury, taught his

4. Increase Mather, *The Latter Sign Discoursed of In A Sermon Preached at the Lecture of Boston in New England; August 31, 1682* (Boston, 1682), p. 19.

5. Nathaniel Gookin, sermon [May or June, 1690], *Sermon Notes, Apr. 24–Aug.13, 1690,* recorded by John Hancock, Harvard University MS, pp. 85, 90–91.

6. Samuel Willard, *The Character of a Good Ruler* (Boston, 1694), p. 5.

7. Increase Mather, sermon of Mar. 21, 1686, *Substance of Sermons delivered by several Ministers in Boston,* recorded by Cotton Mather, Huntington Library MS, p. 76.

8. Thomas Shepard, *The Sincere Convert: Discovering the small number of True Believers, and the Great Difficulty of Saving Conversion* (London, 1672), p. 3.

9. Thomas Shepard, *A Short Catechism Familiarly Teaching the Knowledg of God, and of our Selves* (Cambridge, Mass., 1654), p. 15.

10. Increase Mather, sermon of 1686, *Substance of Sermons,* p. 277.

indigenous flock that "the writings of the Bible are the very Words of God."[11]

The high opinion of the Bible held by the Puritan clergy is not only evident from their belief in its divine authorship, but also from the names and descriptions they used when referring to the Scriptures. In countless sermons the Bible was spoken of as the "Word of God." This appears to have been the clergy's favorite designation for the Bible, although numerous other titles and descriptive phrases were used which also demonstrate the highest regard for biblical authority. Emphasis on the truthfulness of the Word is found in epithets such as "word of truth," "great store-house of truth," and "Scriptures of truth."[12] In other sermon passages the Bible is called "ye eternal word," "the Holy Scriptures," "the Sacred Word," "the infallible Oracles," "his [God's] revealed will," "the Sword of the Spirit," "the RULE," "the purest spiritual milk in the world," "a treasure," and "infinite wisdom."[13]

Direct statements were frequently made in the Puritan clergy's sermons and writings which leave little doubt that biblical infallibility was accepted dogma. Not only was the Bible viewed as the Word of God, but it was also seen as absolutely reliable, accurate, and complete. The Scriptures were "a perfect rule of Faith & Holyness, according to which all doctrines are to be tryed, and all controversies decided."[14] The Word was "a perfect directory, shewing us how we must Serve God, and how we must Serve the Generation wherein we live."[15] Because a holy God had authored the Word it followed logically that the Scriptures were "the infallible Oracles of that God who

11. John Eliot, *Tears of Repentance: Or, a further Narrative of the Progress of the gospel Amongst the Indians in New England* (London, 1653), p. 39.

12. John Cotton, *The Way of Life* (London, 1641), p. 139; Increase Mather, sermons of Mar. 21 and 28, 1686, *Substance of Sermons*, pp. 73, 96; Josiah Flynt, sermon [1670s], Harvard University MS, p. 166; Samuel Willard, *The Mourners Cordial Against Excessive Sorrow* (Boston, 1691), p. 65; Increase Mather, *The Mystery of Israel's Salvation Explained and Applyed* (London, 1669), p. 18.

13. Increase Mather, sermon of 1686, *Substance of Sermons*, p. 277; *Brief Discourse Concerning the Unlawfulness of the Common Prayer Worship, and of Laying the Hands on, and Kissing the Booke in Swearing* (Cambridge, Mass., 1686), p. 6; Cotton Mather, *Optanda* (Boston, 1692), p. 31; Samuel Willard, *Impenitent Sinners Warned of their Misery and Summoned to Judgment* (Boston, 1698), p. 32; *The Barren Fig Trees Doom* (Boston, 1691), p. 76; Urian Oakes, *The Unconquerable, All-Conquering, & more-than-conquering Souldier* (Cambridge, Mass., 1674), p. 26; Cotton Mather, *Early Religion* (Boston, 1694), p. 14; John Eliot, *The Harmony of the Gospels* (Boston, 1678), p. 32; Flynt, sermon [1670s], p. 274; Thomas Shepard, sermon [1641], Harvard University MS, n.p.

14. Shepard, *Short Catechism*, p. 14.

15. Increase Mather, *David Serving His Generation* (Boston, 1698), p. 11.

cannot ly."[16] Cotton Mather referred to "those unerring Oracles" and the "Holy and Just and Good Laws of the Lord." Thomas Shepard called "the voice of the Scriptures, the highest of all"; John Cotton asserted that "the perfection of the Word of God may well be concluded"; and Samuel Danforth preached about "the Holy Scriptures, which are the Authentick and unerring Canon of Truth." John Eliot declared that "the Law of God, written in the Scriptures of the Old and New Testament" is "pure, holy, righteous, perfect, and good . . . the perfect Systeme or Frame of Laws, to guide all the Moral actions of man," and Richard Mather declared that "the Word is never contrary to it self." But perhaps John Davenport, minister at Boston, put it most emphatically as he declared with a biblical citation, "The whole Scripture is breathed of God, and therefore infallible, and stamped with God's own authority in every sentence of it, 2 Tim. 3.16."[17]

The Bible as the Word of God was viewed as a complete revelation, containing everything God would have mankind know about spiritual matters, as well as much in the temporal realm. Any group which was not perceived to share this perspective was anathema to New England's Puritan divines. The Quakers were singled out for special condemnation because of their deficient view of the completeness of the biblical revelation. In 1690 four prominent clergymen collaborated in a written attack against Quakerism, centered on that sect's belief in an "inner revelation" which implied that the Bible did not contain all the Word of God.[18] To be a Quaker was, in Puritan eyes, to believe "that God hath one Rule to direct his people Outwardly, and another Inwardly, or as if God taught us one thing by His Word, and another by His Spirit . . . how perniciously this undermines the Christian faith."[19] In one of his anti-Quaker tirades, Cotton Mather lashed out against the "Grievous Wolves" of Quakerism ready to snap at New England's "Little Flocks." "What religion shall we have," he asked, "if

16. Willard, *Impenitent Sinners*, p. 32.

17. Cotton Mather, *Warnings from the Dead* (Boston, 1693), p. 4; *Humiliations follow'd with Deliverances* (Boston, 1697), pp. 4–5; Thomas Shepard, *Subjection to Christ in all His Ordinances and Appointments, the best means to preserve our Liberty* (London, 1652), p. 153; John Cotton, *Some Treasure Fetched out of Rubbish* (London, 1650), p. 11; Samuel Danforth, *An Astronomical Description of the Late Comet or Blazing Star, Together With a brief Theological Application thereof* (Cambridge, Mass., 1665), p. 16; John Eliot, *The Christian Commonwealth* (London, 1659), pp. 4, 35; Richard Mather, *An Answer to Two Questions* (Boston, 1712), p. 21; John Davenport, *Gods Call to His People to Turn unto Him* (Cambridge, Mass., 1669), p. 7.

18. James Allen, Cotton Mather, Joshua Moodey, and Samuel Willard, *The Principles of the Protestant Religion Maintained* (Boston, 1690), pp. 7, 16, 20–21.

19. Ibid., p. 7.

the Scriptures once come to be vile in our opinion of them? Now to withdraw men from the esteem and study of the Scriptures, has hitherto been the main Design of Quakerism."[20] Such a criticism was doubtless among the worst that could be leveled at anyone in seventeenth-century New England.

Not only was the Bible viewed as God's inspired and complete revelation, but this divine and hence ageless inspiration was also seen as present throughout the entire Old and New Testaments. When it came to Holy Writ, there was "no part unprofitable."[21] The result was the use of sermon texts from all parts of the Bible with little preference being expressed by the clergy as a whole for one Testament over the other. The Bible in its entirety was accepted as the Word of God, a book for all time, applicable as much to the present as it was to the past, in principle if not in every ritualistic detail. Cotton Mather proclaimed that "the blessed suitableness of this miraculous Book unto the Affayrs and Concerns of all men, is to be found . . . in every part thereof."[22] John Cotton testified that "I never yet observed any part of a Scripture . . . but without carnall affectation, or straining of wit, it might holily be applyed both with power and profit, and delight to an honest heart."[23] Samuel Willard, in referring to the relevance of the Bible for the present age, stated that "Scripture Counsels, when directed indefinitely, are for the most part, intended universally; where the Spirit of God doth not set any limitations, neither should we."[24] The Word was binding on the current generation; it was "the Rule according to which we must believe."[25] It was a Word from God containing "particular Instructions to us" with a message valid "to this day."[26] It was acknowledged that although the Bible did not contain a precept for every detail of human experience, general principles were always present and applicable, ready to guide the faithful searcher of the pages of Scripture. When Puritans faced situations not specifically covered in the Bible they maintained that such matters could be clarified by deductions from the Bible.

20. Cotton Mather, *Little Flocks Guarded Against Grievous Wolves* (Boston, 1691), p. 4.

21. John Danforth, *Kneeling to God, at Parting with Friends* (Boston, 1697), p. 5.

22. Cotton Mather, *Military Duties Recommended to an Artillary Company* (Boston, 1687), p. 2.

23. John Cotton, *Of the Holiness of Church Members* (London, 1650), p. 69.

24. Samuel Willard, *Heavenly Merchandize* (Boston, 1686), p. 4.

25. Increase Mather, *David Serving*, p. 10.

26. Nathaniel Gookin, Sermon of May or June, 1690, *Sermon Notes*, p. 87; John Cotton, *A Brief Exposition of the whole Book of Canticles, or, Song of Solomon* (London, 1642), title page.

Scriptural Documentation in Puritan Sermons

The Puritan clergy's complete dependence on the Bible as their authoritative source in matters of faith and practice can be seen in the way they carefully documented their sermon statements with biblical references. Every homily was based on a specific biblical text. To preach a sermon in seventeenth-century New England without such a base would have been unthinkable. The Bible was the source from which flowed all important theological ideas and the body of each sermon generally contained dozens of Scripture citations. Sometimes verses were quoted; at other times chapter and verse references were given. The important thing was to demonstrate that what was said had scriptural grounds and was not of mere error-prone human origin.

Nearly every Puritan divine sprinkled his sermons and treatises liberally with biblical references, but few were more fastidious in this regard than Boston's well-known and respected pastor, John Cotton. In a catechism designed for children, he prepared 62 questions and answers, buttressing the answers with 66 Old Testament passages and 106 citations from the New Testament.[27] In a 13-page tract on the nature of the church, Cotton found it advantageous to employ 105 biblical references.[28] In another treatise on the doctrine of the church, Cotton in 12 pages stated and supported his views on ecclesiology with over 400 different Scripture references.[29]

The Puritan faithful were exhorted from the pulpits of New England that not only was the Bible an authoritative source in matters of faith and practice, but it was the only reliable source. As four ministers in their joint defense of the faith expressed it, "We have no other Rule to inform our selves by, but the Scriptures."[30] Those who succumbed to the ideas of men rather than the sure Word of God were violating a central Puritan tenet. "Such is the lamentable corruption of mens nature," bemoaned Increase Mather, "that they are more apt to be taken with fond, foolish, false prophecies that have nothing of a divine inspiration in them, than with the blessed and holy prophecies contained in the Scriptures of truth."[31] Mather further reminded the saints that "we are not to walk by the opinions of this or that good

27. John Cotton, *Milk for Babes Drawn Out of the Breasts of both Testaments* (London, 1646).

28. John Cotton, *The True Constitution of a particular visible Church, proved by Scripture* (London, 1642).

29. John Cotton, *The Doctrine of the Church, to which are committed the Keys of the Kingdom of Heaven*, 2d ed. (London, 1643).

30. Allen et al., *Principles of the Protestant Religion*, p. 16.

31. Increase Mather, *Mystery of Israel's Salvation*, p. 74.

Man, but by the Scriptures."[32] His son Cotton was of like mind: "The Rule according to which Conscience is to proceed . . . is, the word of God; or what God has revealed in the Sacred Scriptures. Not the opinions and practices of men; nor indeed any suggestions but what are Consonant unto the Faithful sayings of our Bible."[33]

John Wilson, troubled by the "dreamers of this generation," warned his congregation in 1677, "O do not hearken to these Dreamers, but hearken to the holy Word of God. . . . One word from the Lord is to be preferred before all other matters."[34] Increase Mather boldly asserted "the perfection and fulness of the Scripture against all Traditions and Canons devised by men."[35] John Cotton was perturbed by men acting of their own accord "without some light from some Scripture," the unfortunate result of which "is to make a mans selfe wise above that which is written."[36] Urian Oakes of the church at Cambridge admonished fellow clergy and laity alike that in matters of Christian service they had "great reason to examine our selves, and bring all our services to the test and touchstone of the Word of God."[37] Josiah Flynt of Dorchester, Massachusetts, put it bluntly: "Without the word, there is nothing but ignorance, & therefore must needs be unbeleefe."[38]

The Practical Uses of Scripture

Of what use, then, was this divinely inspired, complete, infallible Word of God to the inhabitants of Puritan New England? As the Lord's message to mankind, the Bible was believed to possess great power and utility, able to touch the daily lives of both saints and sinners. Foremost among the powers attributed to the Word was its ability to point the way to salvation through Christ. It did this first by exposing men as God saw them: "The Word of God gives a full demonstration of the natural state of all mankind; it tells us both what we are, and how we came to be so; it declares the wrath of God,

---

32. Increase Mather, *An Arrow Against Profane and Promiscuous Dancing Drawn out of the Quiver of the Scriptures* (Boston, 1684), p. 26.

33. Cotton Mather, *A Companion for Communicants* (Boston, 1690), p. 86.

34. John Wilson, *A Seasonable Watch-Word Unto Christians Against the Dreams & Dreamers Of this Generation* (Cambridge, Mass., 1677), p. 5.

35. Increase Mather, *David Serving*, p. 21.

36. John Cotton, *The Bloudy Tenent Washed, And made white in the bloud of the Lambe* (London, 1647), p. 43.

37. Urian Oakes, *A Seasonable Discourse Wherein Sinceritie & Delight in the Service of God is earnestly pressed upon Professors of Religion* (Cambridge, Mass., 1682), p. 8.

38. Flynt, sermon [1670s], p. 261.

and shews how man came to be subjected to it; it convinceth by clear and plain evidence."[39] The Word was "of singular benefit to discover to people what sinne is" and was likened by Josiah Flynt to a trumpet which was "to be sounded in the ears of sinners" in order to awaken the "secure sinner" to his plight.[40] James Allen spoke of sin being revealed "by seeing your selves in the glass [mirror] of the Word."[41] Cotton Mather also spoke of the Word as "the GLASS, which gives Young People, to see the Uncleanness of their Wayes" and also "the SPUR, which moves Young People, to seek a Cure for the Uncleanness of their Wayes."[42] The Word contained the "great voice of God . . . to every sinner," and it was "the great design of the Scriptures" to declare "that the Sinner who shall turn from all his sins shall live, but the Sinner that will not turn from all his Sins shall dye forever."[43]

The Bible was depicted in less severe terms by John Cotton as he spoke of the "attractive drawing power that is found in the word of truth, and goodnesse of the Gospell of Christ,"[44] and by Increase Mather as he referred to the Bible as "a gracious Letter which Christ has sent from heaven, inviting who will, to come to him and be saved by him."[45] William Adams, amazed at "what heart-breakings and soul-meltings there are under the word of God," believed that the purpose of the Word was to "move and work kindly & sweetly upon the heart to persuade, to draw, to instruct, to correct, to awe, to unite the heart to God."[46] Josiah Flynt proclaimed that the "summe and substance of the Gospell" was to declare the "reconciliation made by Christ for sinners."[47] To the Puritans, God in his sovereignty had ordained that the Word be instrumental in transmitting the message of redemption, making it "the power of God to salvation" and using it for "the pricking of the heart."[48] According to Samuel Willard,

39. Samuel Willard, *Mercy Magnified on a Penitent Prodigal* (Boston, 1684), p. 98.

40. John Cotton, *Christ the Fountaine of Life* (London, 1651), p. 187; Flynt, sermon [1670s], p. 11.

41. James Allen, *Mans Self-reflections is the Special Means to further his Recovery from his Apostacy from God* (Boston, 1699), p. 27.

42. Cotton Mather, *Early Religion*, pp. 14–15.

43. Increase Mather, *The Greatest Sinners Exhorted and Encouraged To Come to Christ, and that Now Without Delaying* (Boston, 1686), p. 45.

44. Cotton, *Way of Life*, p. 139.

45. Increase Mather, *Greatest Sinners*, p. 16.

46. William Adams, *The Necessity of the Pouring out of the Spirit*, in *Dedham Pulpit*, ed. E. Burgess (Boston, 1840), p. 61.

47. Flynt, sermon [1670s], p. 152.

48. Cotton, *Way of Life*, pp. 162, 171.

"the Gospel is the great instrument of Gods Appointment for Conversion."[49]

The Puritan clergy extolled the virtues of the Bible as the way to salvation, and also drew upon it for guidance in daily living. New England Puritanism was a blending of the theoretical and the practical, with attention given to both systematic doctrines and their application. The centrality of the Word in Puritan thought is further demonstrated by the way in which biblical examples and teachings were constantly held up as the standard for a Christian society.

Ministers frequently reminded their congregations of the Bible's usefulness as the rule and example which the people of God were required to follow. John Cotton let his congregation know that the Scriptures were given for instruction, teaching, and admonition, and that the episodes recorded in Holy Writ "are of singular use of direction for the Church of God."[50] Samuel Willard exhorted his flock to value the Word, telling them it would direct them into the right path, be a friend and companion at all times, stay with them through all sorts of adversity, lift their spirits when in deepest dejection, enable them to commune with God himself, and support and carry them through the agonies of death.[51] The Scriptures were, according to Joshua Moodey, "the Christians' Apothecaries Shop where he may go and take freely what his occasions call for. If a man needs reproof, Correction, Doctrine, Instruction, &c. all these are there to be had."[52]

It was the Word of God that was the "ordinary and visible way of Gods teaching"[53] and informed the people of God about "sundry things which else they had not known." The Word not only informed, but also served "to stir them up to do such things which they wel knew should be done."[54] Samuel Willard reminded his church that believers were to "walk in conformity to the Rules of Gods Word, frame their lives in all things according to it."[55] John Norton explained that special attention ought to be given to the examples of biblical characters since God had seen fit to make "a considerable part of the Scripture . . . a divine testimony of what the Faithful have done and

---

49. Willard, *Fig Trees Doom*, p. 25.

50. John Cotton, *Singing of Psalmes a Gospel Ordinance* (London, 1647), p. 36; *Way of Life*, p. 124.

51. Willard, *Heavenly Merchandize*, pp. 76–80.

52. Joshua Moodey, *The Believers happy Change by Dying* (Boston, 1697), pp. 3–4.

53. James Allen, *Neglect of Supporting and Maintaining the Pure Worship of God, By the Professing People of God is a God-provoking and Land-Wasting Sin* (Boston, 1687), p. 7.

54. Cotton, *Christ the Fountaine*, p. 179.

55. Willard, *Fig Trees Doom*, p. 41.

suffered."[56] It was a rare election sermon in seventeenth-century Massachusetts that did not urge the electorate in one way or another to "let your choice be guided by the word of God" when it came to selecting a suitable leader.[57]

It is clear that the Bible was regarded by the Puritan faithful as the rule of faith and practice, the guide to salvation, and a volume filled with examples and teachings to be heeded. The Scriptures had value in other areas as well. The Bible pointed the way to happiness, provided growth and depth in the Christian experience, helped the saints to resist sin, warned the saints of the dangers of disobedience, laid the foundations for a just government, and gave the saints comfort during times of distress. And in a world of wickedness, the Puritan saint could say with Thomas Shepard, "When we are mocked and scorned of men of the World, let us look into the Bible, and we shall find bags of Promises, true treasure, and therein let us rejoyce."[58]

Response to the Word

In light of claims made for the Bible by the Puritan clergy, it is not surprising that considerable emphasis in their sermons was placed on a proper response to the Word. The importance of the regular reading of the Scriptures was stressed. Cotton Mather urged his flock to "let not a Day ordinarily pass you, wherein you will not Read some portion of it, with a due Meditation and Supplication over it."[59] When he became concerned that Bible reading was not being taken with the utmost seriousness, Mather became vehement. While reading the Word, he asserted, God may well meet the deepest longings and greatest needs of the soul. "Can you not read a Bible, as well as a Gazet, or a Romance?" he scathingly queried his congregation.[60] Another congregation was even told that "when you cannot read, be sure you meditate upon some part of Gods Word, every day, and every night."[61]

Not only was the reading of Scripture urged, but so was its memorization. Having the Word hidden in the heart and bringing an appropriate passage to remembrance was "ye best way in ye world" to resist

---

56. John Norton, *Abel being Dead yet Speaketh* (London, 1658), p. 4.

57. James Allen, *New Englands choicest Blessing And the Mercy most to be desired by all that wish well to this People* (Boston, 1679), p. 7.

58. Cotton Mather, *Early Religion*, p. 4; Increase Mather, *Practical Truths Tending to Promote the Power of Godliness* (Boston, 1682), p. 142; sermon of Mar. 14, 1686, and undated sermons, *Substance of Sermons*, pp. 38, 50, 277, 278.

59. Cotton Mather, *Military Duties*, p. 68. See also *Small Offers Towards the Service of the Tabernacle in the Wilderness* (Boston, 1689), p. 26.

60. Cotton Mather, *Unum Necessarium* (Boston, 1693), p. 46.

61. Cotton, *Christ the Fountaine*, p. 207.

temptation.[62] Cotton Mather urged his hearers to take special care to bring their children to a knowledge of salvation and to teach them to memorize Scripture.[63] In one of his published catechisms, Mather began his questioning with "What should young-people count the most necessary or commendable thing that can be spoken of them?" He answered with a passage of Scripture: "2 Tim. 3.15. From a Child thou hast known the holy Scriptures which are able to make thee wise unto Salvation."[64] John Cotton urged his congregation to take the Word and "hide it in our hearts, so that we might not sinne against God, Psal. 119.11."[65] The ideal for young and old alike was "to be ready in the Scriptures, like a ready scribe, that can draw out of his Quiver a fitting arrow for every case."[66]

The saints were urged to give a full measure of concentration to the study of the Bible, both through the private reading of it and the hearing of Bible-based sermons. John Cotton's congregation was urged to "FEED upon the WORD,"[67] while Cotton Mather admonished his flock to "Eat well, that we may Walk well. . . . Let us by a Contemplative Eating chew upon the Word of God."[68] When it came to the hearing of the Word at divine worship, Satan was credited with realizing the importance of the Word being preached, and "it comes to pass that men are most sleepy at Sermon time," said Increase Mather. "Before the sermon began, they were not drowsie, and after the Sermon is ended, they are not so; but just at that season, when they are called to attend the word of God, they are apt to drowse and sleep. This is as Satan would have it."[69]

Other congregations were urged to "digg and dive into the rich Mines of Scripture"; to "be found in, and cleave to the way of the Rule, the way of Gods Word"; to "stick close to the guidance of the Scriptures, and love them"; to "stand in aw of the Word and with Reverence to receive and attend it"; to "let the word of God speake, & doe thou heare what it saith"; and "to study the Lord's will, to be frequent in the Scriptures, searching out the mind of God there, for your direction."[70]

62. Increase Mather, sermon [1686], *Substance of Sermons*, p. 278.
63. Cotton Mather, *A Family Well-Ordered* (Boston, 1699), p. 19.
64. Cotton Mather, *Scriptural Catechism*, p. 1.
65. Cotton, *Christ the Fountaine*, p. 136.
66. Eliot, *Harmony of the Gospels*, p. 63.
67. Cotton, *Christ the Fountaine*, p. 134.
68. Cotton Mather, *Early Piety* (London, 1689), p. 20.
69. Increase Mather, *Power of Godliness*, p. 199.
70. Increase Mather, *The Mystery of Christ Opened and Applyed* (Boston, 1686), p. 43; Richard Mather, *A Farewell Exhortation to the Church and People of Dorchester in New England* (Cambridge, Mass., 1657), p. 6; Jonathan Mitchell,

To those who did not give the Word its proper place, the warnings were dire enough. Increase Mather thundered that those who repeatedly heard the Bible preached and yet did not heed God's Word and become converted would find themselves "at ye Last Day . . . in ye Lowest Hell."[71] A startling example of the heinousness of neglecting the Word comes from the confession of James Morgan, convicted of murder by the Massachusetts government in 1686. In his public confession, recorded by Increase Mather, Morgan admitted to the murder, but that act was not his greatest regret. "The sin which lieth most heavey upon my Conscience, is," he maintained, "that I have despised the Word of God, and many a time refused to hear it preached."[72]

Conclusion

It can be seen clearly from the sermons and writings of the Puritan clergy in New England that the importance of the Bible to Puritan orthodoxy can scarcely be overstated. The Word was held in the highest possible regard by the Puritan clergy throughout the seventeenth century, and well beyond that for most of the ministry. The names the clergy used for Scripture; their absolute faith in its divine authorship, infallibility, and uniqueness; their desire to base their sermons on nothing but Scripture texts properly interpreted; and their exhortations for all to study and follow biblical precepts—these constitute strong evidence of their dependence on, and reverence for, the Bible. Furthermore, no sign of disagreement was found among the clergy concerning the nature and authority of the Bible, at least during the seventeenth century. Theological disagreements in Puritan New England may have arisen over other issues, but the Bible was the unquestioned Word of God.

It should be emphasized that the Puritans' high view of the Bible did not preclude a role for reason in their theological thinking. Miller was correct that reason and logic were important in Puritan preaching, but he failed to recognize that for the clergy, nothing in the realm of human reason ever took precedence over the Bible. For example, miracles, contrary to normal human experience yet recorded in the Word, were accepted at face value. Logical reasoning alone could

---

Nehemiah on the Wall in Troublesom Times (Cambridge, Mass., 1667), p. 27; Thomas Shepard, *The Parable of the Ten Virgins Opened & Applied* (London, 1660), p. 151; William Adams, *God's Eye on the Contrite* (Boston, 1685), p. 4; Flynt, sermon [1670s], p. 54; Samuel Willard, *The duty of a People that have Renewed their Covenant with God* (Boston, 1680), p. 8.

71. Increase Mather, sermon of Mar. 14, 1686, *Substance of Sermons*, p. 53.

72. Increase Mather, *Sermon Occasioned by the Execution of a Man found Guilty of Murder* (Boston, 1686), pp. 27–28.

never have led to many of the theological positions held in all sincerity by the Puritan faithful.

In short, the Bible alone stood as the recognized basis of legitimacy for every aspect of Puritan Christianity, although at times this biblical support was less than explicit, with some passages being interpreted parochially in light of current attitudes. Nonetheless, the clergy and the faithful of Puritan New England were, perhaps to a degree never surpassed before or since, a people of the Word. Only with such an awareness of the foundational role of the Bible can Puritan Christianity in America be properly understood.

4

Theology
Human Nature, Sin, and Christ

While it is clear that Puritan theology was biblically based, there were certain themes and emphases which were given priority in Puritan preaching. The Puritan ministry appear to have sought balance in their preaching and writing in terms of the totality of what the Bible teaches, yet there were certain truths which struck them as foundational. These essential Puritan doctrines will be the focus of this chapter and the next.

The Puritans of New England did not refer to themselves as "Calvinists," for they were wary of following the system of any one man and would have preferred to be known simply as "biblicists." Yet they agreed with Calvin on many points, such that we can reasonably call them Calvinists in the common meaning of the term today.

Human Nature

Calvin taught that depraved humankind can do nothing to earn salvation; it is a gift of God. The Puritans of New England looked at man and saw him as thoroughly depraved, evil and worthless, deserving of nothing other than contempt and damnation. The self-concept of the Puritan saint was low by nearly any standard, and numerous extant diaries from the period attest to a great sense of personal sin and imperfection, as well as to the practice of spiritual self-examination. The purpose of self-examination was to see oneself as much as possible from God's perspective, the result of which would surely be a sense of humility and self-abasement.[1]

Given the sinfulness of human nature, humility was seen as a necessary and very great virtue. In fact, humility and self-abasement became, to the Puritans, indicators of true spirituality. Those who "think modestly, lowly, meanly of themselves," according to William Adams, were truly blessed. The mark of serious saints, he contended, "is their being of a poor and contrite spirit, and trembling at His [God's] Word."[2] One could not be too humble, according to Cotton Mather, who stated that "when we have humbled our selves never so much, Let us count that we have cause to be Humbled over again, for the defects of our own Humiliation."[3]

Not only was the saint expected to display humility, but he was actually required to abhor his sinful nature. This low self-image was theoretically a function of one's relationship to God. As John Cotton expressed it, "the more the heart doth inwardly love Christ, the lesse we do love our selves. . . . This shall you ever finde to be the frame of the spirit of a christian, the more deeply he affects for Christ, the more inwardly he loaths himself. . . ."[4] "He that submits to the Lord Christ," asserted Thomas Shepard, "must loathe himself."[5] William Adams maintained that those in God's favor could not help but be aware of "the infinite Distance and Disproportion that is betwixt God and them." "They are worms to the Lord," he maintained. "All their righteousness they know are but filthy rags." Those saints who kept their lowly positions always in mind were, according to Adams, "the greatest Favourites in the Kingdom of Heaven."[6] Despite the fact that the saints had experienced the forgiveness of their sins and had been made "new creatures" in Christ, Josiah Flynt warned his congregation that these facts should "not hinder or stop your selfe loathing, and abhorrence." "Remember this," he said, "in that white robe, if you turne it up & looke under it, it covers an odious vile fleshye loathsome creature."[7] It would appear that the human race as sinners received more attention from some Puritan clergy than the human race as imagers of God, perhaps even to the detriment of mental health in seventeenth-century New England.

1. See, e.g., Cotton Mather, sermon [ca. 1682], Huntington Library MS, n.p., based on 1 Cor. 11:28, "Let a Man Examine Himself."

2. Adams, *God's Eye*, pp. 4–6.

3. Cotton Mather, *Humiliations*, p. 38.

4. Cotton, *Christ the Fountaine*, pp. 11–12.

5. Shepard, *Subjection to Christ*, p. 51.

6. Adams, *God's Eye*, pp. 14, 18.

7. Flynt, sermon [1670s], Harvard University MS, p. 302.

Sin

The popular characterization of the Puritans as a people obsessed
with an awareness of sin does not totally miss the mark. While the
Puritans did have their lighter moments, their theology of sin was in-
grained even into their young children. Sin, as defined in the Bible,
was perceived as the root cause of the sad state of human affairs and
consequently deserved much attention. Sin was the recipient of the
greatest loathings the faithful Puritan could muster because it threatened the social order, violated reason, and most of all epitomized the
antithesis of that which he professed to love most dearly—the Lord
God and his commandments in the Bible.

Sin was defined in various ways by the clergy, but always from a
biblical perspective. Nathaniel Gookin described it as "ye want of
conformity unto, or ye transgression of gods law in some act of man."
Gookin believed that "every breach of gods Law is a sin."[8] According
to Cotton Mather, "Sin is in the very Nature of it, a Departure from
God: and therefore it is a departure from that Felicity and Fruition
which is most of all to be desired."[9] Increase Mather defined sin as "a
violation of that Law which is expressive of the Holy Will of God. . . .
Sin is rebellion against the Lord." He went on to elaborate upon the
attributes of sin as depicted in the Word: sin "rebells against the Lord
Hos. 13.16," "grieves the heart of God Gen. 6.6," "dishonors God's
name Rom 2.23," and "challenges God Is[aiah] 5.19." In another sermon Increase Mather told his congregation that "Sin is the greatest
Folly in the World. . . . Sin is a departure from the Rule of Wisdom."
Furthermore, Mather maintained, "Sin is Contrary to the Holy Nature
and perfect Will of God."[10] According to Thomas Shepard, "sin is op-
posite to God."[11] For Samuel Willard and others, the essence of sin
was seen as disobedience to God and his Word, the Bible.

The nature of sin was especially heinous when viewed from a divine perspective, which the Puritan clergy found in the Scriptures.
"God hates sin," declared Samuel Willard, "and it is his holy and pure
nature that is displayed in his so doing. . . ."[12] It was Nathaniel
Gookin's opinion that sin existed in varying degrees—that "some sins
are greater in the sight of god than others." Nevertheless, all sin is evil

8. Nathaniel Gookin, sermon [1687], *Sermon Notes, 1687,* Harvard University
MS, pp. 118, 5.

9. Cotton Mather, *Pillars of Salt* (Boston, 1699), p. 10.

10. Increase Mather, *The Folly of Sinning* (Boston, 1699), pp. 13–15; *A Sermon
Wherein Is Shewed That Excess in Wickedness doth bring Untimely Death*
(Boston, 1685), p. 19; *Solemn Advice to Young Men* (Boston, 1695), p. 74.

11. Shepard, *Sound Believer,* p. 48.

12. Willard, *Impenitent Sinners,* p. 4.

and humankind had no excuse to indulge in any sin, especially in New England "where ye word of God, and ye way of uprightness are taught."[13] Samuel Willard, on the other hand, did not acknowledge degrees of sin: "Every Sin is great, as it is against God, and is a violation of his Law; for the least affront offered to that glorious being cannot be small."[14] Thomas Shepard agreed—sin was sin, and "there is as much venom and mischief done against God in the least, as in the greatest sin: and therefore it, and whosoever commits it, deserves death for it, as if they had committed the foulest sin in the world." Shepard further emphasized the seriousness of sin by stating that "in everie sin thou dost strike God, and sting a daggar at the heart of God." He also preached that "the real greatness of sin is seen by beholding the greatness of God who is smitten by sin."[15]

It was because of sin that humankind had become God's enemy.[16] The wrath of God against sinners was necessary because "the Infinite Holiness of the blessed God does punish sin not only from his Will but his Nature. . . . He cannot but hate sin. It is inconsistent with the holy Nature of God to love any sin, or not to hate every sin. "[17] Every time a man sinned, the sin was committed "against God," and oftentimes "against man" as well.[18] Sinners also wronged themselves. Increase Mather preached a sermon in 1674 directed to two condemned murderers in which he warned, "He that sinneth against me [God] wrongs his own soul. The Impenitent Sinner brings ruin upon his own soul. Therefore Sin is folly, and the more sinful the more foolish: The greatest sinners, are the greatest Fools on the world."[19] Cotton Mather warned of the ill effects of sin and denounced it in dramatic form from his pulpit: "Let us Beware of every Sin; for Sin will Turn a Man into a Devil. Oh! Vile SIN, horrid SIN, cursed SIN; or to speak a more Pungent word, than all of That; oh SINFUL Sin; how Pernicious art thou unto the Souls of Men!"[20]

There was no doubt among the clergy that sin had its origin with Satan, and that Satan was still a powerful force influencing men to do

13. Gookin, sermon of Aug. 1687, *Sermon Notes, 1687,* Harvard University MS, pp. 140, 142.

14. Samuel Willard, *A Remedy against Despair* (Boston, 1700), p. 9.

15. Thomas Shepard, *Three Valuable Pieces* (Boston, 1747), p. 14; *Sincere Convert,* p. 178; *Sound Believer,* p. 22.

16. See Shepard, *Sincere Convert,* p. 49.

17. Increase Mather, *Mystery of Christ,* pp. 162–63.

18. Gookin, sermon [1687], *Sermon Notes, 1687,* Harvard University MS, p. 76.

19. Increase Mather, *Excess in Wickedness,* p. 20.

20. Cotton Mather, *The Way to Excel* (Boston, 1697), p. 26.

evil. When it came to sin, "the Devil" was "the Father of it."[21] "Every unregenerate man is under the power of Satan," asserted Josiah Flynt, "& led by him according to his pleasure. Satan is the unregenerate mans God, & holds a godlike power over him."[22] Satan was considered as a being possessed of great power and, working in unison with depraved humankind's inclination to sin, the results were a saint's nightmare. "Satan is one of the Allies of In-dwelling sin," warned Urian Oakes, "and in Confederacy with our own Hearts, which are ready every moment, if there be not a strict watch kept upon them, to betray us up to Him."[23] It was Cotton Mather's concern that "when Men permit Satan, with his Temptations to fill their Hearts, they are in the high road unto all manner of Wickedness and Misery."[24]

Satan needed to do little prodding, since sin was viewed in Puritan theology as imbedded in human nature since the fall of Adam. The clergy's belief in human depravity and its origin was consistent with their literal interpretation of the Bible; Adam was seen as a real man, the one man by whom "Sin entered into the world, and death by sin, and so death passed upon all men, for that all have sinned."[25] The unhappy result was that "original sin hath depraved the whole man. It is a woful Leprosy whereby every member of the body, and all the powers of the soul are tainted and disordered."[26] All humankind were infected by the disease of sin and had a "marvelous propensity" to engage in sinful conduct.[27] Cotton Mather, in a sermon preached on the text of Romans 3:23—"For all have sinned and come short of the glory of God"—stated as his central point that "There is not a man to be found in ye whole world, but he has been guilty of sin in ye sight of god."[28] Thomas Shepard noted that there were "six things that every man is full of: Sin, Darkness, Unbelief, Satan, Self, World." In another sermon Shepard emphasized that "Every natural man and woman is born full of sin . . . every piece of his soul is full of sin; their hearts are bundels of sin. . . ."[29] William Brattle conveyed the idea of original sin to his congregation by saying that "all men are personally condemned in guilt and adams apostacye."[30] "This original sin is a hereditary

---

21. Cotton Mather, *Batteries upon the Kingdom of the Devil* (London, 1695), p. 30.
22. Flynt, sermon [1670s], Harvard University MS, p. 22.
23. Oakes, *Unconquerable Souldier*, p. 10.
24. Cotton Mather, *Batteries*, p. 5.
25. Cotton Mather, *Scriptural Catechism*, p. 9.
26. Increase Mather, *Solemn Advice*, p. 8.
27. Increase Mather, *Sermon Occasioned by Execution of a Man*, p. 26.
28. Cotton Mather, sermon [ca. 1682], Huntington Library MS, n.p.
29. Shepard, *Parable of Ten Virgins*, p. 195; *Sincere Convert*, p. 40.
30. William Brattle, sermon of July 30, 1699, Harvard University MS, n.p.

habituall controversy & enmity of mans nature against the whole will of god," declared Nathaniel Gookin in 1687. "[I]t comes from parents to ye children. So that ye child as soon as he is born has this corrupt principle in him."[31] According to Increase Mather: "Adams sin has brought that misery of Spiritual blindness upon all his Children."[32] Josiah Flynt was in full agreement with his fellow divines on this matter. "Fallen man brings with him into the world a corrupt & defiled creature, having a heart full of evill . . . this the scripture frequently asserts."[33]

These statements of the Puritan clergy concerning original sin clearly conflict with Miller's conclusions. The covenant concept (see chapter 5), which Miller found fascinating, was built on the doctrine of human sinfulness and the need for salvation. Yet, according to Miller, the idea of a covenant between God and man meant that when man failed to live up to his part of the contract, "man has been expelled [from God's favor] for non-payment, he is not spiritually polluted." When Adam sinned and broke the covenant with God, Miller asserted, "the guilt was 'imputed' to his constituents as a legal responsibility, not inherited as a cancer or a leprosy."[34] According to the Puritans' own testimony, which clearly indicates that sin is an inherent condition of spiritual pollution, Miller has misconceived a fundamental Puritan doctrine. The Puritans did not arrive at their position by intellectual reasoning; they accepted the Bible as their authoritative doctrinal source.

Puritan theology clearly recognized that all men were born in sin as a result of the fall of Adam and Eve. Furthermore, the only way to remove this guilt was by faith in the person and work of Christ. Salvation and its accompanying forgiveness did not, however, preclude the saints from future misdeeds. Even after conversion, the earthly saint was burdened with his old sinful nature, which he was now supposed to control. Samuel Willard urged his congregation to reject any thoughts of perfection this side of heaven since "original sin remains in God's people as long as they shall live." Willard likewise warned them that "the Children of God may sometimes fall into very Great Sins."[35] Josiah Flynt conveyed the same idea to his congregation at Dorchester: "We must not expect heaven in its perfection upon the

31. Gookin, sermon of June, 1687, *Sermon Notes, 1687*, Harvard University MS, p. 112.

32. Increase Mather, *Solemn Advice*, p. 82.

33. Flynt, sermon [1670s], Harvard University MS, p. 59.

34. Miller, *New England Mind*, pp. 400–401.

35. Willard, *Remedy against Despair*, pp. 9–10.

earth, saints have their darke sides, their infirmityes, & will have as long as they are in this tabernacle [physical body]. . . ."[36]

The Sin of Hypocrisy

While agreeing with Calvin that sin could not cancel the salvation of the elect who had put their faith in Christ, the Puritan ministry was quick to denounce sin repeatedly from the pulpit. They preached that not only did sin offend a holy God, but it also caused others to stumble, caused much misery in this life, and caused a forfeiture of rewards in the life to come. A sin that was attacked with special vehemence and regularity was the sin of hypocrisy—a general term used to describe the possession of the outward forms of religion without its true substance. Cotton Mather defined the hypocrite as "one who does pretend Religion, and but pretend it." "Hypocrisie is properly a counterfeit of Religion," he asserted. "[A]n Hypocrite acts the part of a Saint while he is but a Sinner still."[37] Puritan Christianity may have unwittingly encouraged hypocrisy by its dual stress on internal belief as well as an external profession and lifestyle, as called for by the covenant system. From the numerous sermons of the period dealing with the problem of hypocrisy, one may conclude that there apparently were many individuals in seventeenth-century New England who found it advantageous or even personally satisfying to conform outwardly to expected religious forms while missing the true essence of the faith.

This sin of hypocrisy was seen by the clergy as a very great problem, for to the devout Puritan religion was not a mere outward show and assent to biblical doctrines, but a personal belief in Christ and an internalization of his Word. The most outwardly pious communicant, if not truly converted, was no better off than the worst of sinners; in fact, he was probably further from salvation. "The portion of Hypocrites," declared Cotton Mather in a sermon fittingly entitled *The Stage-Player unmasked,* "is a very miserable portion."[38] Hypocrites were far from salvation because in many cases they had succeeded in deceiving themselves and hence were no longer seeking God.[39] In Samuel Willard's words, hypocrisy was a sin of "unspeakable folly," because hypocrites "deceive their own Souls, but God is not to be mocked. . . ."[40] Outwardly moral but inwardly unregenerate persons were described by Thomas Shepard: "They can hear all Sermons, no

---

36. Flynt, sermon [1670s], Harvard University MS, p. 340.
37. Cotton Mather, *Batteries,* p. 71.
38. Ibid., p. 70.
39. Shepard, *Sincere Convert,* p. 98.
40. Willard, *Fig Trees Doom,* p. 69.

wind will shake them, no searching, threatening truths concern them; they are so good, that they think the Lord means not them." Shepard went on to say that "the most convincing hypocrites find themselves helpless and useless before God in the end."[41]

Throughout the seventeenth century ministers warned their flocks that "there will be a number of Hypocrites mingling themselves with the purest Churches."[42] John Norton preached in 1657 that some New Englanders only thought they were saved; "there are many that partake of the dispensation of the promise who fall short of the good of it."[43] Samuel Willard told his congregation in 1684 that "outward careful attendance upon the visible service of God, is no sure sign of a sincere Christian."[44] It was Josiah Flynt's contention that "the priviledges of the gospel enjoyed, cannot in themselves save sinners from hell & wrath . . . a people never soe hyghly exalted in ye enjoyment of the Gospell & ordinances, or a person, may yet be for all this in a miserable & soule damning condition." Flynt emphasized that mere ordinances without inward sincerity were valueless: "thy Baptisme of water is nothing, unlesse thy soule be washed in the Laver of Regeneration: thy hearing ye word preached is nothing, unlesse thou art inwardly taught of God."[45] In a sermon preached against hypocrisy in 1685, William Adams of Dedham said, "Men may (and would to God there were none here that did so!) live under the most clear Gospel Light, in the pure, peaceable, free Enjoyment of Gospel Order and Ordinances . . . have great knowledge of Religion, and make high profession . . . and yet live in some sin openly or secretly, be enslaved to some base defiling lust, wherewith they not only pollute themselves, but others also." Adams, apparently disillusioned with his entire generation, saw hypocrisy everywhere and labeled New Englanders in general as "a visibly professing people under spiritual declension and defection."[46] Within fifteen years of the founding of Boston, Thomas Shepard was already warning his congregation that "if a man be outwardly holy, but not within, he is not sanctified, no more than the painted sepulchres of the proud Pharisees." Shepard was convinced that hypocrisy was rampant in early Massachusetts, that "they that in respect of Church estate, and outward Covenant,

41. Shepard, *Parable of Ten Virgins*, pp. 139, 152.
42. Ibid., p. 115.
43. John Norton, sermon of Oct. 11, 1657, Boston Public Library MS, n.p.
44. Willard, *Mercy Magnified*, p. 365.
45. Flynt, sermon [1670s], Harvard University MS, pp. 136, 143.
46. Adams, *God's Eye*, pp. 11, 2.

and profession, are outwardly . . . Saints, are many times inwardly, and really unsound."[47]

The clergy attempted to show God's displeasure over the sin of hypocrisy, and warned their congregations of the dim view Christ took of hypocrites in the New Testament. Samuel Willard reminded his hearers that Christ had strong words for those who honored God with "Lip Service, whilst their hearts were absent."[48] John Cotton urged his Boston congregation to avoid hypocrisy because of "how loathsome it is to Christ, hee never speakes worse word than this, o yee hypocrites, when hee speakes with most detestation, yet this is the worst word hee speakes of any men, o yee hypocrites. . . . Abhore you all seeds of hypocricie, it is very loathsome to God. . . ."[49] Thomas Thacher preached on a public day of fasting in Boston in 1674 and urged his hearers to have pious attitudes as well as actions. "God cares not for external performances without the heart," he maintained; in fact, it was a "high abomination" to profess religion outwardly while not having "a suitable heart."[50] God could not stand hypocrisy, according to Nathaniel Gookin, because He knows and values "ye thoughts of men as well as their words and actions."[51]

Since the sin of hypocrisy found such disfavor in the sight of God, the clergy not only warned against it, but also tried to help their congregations discern hypocrisy in their midst and in themselves. To begin with, the motives of the hypocrite were faulty. According to Samuel Willard, "However they hope to recommend their lives to men, they do not approve their hearts to God: they labour, but it is to make a Spiders web: their aims are wrong set, they seek not the glory of God, but to be seen of men; and they have all their reward when they have gotten the applause they desired, for God will reject them."[52] Thomas Shepard noted that "one of the greatest differences betwixt a child of God and a hypocrite. . . . In their obedience the one takes up duties out of love to Christ . . . the other out of love to himself. . . ." Although to all outward observers there may be little difference, "there is a vast and great internal difference between those that are sincere, and the closest Hypocrites."[53] Samuel Willard believed

47. Shepard, *Sound Believer*, p. 236; *The Church Membership of Children, and Their Right to Baptisme* (Cambridge, 1663), p. 2.

48. Samuel Willard, *The Sinfulness of Worshipping God With Men's Institutions* (Boston, 1691), p. 3.

49. John Cotton, *The Saints Support & Comfort, In the Time of Distress* (London, 1658), p. 135.

50. Thomas Thacher, *A Fast of Gods chusing* (Boston, 1678), p. 9.

51. Gookin, sermon [1687], *Sermon Notes, 1687*, Harvard University MS, p. 22.

52. Willard, *Fig Trees Doom*, p. 78.

53. Shepard, *Sincere Convert*, p. 29; *Parable of Ten Virgins*, p. 131.

that hypocrites could be spotted by their reactions to persecution and adversity. "Hypocrites cannot long endure the fiery trial," he explained, "but when it grows hot upon them, they relinquish their Religion, and comply with the World, to avoid trouble."[54] Urian Oakes believed that the "saucy spirit" in all hypocrites would eventually expose them to the discerning eye.[55]

Those guilty of hypocrisy could expect harsh judgment, according to the Puritan clergy. God's wrath was kindled, said John Cotton, against "damnable Ignorance, and Superstition, Idolatry, and Hypocrisie. . . ." "God will cut off false brethren."[56] Cotton Mather vividly depicted the ultimate plight of the unregenerate hypocrite: "when the body of the Hypocrite shall have snakes and worms in a cold grave crawling about it, then shall the Spirit of him in an hot Hell be under the gnaws of the worm, the snake which never dyes."[57] Eternal suffering might be the portion of the hypocrite but hypocrisy, if unchecked, had severe consequences for the present as well. If admitted to "the priviledges due here to visible Saints," John Oxenbridge warned, hypocrites "will be likely to eat out the heart of liberty and religion."[58]

Miller has concluded that the clergy were prepared to make a "frank admission that many of their visible saints were hypocrites, and that hypocrisy had a positive function in their system." He maintained that the clergy participated in "an eminently practical utopia" which "exact[ed] nothing beyond human possibilities." Miller was correct in stating that the clergy were aware that visible sainthood (the living of an outwardly good life) was not equated with regeneration, and that the clergy were also aware of their limitations in probing for true sainthood. According to Miller, hypocrites were at least "serviceable and useful in their callings" and the ministry "became committed to a proposition of which [they] never thereafter lost sight: the land is full of hypocrites, but they have their uses." In Miller's interpretation, the clergy believed that although hypocrites may be insincere, what they profess is true and they furthermore may have talents that are of value to society.[59] Miller does not appear to have recognized the seriousness of the attacks made by the clergy

54. Samuel Willard, *The Fiery Tryal no strange thing* (Boston, 1682), pp. 8–9.

55. Oakes, *Seasonable Discourse*, p. 7.

56. John Cotton, *The Powring out of the Seven Vials* (London, 1642), p. 15; *Holiness of Church Members*, p. 28.

57. Cotton Mather, *Batteries*, p. 78.

58. John Oxenbridge, *New England Freemen Warned and Warmed, to be Free indeed, having an Eye to God in their Elections* (Cambridge, 1673), p. 26.

59. Miller, *The New England Mind from Colony to Province* (Cambridge, Mass., 1953), pp. 71–72, 75, 79–80.

against hypocrites. The clergy viewed hypocrites as the worst of sinners; they were dangerous and not useful, and received the ministry's harshest denunciations.

The Results of Sin

Hypocrisy was by no means the only sin singled out for severe condemnation, although it was frequently mentioned.[60] Numerous other sins were denounced from New England pulpits in the seventeenth century which were either condemned directly in the Bible or indirectly according to the clergy's interpretations. Increase Mather articulated a principle of biblical interpretation regarding sin which made it possible to use Scripture to attack practices deemed undesirable although not expressly condemned in the Bible. He said, "It is an Eternal Truth to be observed in expounding the commandments, that whenever any sin is forbidden, not only the highest acts of that sin, but all degrees thereof, and all occasions leading thereto are prohibited." Thus he was able to preach against "Profane and Promiscuous Dancing" by identifying it as a step toward violation of the commandment which forbade adultery.[61] Mather also set forth the principle that things not wrong in themselves were to be shunned "when they become an occasion of sin."[62]

While the clergy often denounced specific sins in their sermons, the negative effects of all forms of sin were frequently pronounced from Puritan pulpits, with necessary documentation from the Word. The devastating effects of sin were seen as significant to three groups—individual unbelievers, individual saints, and the community as a whole.

Unregenerate sinners were given the repeated warning from the pulpit that "there shall be a day of judgment, and those rejecting the Gospel shall be condemned. . . . The Scripture does abundantly bear witness to this truth." The Bible stated "that every Sinner shall dye, Gen. 2.17." Therefore the only thing to be expected by sinners who broke God's commandments was "vials of Divine wrath." The torments of hell were reserved for the unregenerate, and "no unbeliever in all the World shall escape . . . that dreadfull day. 2 Cor. 5.10." Each sinner would then be forced to acknowledge that "I am the man with

60. See Allen Carden, "The Ministry and the Word: The Clergy, the Bible, and Biblical Themes in Five Massachusetts Towns" (unpublished doctoral diss., University of California, Irvine, 1977, app. C).

61. [Increase Mather], *Profane and Promiscuous Dancing*, p. 2.

62. Increase Mather, *A Testimony Against several Prophane and Superstitious Customs Now Practised by some in New England* (London, 1687), p. 36.

whom the Eternal GOD, the Soveraign of the whole World is angry."[63]
Sin would inevitably result in judgment and life for the unbeliever
was pictured as precarious: "They are ready every moment to drop
into hell. God is a consuming fire against thee, and there is but one
paper wall of thy body between thy soul, and eternal flames. How
soon may God stop thy breath, there is nothing but that between thee
and hell; if that were gone, then farewell all."[64] Josiah Flynt gave
solemn warning to his congregation that "as soon as ever the unregenerate sinner dyes, he goes to hell and there he is tormented . . . we
see them leape out of the frying pan: I mean, depart from the miseryes
of this present life; but we see not the fire that they goe into." The
truth of this doctrine, Flynt maintained, "may be demonstrated . . .
from plain scripture testimony. . . ." In a subsequent sermon Flynt
again emphasized that "the damned sinner in hell shall suffer unspeakable torments to all eternity" and he addressed the saints, asking
them to consider "what a powerful motive is here for us, to bee
earnest for & with poor sinners, that they may be converted &
saved."[65] Increase Mather described the torments of hell and proclaimed to the unconverted that "This! This! will be thy portion as
sure as this Bible is the Word of God. . . ." In another sermon Mather
warned the unregenerate ones in his congregation of their certain
doom in terms very similar to those employed by Jonathan Edwards
nearly fifty years later in his famous sermon, *Sinners in the Hands of
an Angry God:* "O Christless Sinner, look about thee and see where
thou art! Thy soul is hanging over the mouth of hell by the rotten
thread of a frail life: if that break, the devouring Gulf will swallow
thee up for ever. . . . If a few sparks of this wrath are so fearful, can
thine heart endure when thou shalt be thrown in the Ocean of Fire
never to be quenched? Yet this is that which every Christless Sinner
is doom'd unto."[66] Sometimes the clergy took a less harsh approach to
the issue of the fate of unbelieving sinners. Jonathan Mitchel, for example, chose to portray the unregenerate as missing the glories of
heaven instead of writhing in the torments of hell.[67]

63. Increase Mather, *The Times of Men are in the hand of God* (Boston, 1675),
p. 4; *Greatest Sinners*, pp. 66–67; William Brattle, *Public Thanksgiving*, Nov. 22,
1699, Harvard University MS, p. 7; Cotton Mather, *Warnings from the Dead*, p. 4;
Increase Mather, *Solemn Advice*, p. 33; Joshua Moodey, *An Exhortation to a
Condemned Malefactor* (Boston, 1686), p. 64.

64. Shepard, *Sincere Convert*, p. 59.

65. Flynt, sermon [1670s], Harvard University MS, pp. 82, 91, 98, 105.

66. Increase Mather, *Folly of Sinning*, p. 45; *Mystery of Christ*, pp. 144–45.

67. Jonathan Mitchel, *A Discourse of the Glory To which God hath called
believers by Jesus Christ* (Boston, 1721), p. 149.

Not only could the unregenerate sinner count on divine retribution in the world to come; it was also likely that he would experience a foretaste of God's wrath and judgment in this life as a result of his sin. Sinners were presently "under the power of darknesse . . . in bondage unto their spirituall enemies untill they are delivered therefrom by the power of god."[68] Sin also had damaged humankind, preventing the human race from being and achieving what God intended. Sin had "defaced his beauty and covered him with deformity" in the present world.[69] The presence of the Lord was "farre from the wicked" and such sinners could expect "a miserable death after a sinful and mad life."[70]

It was acknowledged by the clergy that the saints themselves were not immune from sin and therefore could expect to suffer certain consequences. Increase Mather noted that "there is sin and corruptions in the hearts of the best and it will be vain to expect that the Saints shall be freed from all suffering, untill such time as they are freed from sin."[71] While all true believers could anticipate "Life Eternal" after physical death, God would nevertheless "chastise believers" for their sins in this present life "because he loves them."[72] While sinless perfection was not attainable in this present life, much sin and heartache could be avoided, John Cotton assured his congregation, by hiding God's Word in one's heart and applying it wisely to life.[73]

Corporate Sin

The Puritans believed that God dealt not only with sin in individuals, but also corporately with New England's sins. Therefore, a community obligation existed to please God by avoiding sin, for if his wrath were kindled, all would suffer. Even "one murdered may Expose a whole Land to ye Displeasure of God."[74] Cotton Mather warned that New England was trying God's patience by sinning, and on occasion his patience wore thin.[75] To the devout Puritan, nothing happened by

68. Gookin, sermon of Sept., 1687, and May 15, 1687, *Sermon Notes, 1687,* Harvard University MS, n.p. and p. 60.

69. Willard, *Mercy Magnified,* p. 235.

70. Jonathan Mitchel, sermon of 1653, Massachusetts Historical Society MS, n.p.; Flynt, sermon [1670s], Harvard University MS, p. 73.

71. Increase Mather, *The Day of Trouble is Near* (Cambridge, 1674), p. 5.

72. Cotton Mather, *Terribilia Dei* (Boston, 1697), p. 12; Gookin, sermon [1687], *Sermon Notes, 1687,* Harvard University MS, p. 13.

73. Cotton, *Christ the Fountaine,* p. 136.

74. Increase Mather, sermon of Mar., 1686, *Sermon Notes, 1687,* Harvard University MS, p. 37.

75. Cotton, *Christ the Fountaine,* p. 86.

chance. When God sent trials and tribulations to the community he was either testing his people's faithfulness or punishing them for their corporate sins. Samuel Willard distinguished between trials and punishments by stating that if God's people are faithful and still undergo adversity, then it is a trial and spiritual lessons may be learned from it. If adversity strikes while decay and "general declinings" are present, then "God is angry" and "he is now punishing them. . . ."[76] It was William Adams' opinion that "had we sinful and foolish people in New England been wise in season, and taken those solemn warnings [from the Word] which have been given us, much of that sorrow and misery which we have felt and do feel in war, sickness and other shakings might have been escaped. . . ."[77] Cotton Mather noted that "the Scourges of Heaven have long been Employ'd upon us, for our crimes against the Holy and Just and Good Laws of the Lord our God. . . . We have been sorely Lashed, with one Blow after another, for our Delinquencies."[78] The clergy taught that God dealt blows to New England hoping to stir the hearts of the people to repentance. However, if repentance was not forthcoming, God could be expected to "return with greater strokes."[79] Indeed, a similar argument had been used years earlier to encourage Puritans to leave England for America before judgment fell on the homeland.

The New England experience with sin and judgment was perceived as closely paralleling the history of Israel in the Old Testament. In both situations, the people were in a constant cycle of falling into sin, being judged, repenting, receiving mercy, and falling into sin again. One problem experienced by New England was that sins occurring "after great and eminent Salvations, Deliverances, and mercies . . . pull down greater Judgments."[80] One of the heaviest judgments to befall New England, in the eyes of Urian Oakes, was the death of her spiritual leaders. In his *Elegie Upon the Death of the Reverend Mr. Thomas Shepard*, Oakes said,

See what our sins have done! what Ruines wrought:
And how they have pluck'd out our very eyes!
Our sins have slain our Shepard! we have bought

76. Samuel Willard, *Rules for the Discerning of the Present Times* (Boston, 1693), pp. 16–17.
77. Adams, *Pouring Out of the Spirit*, in Burgess, ed., *Dedham Pulpit*, p. 38.
78. Cotton Mather, *Humiliations*, pp. 4–5.
79. Nathaniel Gookin, sermon of July, 1690, *Sermon Notes, Apr. 24 – Aug. 13, 1690*, Harvard University MS, p. 70.
80. James Allen, *Serious Advice to delivered Ones* (Boston, 1679), p. 2.

And dearly paid for, our Enormities.
Ah Cursed sins! that strike at God, and kill
His Servants, and the Blood of Prophets spill.[81]

It was the community's task to "Labour to find out ye sin that doth procure judgment. . . ."[82] The remedy for public judgment was nothing short of "True and General Repentance."[83]

The Saintly Struggle

In light of the havoc wreaked by sin, the saints were urged from the pulpit to respond to sin with great aversion. "It is not enough for the Christian only to abstain from evil," declared John Allin, but he must also "abhorre it."[84] According to Increase Mather, "the consideration of what Christ suffered for our Sins, should make us afraid of the least Sin, and not to make a light matter of any Sin."[85] Joseph Belcher preached that "whosoever will be a friend of Christ, will be an enemy of sin. . . ."[86] Since "Sin is a most odious thing . . . Men ought to hate every Sin: They have Infinite reason so to do."[87] Richard Mather urged that the saints "mourn for their sins, as the cause of Christs sufferings."[88] The devout Puritan was urged to speak out against evil wherever he found it—not to merely quietly abstain from it.[89]

The violation of the commandments in the Word of God was a constant source of anxiety and tension in the Puritan world of seventeenth-century New England. The battle against sin was seen as a life-and-death struggle and the social pressures to be constantly victorious over sin must have been immense. Yet the clergy knew and openly acknowledged that a sinless life was an earthly impossibility. This paradox may perhaps be reflected in the fact that although sins such as adultery were crimes punishable by death, court records indicate that the maximum punishments were only rarely executed.

81. Urian Oakes, *An Elegie Upon the Death of the Reverend Mr. Thomas Shepard* (Cambridge, 1677), p. 15.

82. Increase Mather, *Solemn Advice*, p. 78.

83. Allen, *Neglect of Pure Worship*, p. 4.

84. John Allin, sermon of Aug., 1651, Massachusetts Historical Society MS, p. 24.

85. Increase Mather, *Folly of Sinning*, p. 23.

86. Joseph Belcher, *The Worst Enemy Conquered* (Boston, 1698), p. 14.

87. Increase Mather, *Solemn Advice*, p. 74.

88. Richard Mather, *Farewell Exhortation*, p. 3.

89. John Norton, sermon of Oct. 22, 1657, Boston Public Library MS, n.p.

The Person and Work of Christ

The Puritans had no doubt that the answer to the problem of humankind's sinfulness was found in Christ. In fact, if anything deserves to be termed "the marrow of Puritan divinity," it is the doctrine of the person and work of Christ. Since the Bible, viewed as the written Word of God, was interpreted as being Christ-centered in both Old and New Testaments, it is not surprising to find so many Puritan sermons focused on Christ. If there were anything to be more revered by the devout Puritan than the written Word, it was Christ, the living Word. The Scriptures were important for the information they contained concerning Christ, but were not in themselves an object of worship. The written Word was sent "to reveal the Lord Jesus,"[90] but only "God in Christ is the object of Divine Worship."[91] As Thomas Shepard pointed out, the Bible was very important, particularly in Christ's physical absence: "Christ is now gone, and we have no immediate speech with him, but in his Word. . . ."[92] Increase Mather explained to his congregation that "If we would have a right understanding of those Truths which concern the Person of Christ the Son of God, we must attend the Means which the Lord hath appointed in order to the attaining that Knowledge, e.g. Searching the blessed Scriptures: therefore Christ said; Search the Scriptures for they testify of me."[93]

A thorough and accurate understanding of Christ was crucial to the Puritan system because without knowledge of and belief in "fundamental Truths, about ye Lord christ" the unconverted sinner "cannot be saved." According to Increase Mather, saving belief in Christ included the following aspects:

That Jesus of Nazareth is ye true Messiah, Joh. 8.24

That Jesus christ is ye Eternal son of god.

That Jesus christ is Man as well as god.

That Hee is ye only mediator [between God and man].

That salvation is obtained only from Him, and from ye merit of His Righteousness.[94]

90. Shepard, *Short Catechism*, p. 10.

91. Joshua Moodey, *The Great Sin of Formality in God's Worship* (Boston, 1691), p. 38.

92. Shepard, *Parable of Ten Virgins*, p. 138.

93. Increase Mather, *Mystery of Christ*, pp. 38, 42.

94. Increase Mather, sermon of Mar. 21, 1686, *Substance of Sermons*, Huntington Library MS, p. 77.

"Unless we preach who Christ is," stated William Brattle, "it is in vain to preach faith, for none can believe in him they know nothing of." This knowledge was critically important in Puritan eyes, because "they that remain ignorant of Christ, must needs be in danger of death, yea of eternal Death."[95]

A survey of the sermon literature of the seventeenth century leads to the conclusion that the Puritan clergy were unwavering in their acceptance of Christ's dual nature—he was both human and divine. John Cotton's catechism of 1646 stated the doctrine plainly: "Qu. Who is Jesus Christ? A. The eternall Son of God, who for our sakes became man, that he might redeem and save us."[96] The dual nature of Christ was vigorously proclaimed and the characteristics of deity as well as humanity attributed to him. Christ was referred to as "the Son of Man, that Man Christ Jesus, who was not a meer man, but the eternal Son of God, and God manifest in the flesh. . . ."[97] In various ways Christ was repeatedly referred to as "no less than the Eternal Son of God"[98] and of the same essence as God the Father. Christ's nature was unique—"There is no such person in heaven or earth concerning whom it may be said, That person is both God and man, excepting only the Man Christ Jesus."[99]

Increase and Cotton Mather were perhaps the most outspoken of all New England ministers concerning the deity of Christ. "The Father is the Fountain of the Deity," Cotton Mather asserted, and "the Son is the Express Image of the Fathers Person, or God Essentially Representing God."[100] Christ was, in Cotton Mather's view, the antitype of the Jewish temple, "the true Temple of God; it is in Him that there dwells the Fulness of the God-Head Bodily."[101] To be truly among God's saints, he asserted, "we must Believe Him [Christ] to be no less than, the Lord God of Truth; to be God as well as Man, to be God and Man in one person."[102] Increase Mather attributed the efficacy of Christ's death for the saving of sinners to the fact that "the Blood of christ is not ye Blood of a man only. No, tis ye Blood of

95. William Brattle, sermon of Sept. 17, 1699, *Sermon Notes, Aug. 3, 1699–July, 1706*, Harvard University MS, n.p.; Increase Mather, *Mystery of Christ*, p. 42.

96. Cotton, *Milk for Babes*, p. 7.

97. Belcher, *Worst Enemy Conquered*, p. 6.

98. Cotton Mather, *Companion for Communicants*, p. 66.

99. Increase Mather, *Mystery of Christ*, pp. 78–79.

100. Cotton Mather, *Blessed Unions* (Boston, 1692), p. 48.

101. Cotton Mather, *The Day & the Work of the Day* (Boston, 1693), p. 15.

102. Cotton Mather, *A Good Man making a Good End* (Boston, 1698), p. 26. See also sermon of May 25, 1687, Harvard University MS, pp. 90–91.

god, & so may purchase millions of souls."[103] Christ was "the Son of God before his coming into the world." Increase Mather also emphasized that "though God the Father and the Son are personally distinct, they are essentially One." "Christ . . . doth partake in the same Nature with the Father, and so is equal with God, and thence is to have equal Honour with Him."[104] Mather placed tremendous importance on the doctrine of Christ, urging his congregation to "Believe this Truth, that Jesus Christ is the Son of God" because "All Religion, yea whole Christianity would fall to the ground if this Principle should be plucked up. The Summe of the Gospel is contained in this great Truth."[105]

In sermons far too numerous to quote here, the Puritan clergy of New England made clear their commitment to the divinity of Jesus Christ, both in direct statements and in their attributing to Christ the names and characteristics of deity. Christ was described in various sermons as "Holy," as possessing the "Wisdom of a Prophet, the Holiness of a Priest, the Power of a King," as having "omniscience that knows all our needs and dangers, and how and when to supply; and . . . omnipotence whereby he is able to do it," as well as being "in every respect the most suitable object of faith, being so all-sufficient, faithful, compassionate and loving."[106] John Cotton labelled Christ the "Redeemer," the "King, Priest, and Prophet; and all these things he received from the hand of the Father, Col. 1.19 for it pleased the Father that in him should all fulness dwell."[107] Christ was called "our peace," the "author of peace" and "the great King that creates peace . . . hence called the prince of peace."[108] Jonathan Mitchel enumerated among Christ's attributes his "glory, excellency, worth, sweetnesse, amiablenesse" and stated that "the Lord Jesus Christ our redeemer is full of grace and truth."[109] John Eliot asserted that "Christ . . . hath all power."[110]

The Puritan clergy's belief in the sinless perfection of Christ was an especially significant evidence of deity inasmuch as they were exceed-

103. Increase Mather, sermon of Apr. 2, 1686, *Substance of Sermons*, Huntington Library MS, p. 171.

104. Increase Mather, *Mystery of Christ*, pp. 22–23, 27, 29, 31, 50.

105. Ibid., pp. 44–45.

106. Cotton Mather, *Terribilia Dei*, p. 52; Increase Mather, *Mystery of Christ*, p. 127; John Allin, *The Lord Jesus, His Legacy of Peace, to Arm his Disciples Against Trouble and Fear*, in Burgess, ed., *Dedham Pulpit*, p. 7.

107. John Cotton, *A Treatise of the Covenant of Grace* (London, 1659), p. 28.

108. Flynt, sermon [1670s], Harvard University MS, pp. 5–6.

109. Jonathan Mitchel, sermon of Aug. 1651, Harvard University MS, p. 15; sermon of May 1, 1653, Massachusetts Historical Society MS, n.p.

110. John Eliot, *Communion of Churches* (Cambridge, 1665), p. 4.

ingly conscious of sin and the impossibility of earthly perfection in themselves and everyone else. Nathaniel Gookin, in a sermon in 1687, explained that "there is no man that sinneth not" and made it clear that "when it is said there is no man that sinneth not ye man Christ Jesus is to be excluded . . . ye man Christ Jesus never sined."[111] Increase Mather left no room for doubt about the absolute impeccability of Christ's life and his ability to obey the precepts contained in the Old Testament. "The man christ Jesus," affirmed Mather, "was Righteous to ye utmost extent of ye Law of Righteousness. . . . He never transgressed ye Law of god in any particular in any degree."[112] John Cotton stated that Christ was called "the Lamb" in Scripture because of his innocence.[113] Christ's sinless life was theologically important to the Puritan clergy because of the belief that only a perfect sacrifice could expiate sin. According to Cotton Mather, "our Lord JESUS CHRIST, who Knew no Sin, hath been made a Sacrifice; a Real, Proper, Expiatory Sacrifice to God, for our Sin. . . . Christ never was a Sinner; If He had been a Sinner He could not have been a Saviour."[114]

Another of Christ's attributes which gave credence to his goodness and deity was the love he displayed in his life and death on behalf of mankind. Only God was capable of forgiving sins, and only God, in the person of Christ, possessed the degree of love necessary to carry out the plan of salvation which called for the ultimate sacrifice of death and the bearing of the sins of the world. The doctrine John Norton emphasized to his congregation on May 2, 1657 was precisely this—"That Christ out of the aboundance of his Love in way of satisfaction of divine Justice gave up himselfe to suffer the punishment due to his redeemed." In his sermon the week before, Norton had urged his hearers to accept the fact that in love "Christ gave himselfe for us" and that such love "constrayneth us" to godly living.[115] Nathaniel Gookin impressed upon his flock the "matchless & unspeakable Love that is in the heart of Christ."[116] Christ proved his divine love for mankind in that he "did voluntarily bear for us the reproaches, cruel mockings, derisions, scoffs, and despisings of the

111. Nathaniel Gookin, sermon [June 1687], *Sermon Notes, 1687,* Harvard University MS, p. 117.

112. Increase Mather, sermon of Apr. 2, 1686, *Substance of Sermons,* Huntington Library MS, p. 125.

113. Cotton, *Saints Support & Comfort,* p. 43.

114. Cotton Mather, *A Present from a Farr Countrey* (Boston, 1698), pp. 28, 32.

115. John Norton, sermons of Apr. 25, 1657, and May 2, 1657, Boston Public Library MS, n.p.

116. Nathaniel Gookin, sermon of Sept., 1687, *Sermon Notes, 1687,* Harvard University MS, p. 33.

People."[117] Urian Oakes comforted his congregation with the assurance that "Christ . . . loveth you a thousand times more than you can love him, and loved you above his own Life, and will love you to Eternity. . . ."[118] In the clergy's view, the love of Christ for mankind was unconditional. However, such love by no means meant that salvation was universal. Individual men and women had to respond personally in faith to Christ's love and enter the covenant of grace before this love would be of benefit to their souls.

The frequent sermon references to Christ and his perfect human existence are all the more understandable when it is considered that he was held up as the model for the saints to emulate. The Bible was the Puritans' guide for living, and Christ was at the heart of the guidebook. He was sent not only to be mankind's Savior from sin, but also to transform those who believed into his likeness.[119] Christ demonstrated through his sinless earthly life the high potential in human nature, if sin only could be eliminated. "The human Nature of Jesus Christ," stated Increase Mather, "is of all created Objects the most excellent and glorious." "Furthermore," he maintained, "the Son of God has dignified human nature, and therefore for any to abuse or abase it, must needs be an horrid thing. This sheweth us how great an evil it is to wrong any man."[120] John Eliot saw one of the purposes of Christ's rejection by the Jews and his sufferings as being "to set us a Copy and pattern of patience, that we might learn of him how to carry our selves under such injuries."[121] To know the ways of Christ was beneficial, according to Cotton Mather, because it "will fill us with a blessed variety of other knowledge. . . . He [Christ] has been a compleat copy and a perfect Pattern for us; and His Call unto us is, Look on me and do likewise." "Let us Tread in the Steps of the Lord Jesus Christ," Mather exhorted.[122] Christ was for the Puritan saints "a leader to go before them as their Prince and Captain, and a Commander to give them Laws and Rules for their obedience."[123]

Christ was of prime importance to Puritan theology not only because of who he was, but also because of what he had done in the past, what he was presently doing on behalf of the saints, and what he

117. Eliot, *Harmony of the Gospels*, p. 53.
118. Urian Oakes, *The Soveraign Efficacy of Divine Providence* (Boston, 1682), p. 26.
119. Cotton, *Way of Life*, p. 3.
120. Increase Mather, *Mystery of Christ*, pp. 184, 112.
121. Eliot, *Harmony of the Gospels*, p. 53.
122. Cotton Mather, *Addresses to Old Men, and Young Men, and Little Children* (Boston, 1690), pp. 9–10; "The Walk of Holy and Happy Men," in *Early Piety*, p. 18.
123. Belcher, *Worst Enemy Conquered*, p. 21.

would do in the future according to the Word. The creation of the world and all it contains was attributed to Christ. His work in guiding the authors of Scripture was often recited. His ability to perform miracles while on earth was seen as a significant evidence of his divine power.[124] Among the miracles of Christ recorded in the Word, the greatest was "the Resurrection of our dear Jesus from the Dead," which served as "an Incontestable Demonstration, That this His Religion, must be the way of Truth, and the Truth of God."[125]

The living Christ was credited with the performance of various functions on behalf of the saints including headship of the church (see chapter 6). Christ was portrayed, with biblical support, as currently seated "at the right hand of God . . . in a state of glory next to the glory of God himself."[126] In this position of power and authority, Christ exercised "all Soveraign & Supreme Power of Government" and it was through him that "all the Changes of this World, are Ordered and Managed."[127] The Puritan saint could rest assured that "the affairs of providence are in the hands of Christ. . . . He has a perfect understanding of all affairs and transactions upon the earth."[128]

The believer in Christ was furthermore blessed by experiencing "peace within us" because of Christ's "pardon of our sin . . . it is ye peace which passeth all understanding."[129] With Christ as the saints' "friend & advocate," they could experience "ever perfect peace." Christ was eager to "bestow rest upon all those that under the weight & burden of sin come to him in faith."[130] According to John Cotton, Christ was able to grant liberty from fear—the fear of enemies, sin, death, and hell.[131] Additionally, Christ served as the believers' high priest, offering prayers to God the Father on their behalf.[132] He was depicted as the saints' "Blessed Helper,"[133] the only one "that is able to help ye when all thinges faile. . . ."[134]

124. Increase Mather, *Mystery of Christ*, pp. 66, 68.

125. Cotton Mather, *A Pastoral Letter to the English Captives in Africa* (Boston, 1698), p. 6.

126. Norton, *A Brief Catechism Containing the Doctrine of Godliness* (Cambridge, 1660), p. 10.

127. Richard Mather, *An Answer to Two Questions*, p. 9; Cotton Mather, *Observanda* (Boston, 1695), p. 12.

128. Increase Mather, *The Doctrine of Divine Providence Opened and Applyed* (Boston, 1684), pp. 3, 6.

129. James Allen, sermon of May 1, 1690, *Sermon Notes, Apr. 24–Aug. 13, 1690*, p. 37.

130. Flynt, sermon [1670s], Harvard University MS, pp. 313, 229.

131. Cotton, *Christ the Fountaine*, p. 65.

132. Cotton Mather, sermon of May 25, 1687, Harvard University MS, p. 90.

133. [Cotton Mather], *The Bostonian Ebenezer* (Boston, 1698), p. 13.

134. Jonathan Mitchel, sermon of Oct., 1651, Harvard University MS, p. 79.

The Lord Jesus Christ was believed to be especially helpful at the time of the believer's death. The fact that at the expiration of life "Christ will receive our Souls unto Himself" should be, according to John Norton, a great consolation for the sufferings of this life. Thereafter, the departed saint would enjoy "the presence of Jesus [which] is the place of blessedness"[135] and would throughout eternity experience "glory in the world to come" where Christ's "face shall be seen, and his company enjoyed by the Saints in Heaven. . . ."[136]

A Call for Commitment to Christ

In light of Christ's divine authority and majesty and his work on behalf of the elect, the Puritan clergy maintained that a response was called for on the part of the saints beyond a mere mental assent to biblical accounts of his life. The saints were exhorted to "give up our selves to Christ, and to him alone, utterly renouncing our interest and trust in all other things . . . cleave unto him with full purpose of heart, to be for him, and for no other."[137] The end of civil government "should be to exalt Christ," according to John Davenport.[138] Unfortunately, in the eyes of James Allen, many had forgotten this objective and "will not yield professed obedience unto ye Lord Jesus Christ, this was ye Errand into this willderness; man forgott this Errand."[139] The faithful were urged to recognize Christ's matchless worth and to acknowledge that he is "the most precious thing imageinable" and "precious unto every true believer."[140] John Cotton on many occasions emphasized the supreme importance of Christ above all that the world had to offer: "What is it for a man to have a good wife, or a good husband, or beautiful children? What if he had rich kindred and acquaintance? What if he had all the world, and have not Christ, he hath no life."[141]

The clergy preached that dependence on Christ should be at the center of the saints' existence and affections. To have Christ was to have everything; all else was "losse, and drosse, and dung" when

---

135. John Norton, *Three Choice and Profitable Sermons* (Cambridge, 1664), pp. 18, 23; Cotton Mather, *The Thoughts of a Dying Man* (Boston, 1697), p. 19.

136. Mitchel, *Discourse of the Glory*, pp. 4, 27.

137. Samuel Willard, *The Child's Portion* (Boston, 1684), p. 13.

138. John Davenport, *A Sermon Preach'd at the Election of the Governour, at Boston in New England, May 19, 1669* (Cambridge, 1670), p. 10.

139. James Allen, sermon of May 1, 1690, *Sermon Notes, Apr. 24 – Aug. 13, 1690*, Harvard University MS, p. 43.

140. Cotton Mather, *Thoughts of a Dying Man*, p. 17.

141. Cotton, *Christ the Fountaine*, p. 172.

compared to him.[142] John Allin asked, "Can you lean and stay upon him alone, and say, he is my Rock, my only Refuge? Have you chosen him as your portion? your all in all? Are all things dung and dross in comparison of him? Can you suffer the loss of all for him? This is a true leaning upon Christ as your Beloved."[143] God would reward submission to Christ's authority by making the saints' relationship with Christ such that "no Delights in this world" could compare to "what are in an entire Resignation of ourselves, and Lives, and all to ye will and service of Jesus Christ. The man that does this is half in heaven."[144] Finally, those who believed and were cleaving to Christ for salvation ought to be "in a constant or continual readinesse to meet Christ." In light of the secure future of the believer in Christ, the saint should be "ready to welcome Death."[145]

It is apparent that the seventeenth-century Puritan clergy gave Christ the central place in their theological system. He was at the core of their faith—the only way for man to bridge the gap that sin had created between God and humankind. Christ was the mediator, the God-man, the sacrifice for sin, and he was portrayed as alive and active, not merely a historical personage. Miller made little distinction in the triune roles of the Puritan's God—Father, Son, and Holy Spirit—dealing more with God as a single force or concept than as a personality. By distinguishing among the three persons of the Trinity and emphasizing Christ the Son, the Puritan ministry related to a personal God, one who had not only created humanity but had experienced humanity. The later Unitarian Churches of New England, while claiming direct descent from the Puritan Congregational Churches of the seventeenth century, would no doubt have been thoroughly repudiated by the seventeenth-century ministry for their rejection of the Trinity and Christ as God in the flesh. By ignoring or minimizing the role of Christ in Puritan theology, Miller and other scholars of Puritan intellectual history have missed a key concept. The Puritan clergy were not committed merely to a creed. They were committed to a person whom they perceived to be the living Son of God, whom they believed could be known through the revelation of the Scriptures, that Word from God that gave the human race a dismally accurate view of itself, and gave knowledge of the remedy provided by Christ.

142. Ibid., p. 22.
143. Allin, *Legacy of Peace*, p. 12.
144. Joshua Moodey, sermon of Mar., 1686, *Substance of Sermons*, Huntington Library MS, p. 108.
145. Shepard, *Parable of Ten Virgins*, p. 40.

5

Theology
The Covenant, the Pursuit of Holiness, and the Coming Kingdom

The Puritans of New England were convinced that God was dealing with them as a special, chosen people, just as he had dealt with Israel in the days of the Old Testament. Since the coming of Christ the way of salvation had been made plain and the Puritans recognized that they differed from the Jews—they were no longer subject to the law of Moses. Yet, the Puritans retained a link with the past and maintained a hope for the future through the same kind of agreement (the covenant) which God had established with the Jews. The covenant was viewed as a formal contract or promise, with legal validity, between God and man. New England theology was given practical application through means of this covenant idea, a concept with Old Testament roots, which was full of social as well as spiritual implications. Puritan biblical interpretation conceived of this covenant between God and his faithful as having two dimensions, an outer covenant of works and an inner covenant of grace.

The Covenant of Works

The covenant of works, sometimes referred to as the external covenant, necessitated that humankind follow exactly the laws of God in order both for God to bless the human race and for believers to enjoy fellowship with God. It was this covenant that God set before Adam and which Adam violated through his disobedience, thus tainting all of humanity. Failure to comply with this aspect of the covenant (and everyone did fail sooner or later) resulted in divine wrath and eventual damnation.

But in a less cosmic sense, the covenant of works had a very practical application in the towns, churches, and families of Puritan New England. It was understood that the community as a whole prospered or suffered at the hand of God in correlation with how faithfully the populace fulfilled the covenant, a voluntary agreement written up by towns and churches based on biblical commands and exhortations. The covenant as it related to the community was an external covenant strictly of works; if the right deeds were performed, blessings or at least the absence of punishment could be anticipated. Both towns and churches in New England were organized by means of covenants, voluntary agreements outlining goals and promises of those entering into the community at hand. Indeed, the Massachusetts Bay Colony was seen as a covenanted society in its entirety, while being composed of smaller covenanted units (families, churches, and towns),[1] although it took a few years for this community and "national" covenant concept to be fully developed and articulated. The external covenant had more social value than spiritual value—it served as a cohesive force in maintaining law and order and a sense of community but it did not guarantee salvation for the soul. This aspect of the covenant enhanced a sense of mission and "chosenness" which kept most folks in line, and when some dared to question God's special relationship with New England, as did Roger Williams, they found that life could be most unpleasant. Both Edmund S. Morgan and Stephen Foster have recognized the Puritan reliance on a voluntary, covenant relationship with God and each other as a form of "tribalism" which tightened the bonds of community even as it it excluded "undesirables."[2]

The covenant of works had its uses, but fallen humanity was unable to fulfill this covenant and earn salvation through its own merits. To remedy this situation, God in his mercy and love instituted a new covenant of grace, totally undeserved by mankind, whereby "God demands of him now not a deed but a belief, a simple faith in Christ the mediator." "If he can believe," Miller states, "he has fulfilled the compact; God then must redeem and glorify him." This concept was biblical rather than Puritanical in origin, yet the Puritans laid

1. Stephen Foster, *Their Solitary Way: The Puritan Social Ethic in the First Century of Settlement in New England* (New Haven, 1971), p. 57.

2. See Edmund S. Morgan, *The Puritan Family* (New York, 1966), pp. 161–86; Foster, *Their Solitary Way*, p. 58.

such stress on the covenant that Miller called it "the marrow of Puritan Divinity."[3]

The Covenant of Grace

The Puritan clergy spoke often of the covenant and its dual aspects. It was "a double Covenant," Thomas Shepard explained, "1. External and outward: 2. Internall and inward."[4] Local church congregations were encouraged periodically to renew their covenants.[5] Such a renewal referred to the external community covenant only since the covenant of grace (personal salvation through faith), once entered, could never be broken since it was not dependent on human effort. According to Increase Mather, those who have experienced personal salvation "cannot fall totally and finally, yet they may be subject to partial apostacyes from God, and from his blessed wayes." While the community aspect of the covenant was a frequent theme in Puritan sermons, it did not receive as much emphasis as did personal salvation—the covenant of grace applied to individual souls. Individual salvation was recognized as more important than the external community covenant for it guaranteed forgiveness of sins and eternal life, rewards unattainable by works. Increase Mather pointed out to his congregation in 1680 that "they that are the Lords People in respect of a visible Covenant Interest only, may fall totally and finally."[6]

The importance of personal salvation was driven home repeatedly to New England's Puritan congregations by pastors who recognized that by no means had their entire flocks undergone true conversion. Christ's redemptive work was desperately needed since "all flesh is corrupt" and "all men by nature do need salvation."[7] "We are all by nature children of wrath and Enemies [of God]," according to William Adams, "but they who are gotten into Christ they are thereby reconciled, Col. 1.21,22."[8]

The plan of salvation through Christ, or the covenant of grace, was seen by the Puritan clergy as being at the core of the Scriptures and was the principal ministry of Christ to mankind. It was a plan upon which God the Father and Christ the Son had agreed before the world

3. Perry Miller, "The Marrow of Puritan Divinity," *Publications of the Colonial Society of Massachusetts* 32, pp. 258 n., 260–61.

4. Shepard, *Church Membership of Children*, p. 1.

5. For a good example of this type of sermon, see Increase Mather, *Returning unto God the great concernment of a Covenant People* (Boston, 1680).

6. Ibid., pp. 2–3.

7. Cotton, *Christ the Fountaine*, p. 168; William Brattle, sermon of July 30, 1699, *Sermon Notes*, Harvard University MS, n.p.

8. Adams, *Pouring out of the Spirit*, p. 38.

was even formed.[9] "It was the great businesse upon which Jesus Christ came into the world," asserted Josiah Flynt, "too seeke up, & save lost sinners: this was the verye design upon which he assumed our humanity: the cause why the son of God became the son of man."[10] Tracing God's plan of salvation back to the patriarchs, John Cotton preached that "in the Covenant which God made with Abraham, God gave himself to be a God to him and his seed; and received Abraham and his seed to be a people unto himself; and the chiefest of this seed, the Lord Jesus Christ, he took to be the Mediator or Surety of this Covenant between them both."[11] Cotton Mather reminded his hearers that God the Father deals with man through Christ—that "All the Mercy of God unto us comes thro' the Hand of the Lord JESUS CHRIST, the God man, and the Mediator between God and Man."[12] Josiah Flynt urged his congregation to "Fly under the wings of Christ, hee is the one Mediator and there is no other, believe in him. . . ."[13]

When it came to the way of salvation, the Puritan clergy were adamant—there was only one way, and that was through Christ. The Puritans followed in the Reformers' belief that there was absolutely no other way to find forgiveness of sins and favor with God. "It only is the Lord Jesus that can give eternall life," asserted John Cotton. "Nay Heaven and earth cannot save thee without Christ. None but Christ can deliver from the Wrath to come," agreed Increase Mather.[14] Christ was referred to as the symbolic "door" leading to salvation and eternal life, and Christ himself was quoted from the Word as saying, in John 14:6, "I am the Way; no man comes unto the Father but by me."[15]

The details of God's redemptive covenant of grace through Christ were spelled out in numerous sermons in order that the role of Christ and the proper response of the unregenerate heart would be clearly understood. The death of Christ was given considerable emphasis by the clergy because this was seen as the central act in the plan of salvation whereby the sins of men were laid on Christ the Son of God. It was "by his death he wrought out glorious redemption for his elect . . . he by his death obtained victory over ye great enemy Satan." Christ's death was necessary because "nothing less could satisfy for our sins

---

9. Increase Mather, *Mystery of Christ*, p. 6.

10. Flynt, sermon [1670s], Harvard University MS, p. 178.

11. Cotton, *Covenant of Grace*, p. 3.

12. Cotton Mather, *The Christian Thank-Offering* (Boston, 1696), pp. 7–8.

13. Flynt, sermon [1670s], Harvard University MS, p. 164.

14. Cotton, *Christ the Fountaine*, p. 5; Increase Mather, *Greatest Sinners*, p. 32.

15. Cotton Mather, *Work Upon the Ark* (Boston, 1689), p. 4; Cotton, *Saints Support & Comfort*, p. 4; Cotton Mather, *The Day*, p. 14.

than death, even the death of him who was god as well as man."
Christ, by sacrificing his own life, fully met the requirements of the
covenant of grace. All that was required of humankind was belief—
saving faith. Christ's death, because of his virtuous and sinless life,
"has paid ye debt of all ye elect of god. . . ."[16] The Old Testament
blood sacrifices were seen as foreshadowings of Christ, whose blood
was "Sin Pardoning . . . Soul-Purifying and Heart-softening blood."[17]
"Sin leaves a guilt upon ye soul and an horrid stain there," preached
Increase Mather, "that nothing in ye world can get out. . . . But ye
Blood of Christ will fetch it out, yea, though ye soul be made by sin as
black as Hell."[18]

Through his death Christ "became Responsible for all our Sins; All
our Debts, He took upon Himself." That God would put his Son
through such torment for the sake of sinful man in order to "quench
His Burning Displeasure" against sin was, in the eyes of Cotton
Mather, a sign of the great "Goodness of God" toward the human
race.[19] John Eliot explained Christ's role on behalf of the elect in the
redemptive process as follows:

> Jesus Christ undertakes to perform for them and in their stead
> those two great works which they are never able to perform for them-
> selves. Jesus Christ undertakes as their surety to keep and fulfill the
> holy Law and covenant of works, to obtain from them the reward of
> justice, and also to suffer for them, and in their stead the penalty of
> the Law, which is, to dye, and thereby to satisfy the vindictive justice
> of God. . . . The sufferings of Jesus Christ fully satisfied vindictive
> justice, and the active obedience of Jesus Christ did fully satisfie re-
> warding justice, every act of Jesus Christ was pure, perfect and meri-
> torious, God saith, in him I am well pleased Mat. 3.17.[20]

It is interesting to note the relative scarcity in Puritan preaching of
references to the resurrection of Christ, a central doctrine of the faith.
In Puritan sermons Christ was portrayed as alive and active on behalf
of the saints. In Puritan theology the atoning death of Christ was
of utmost significance to the plan of salvation; since Christ was God,

16. Nathaniel Gookin, sermon of May 29, 1687, *Sermon Notes, 1687,* Harvard
University MS, pp. 100, 103, 124.

17. Cotton Mather, *Speedy Repentance Urged* (Boston, 1690), p. 75.

18. Increase Mather, sermon [1686], *Substance of Sermons,* Huntington
Library MS, p. 49.

19. Cotton Mather, *Present from a Farr Countrey,* pp. 32, 45.

20. Eliot, *Harmony of the Gospels,* pp. 1, 3.

his resurrection was expected as a "natural" ending to his earthly ministry.[21]

The work of Christ in the plan of salvation was completed, but it remained for men to hear the gospel message and to respond to it. "The Lord Jesus Christ in His Gospel graciously and earnestly Inviteth all the Children of men to LOOK unto Him by Faith upon Him for SALVATION," declared Cotton Mather.[22] The third person of the Trinity, the Holy Spirit, was also involved in attracting men to Christ, according to John Cotton.[23] John Norton saw Christ calling men to salvation both through "the ministry of the word and efficacy of the spirit" and bringing a message of salvation which "quickens and satisfies the hungry soull of a sinner."[24] The result for those who believed was to turn sinners into saints and to experience "spiritual freedom" instead of "spiritual bondage."[25] The soul who entered into the covenant of grace became a "son [of God] by Christ," and was in the position of knowing that "God forgives all his Transgressions, and accepts him as righteous, imputing the Righteousness of Jesus Christ into him."[26] Finally, every sinner believing in Christ, according to Thomas Shepard, is "instantly transformed into a most blessed and happy Estate John 5.24."[27]

Salvation provided blessings and riches in the life to come, if not in the present. It was worth more, Cotton Mather asserted, than "Thousands of rums and ten Thousands of Rivers of Oyl."[28] Another important factor was the judgment which awaits those who reject Christ. Increase Mather warned the unregenerate that "thou wilt lose thy soul for ever if thou dost not come to Christ." In another sermon Mather warned of the shortness of life and the certainty of death and stressed the eternal importance of salvation. It was necessary, he maintained, to examine oneself in order to ascertain "Am I a true Believer, yea or no? Am I a Regenerate Person . . . it is not material to a mans Salvation whether he be a Learned or an Unlearned man, but

---

21. An important statement of the doctrine of the resurrection of Christ is found in Norton, *Brief Catechism*, p. 10.

22. Cotton Mather, *Call of the Gospel Applyed unto All men in general and unto a Condemned Malefactor in particular* (Boston, 1686), p. 5.

23. Cotton, *Way of Life*, p. 15.

24. John Norton, sermon of Jan. 17, 1658, Boston Public Library MS, n.p.

25. Samuel Willard, sermon of 1679, Massachusetts Historical Society MS, n.p.

26. Jonathan Mitchel, sermon notes MS, p. 120; Cotton Mather, *Call of the Gospel*, p. 13.

27. Shepard, *Sound Believer*, p. 204.

28. Cotton Mather, *Call of the Gospel*, p. 41.

whether he is in Christ and a new Creature."[29] "Without Regeneration," Cotton Mather declared, "men cannot enjoy the Kingdom of God." The prospect of the judgment of the unconverted should create fear in them, he maintained, and it was his opinion that "without the use of some Fear, no Real Religion can be exercised." The proper fear of God, Mather asserted, could "carry us to the God, who is therein Our Fear: To Fear God is to Choose Him, to Love Him, to Trust Him, to Seek Him, and to Draw Near unto Him."[30]

Fear of damnation was one factor used by the Puritan clergy to motivate men to seek participation in the covenant of salvation. Another was God's goodness and love. God's wrath and mercy could both be used to bring men to salvation. According to Nathaniel Gookin, "In the dispensations of god towards sinful men, there are two things which he uses to bring them to repentance, Judgments and mercy. . . . He will break them with ye hammer of affliction, and he will draw them by his love."[31] The greatest thing celebrated in the Scriptures, according to Samuel Willard, was "the unparalleled and Incomprehensible Love of God to Sinful Man, displayed in the wonderful Affair of his Redemption and Salvation."[32] According to Thomas Shepard, love was the strongest force which drew men to salvation. "Let a man believe in Christ, and accept the offer of Christ when he can," Shepard urged, "but he can never do it, untill . . . drawn to the Lord Jesus; and that not violently only by terrour, but by stronger cords, even the cords of Love. . . ."[33] It was also pointed out that the Puritans had a God "that delights in mercy. Not only can he be merciful, but it is that in which he taketh great pleasure."[34]

One further motivation for frequent preaching about salvation was a fervent belief that the time for making such a life-and-death decision was limited. The brevity of life was often mentioned, and it was further believed that individuals reached a point in their lives where their own sinfulness and stubborn refusal to come to Christ in faith made salvation increasingly unlikely and eventually impossible. John Allin warned the resisters of grace in his congregation to "think oft of

29. Increase Mather, *Greatest Sinners*, p. 19; *A Discourse Concerning the Uncertainty of the Times of Men, and the Necessity of being Prepared for Sudden Changes and Death* (Boston, 1697), pp. 36–37.

30. Cotton Mather, *Unum Necessarium*, p. 5; *Terribilia Dei*, pp. 1, 4.

31. Nathaniel Gookin, sermon of July 10, 1690, *Sermon Notes, Apr. 24–Aug. 13, 1690*, Harvard University MS, pp. 65–66.

32. Samuel Willard, *The Doctrine of the Covenant of Redemption* (Boston, 1693), p. 1.

33. Shepard, *Parable of Ten Virgins*, p. 184.

34. Samuel Willard, *Spiritual Desertions Discovered and Remedied* (Boston, 1699), p. 142.

this scripture [John 3:16] and consider of the means of grace God hath so long afforded you, and how oft he hath been calling upon you, and knocking at the door of your hearts. Oh, take the season while it lasts! Oh, to-day! today! . . . harden not your hearts, lest God swear in his wrath that ye shall never enter into his rest."[35]

The Word and the Spirit in the Salvation Process

The clergy, in light of the importance given to salvation in the Word and in their own thinking, strove to acquaint their congregations with the details of the conversion experience. According to Josiah Flynt, this matter of "how a child of wrath may be saved" was the "greatest question in the world." The necessary ingredients and steps in the process of salvation were set forth, but members of the clergy did not always completely agree.

The importance of the Scriptures in the process of salvation was, however, acknowledged without question. God in his sovereignty had chosen the preaching of the Word as a major means of salvation. Christ was portrayed as most accessible to sinners during the preaching of his Word. As the clergy preached the Word, the converted sinner had "a blessed opportunity to find him [Christ], and to enjoy him for ever."[36] John Cotton asserted that salvation is usually preceded "by a diligent hearing [of] the Word of God" and that the Spirit of God works on the heart of the sinner "by the breath of his Word." Cotton's advice to those desirous of experiencing salvation was to "First hearken to the Word of God." His second plea was to "Apply the word unto your hearts . . . lay your own estate to the word." The effectiveness of God's Word was not doubted by Cotton, who maintained further that "whatever is expounded to them [the unregenerate] from this Word, may be effectual to bring them on to salvation."[37] Christ "inviteth and calls Sinners to come to him by his written Word, the holy Scriptures . . . ," declared Increase Mather.[38]

Many of the clergy acknowleged in their sermons that, even though the message of the Word was quick and powerful, it was insufficient in itself to bring a person to salvation. The involvement of the Holy Spirit was deemed necessary to make the Word clear and applicable and to interact with the unregenerate soul to bring about a true conversion. Thus the Word and the Spirit were partners in wooing the unregenerate into a state of grace. It was "the power of his Word and

35. Allin, *Legacy of Peace,* in Burgess, ed., *Dedham Pulpit,* p. 13.
36. Increase Mather, *Power of Godliness,* p. 43.
37. Cotton, *Way of Life,* pp. 12, 184–85; *Christ the Fountaine,* p. 187.
38. Increase Mather, *Greatest Sinners,* p. 16.

Spirit" which God employed to "bring us to Christ," John Cotton stated. "What is faith?" he asked. "It is a work of God's Almighty Quickening Power wrought by the Ministry of the Word and Spirit of God. . . ."[39] When it came to the act of conversion, Richard Mather declared that "the word of it self can not do it, without the work of god himself by his spirit."[40] John Norton flatly declared that without the influence of the Spirit, men are not brought to the point of "conviction unto christ."[41] Josiah Flynt described to his congregation the interaction of the Word and the Spirit: "The spirit goes not without the word and ordinances . . . where-ever hee comes hee brings the word along with him, & accompanies it home to the soule . . . he rides upon the word of truth, this is the instrument by which he divides sinners from their sins."[42] William Adams saw the Holy Spirit as an active force in the process of salvation, being sent by God "to convince, awaken, convert, regenerate, and sanctify sinners . . . to open their eyes, to turn them from darkness to light and from the power of Satan unto God."[43] Thomas Shepard preached that without the illumination of the mind by God's Spirit the Word would be of no value, "no more than a Book written in the fairest hand or print, can be seen without light to see it by."[44] John Cotton perhaps most eloquently expressed the interdependence of the Word and the Spirit in bringing men to salvation: "But how is it, or why doth God make his Word so piercing? By ordaining the breath of the word, to be the breath of the Spirit . . . which sets an edge upon it, so as they shall sinke deeply; It is the Spirit of God that gives it a point, and this God hath vouchsafed to his whole word. . . ."[45]

The Conversion Experience

Many of the clergy identified the specific ingredients and procedures which they believed would culminate in conversion. Although various ministers portrayed the steps to salvation in somewhat differing ways, their descriptions tend to complement rather than contradict one another. There were certain key ingredients that all Puritan

39. Cotton, *Milk for Babes*, p. 7; *A Treatise of Faith* [Boston, 1713], p. 3.
40. Richard Mather, *The Summe of Certain Sermons Upon Genes: 15.6* (Cambridge, 1652), p. 4.
41. John Norton, sermon of June 30, 1657, Boston Public Library MS, n.p.
42. Flynt, sermon [1670s], Harvard University MS, p. 166.
43. William Adams, sermon of Sept. 21, 1678, in Burgess, ed., *Dedham Pulpit*, p. 47.
44. Shepard, *Parable of Ten Virgins*, p. 141.
45. Cotton, *Way of Life*, p. 163.

clergy accepted as necessary for salvation, although the degree of emphasis was likely to vary from minister to minister.

One such ingredient was repentance. Repentance involved "a turning of the whole man from sin unto God . . . a leaving off the old wayes of sin to take up a new life of holiness."[46] In calling men to repent, God was urging them to "lay aside all wicked imaginations and sinnefull lusts. . . ."[47] According to Increase Mather, "Repentence is nothing else but a Turning from all Sin unto God. It implyeth a change of the whole man. The mind is renewed." The clergy's emphasis on internalized belief is demonstrated as Mather explained, "that turning from sin which the Word of God requireth, is to be both External and Internal. . . . When a mans heart within him is turned and set against sin, then he has truly experienced that conversion which the Word of God requireth."[48]

Repentance involved a certain agonizing of the spirit. Josiah Flynt portrayed the development of saving faith in the life of an unregenerate soul as follows:

> The sinner finds and feels himselfe a poor, miserable, undone creature. . . . He finds himself a law breaker. . . . He feels the wrath of God resting on him for sin. . . . This makes his sin bitter to him. . . . The poor forlorn wretch can no longer ly still in this condition. . . . He sees that there is an absolute necessity of his perishing where he is. . . . Now he would faine do something, if he knew what, to free himselfe from this distresse. . . . He sees the emptinesse of the world and all things in it. . . . He sees the insufficiencye of his one [own] endeavors. . . . Now is the Lord Jesus Christ set before the soule as a compleat and alsufficient savior, in the discoveryes of the Gospell he is presented, and the spirit of god opens his eyes to discover him. . . . Now the soule enters into Christ, and takes possession of him.[49]

The Role of Faith and Works in Salvation

Faith was a key ingredient in the Puritan theology of salvation which has been unfortunately minimized by Miller and others who have portrayed the Puritans as supremely reasonable and logical. Miller admired the Puritans for what he perceived as the finely tuned logic of their intellectual system. The Puritan clergy were indeed men of reason, but they were first and foremost men of faith. From the perspective of the ministry, salvation without faith was an impossibility.

46. Willard, *Mercy Magnified*, p. 157.
47. Cotton, *Saints Support & Comfort*, p. 69.
48. Increase Mather, *Returning unto God*, p. 6; *Greatest Sinners*, p. 43.
49. Flynt, sermon [1670s], Harvard University MS, pp. 204–6.

The Bible, central to the Puritan Way, was painstakingly translated into the previously unwritten language of Native Americans by John Eliot, although Puritan missionary zeal toward them was generally lacking. (By permission of the Houghton Library, Harvard University)

WUSKU
WUTTESTAMENTUM
NUL-LORDUMUN
JESUS CHRIST
Nuppoquohwussuaeneumun,

CAMBRIDGE:
Printed by *Samuel Green* and *Marmaduke Johnson*
MDCLXI.

Seal of the Massachusetts Bay Colony, from *The General Laws and Liberties of the Massachusetts Colony* (Cambridge, 1672). A Native American asks English-men to Christianize and civilize his people—an unlikely request. (Massachusetts Historical Society)

THE
HOLY BIBLE:
CONTAINING THE
OLD TESTAMENT
AND THE *NEW*.

Translated into the

INDIAN LANGUAGE,
AND
Ordered to be Printed by the *Commissioners of the United Colonies*
in *NEW-ENGLAND*,

At the Charge, and with the Consent of the

CORPORATION IN *ENGLAND*
For the *Propagation of the Gospel amongst the* Indians
in New-England.

CAMBRIDGE:
Printed by *Samuel Green* and *Marmaduke Johnson*.
MDCLXIII.

John Winthrop, founding governor of the Massachusetts Bay Colony (ca. 1629). (Courtesy, American Antiquarian Society)

Reverend Increase Mather, painted by Jan van der Spriett in 1688. Puritan ministers were expected to be scholars, yet preach the Word in "plain style" easily understood by their congregations. (Massachusetts Historical Society)

BOSTON'S FIRST TOWN-HOUSE
1657~1711

Drawn from the Original
Specifications for
Thomas Joy and Bartholomew Barnard
1657

Charles A. Lawrence – 1930

The Boston Town House, center of city government. Erected in 1657, the building is no longer extant. (Courtesy of the Bostonian Society)

This portrait of Elizabeth Paddy Wensley, painted between 1670 and 1680 in Boston, shows Puritan interest in fine clothing, considered acceptable as long as it befit one's station in life and did not detract from devotion to God. (Courtesy of The Pilgrim Society, Plymouth, Mass.)

The Parson Capen house in Topsfield, Mass., built in 1683. (Photo by the author)

A joined oak chair from Ipswich, Mass., made in the 1660s. Simplicity of life and Christian devotion did not preclude an appreciation for style. Material possessions, even fine ones, were not inherently evil as long as spiritual concerns had top priority. (Bowdoin College Museum of Art, Brunswick, Maine)

A joined cupboard made for Peter Woodbury of Beverly, Mass. (1680). (Courtesy, The Henry Francis du Pont Winterthur Museum)

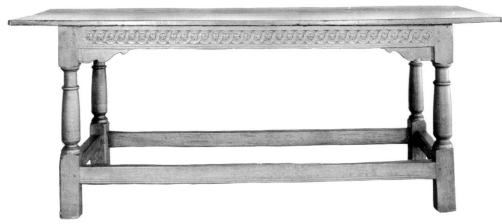

A joined oak table from Salisbury, Mass. (1660–1700). (Wadsworth Atheneum, Hartford. The Elizabeth B. Miles Collection)

A brightly colored turkey-work couch made in England (1690–1695) and transported to New England. (Courtesy of the Essex Institute, Salem, Mass.)

It was this subject of faith, coupled with works, however, that created some disagreement in Puritan clerical ranks. The relationship between faith and works in the process of salvation was a central issue in the antinomian controversy of 1637 (see chapter 13) and was frequently discussed during the seventeenth century.

Faith, defined as belief in and acceptance of God's promises in the Word, was mentioned nearly every time the subject of salvation was discussed in any detail. As vital as the Scriptures were to salvation, "the word preached profits not, when it is not mixed with faith in them that hear it," remarked Samuel Danforth.[50] Increase Mather declared that "Faith is that grace whereby a man doth receive jesus Christ as offered in ye gospel." Mather went on to say that "Faith and Repentance are the great duties required in the Gospel. This was the Scope and summe of all the Apostles preaching."[51] In order for Christ to "sustain you" and "carry you up to Eternal Glory," sinners must "cast your selves on him by Faith."[52] Furthermore, it was believed that the faith required for salvation went beyond anything that mere human wisdom and logic could explain. It was not that the Puritans' faith was unreasonable or illogical in their eyes, but that in certain aspects it transcended human reason and logic. Salvation was a divine and not a human concept: "Every believer is born of god not of man, not of flesh and blood," preached Jonathan Mitchel in 1652. "Faith is a supernaturall thinge. . . ."[53]

None of the clergy belittled the role of faith in salvation, but there were a few who also saw some role for human endeavor in the process of regeneration. This could take the form of preparation for salvation, or of actual good works. Some clerical division of opinion existed over these matters. Thomas Shepard, for example, stated the necessity of feeling "misery" for sin before grace could be received.[54] John Cotton, an outspoken critic of the belief that good works were necessary for salvation, nonetheless saw room for a degree of preparation which he based on Isaiah 40:3 ("Prepare ye the way of the Lord . . ."). Through the abasement and emptying of self, he maintained, "we are made fit for Christ to come into us." In an earlier treatise, however, Cotton had written, "Q: Are there any conditions or qualifications necessary before the soul can experience faith?" He answered negatively, his reason being "if there be any gracious conditions, or qualifications

50. Samuel Danforth, *A Brief Recognition of New England's Errand Into the Wilderness* (Cambridge, 1671), p. 15.

51. Increase Mather, sermon of May 23, 1686, *Substance of Sermons,* Huntington Library MS, p. 214; *Greatest Sinners*, p. 42.

52. Mitchel, *Discourse of the Glory*, p. 188.

53. Jonathan Mitchel, sermon of Jan., 1652, Harvard University MS, p. 138.

54. Shepard, *Sound Believer*, pp. 70ff.

wrought in us before union with Christ, then we may be in a state of grace and salvation before we be in Christ: but that cannot be: Acts 4.12."[55] In 1641 Cotton denounced as "Papist" the idea that "when men are converted, they are prepared for it, by some good fore-going works, some merit . . . what preparation is there in a blind man to see, or in an ignorant man to understand?"[56]

Over against John Cotton's view we find the ideas of Josiah Flynt, minister at Dorchester in the 1670s. Flynt hinted that he viewed works as important in the plan of salvation. To ascertain if one possessed "any grounded hopes of salvation," Flynt believed one must answer affirmatively the question, "Dost thou walke in the narrow way? dost thou lead a life of holinesse?" "Those that are true believers," he maintained, "are soe strict & carefull in the regulating, & ordering of their lives. . . . Heaven is not to be had without striving, God will not save us, without our owne endeavors. . . ."[57] Increase and Cotton Mather appear at times to come close to a "works" philosophy, but they qualified their remarks sufficiently to remain orthodox Calvinists. Increase Mather was convinced that "Where there is true christianity, there will be works of obedience. . . . There will be works of charity as well as of piety, according to ones ability, where there is fruit . . . so, if there bee not such things in a man, how is christ in him?"[58] According to Cotton Mather, "Tis a vanity in any man to Profess, that he has a True Faith in the Lord Jesus Christ, if his Faith be not Fruitful in those Good Works, which may Justify the mans Profession." He went on to state clearly, however, that "It is the Blood of Christ, and not our Good works, that must be of any value. . . . They that build their faith on Good works, Build on a Sandy Foundation."[59] John Davenport listed a mere profession of religion, godly parents, and the performance of all religious duties as unacceptable foundations upon which to build hope of salvation.[60] The futility of man trying to work for his own salvation was pointed out by Samuel Willard in a 1691 sermon in which he said, "man indeed is in himself without strength, he cannot serve God, his Moral Powers are enervated, and altogether disabled by Original sin. . . ." Five years earlier Willard had compiled over two hundred pages of sermon notes into a treatise called *A Brief* (?) *Discourse of Justification* in which he

55. Cotton, *Christ the Fountaine*, p. 41; *Gospel Conversion* (London, 1646), pp. 1–4.

56. Cotton, *Way of Life*, p. 182.

57. Flynt, sermon [1670s], Harvard University MS, pp. 222–23, 225.

58. Increase Mather, sermon of Apr. 4, 1686, *Substance of Sermons*, Huntington Library MS, p. 116.

59. Cotton Mather, *Faith at Work* (Boston, 1697), pp. 6, 20.

60. Davenport, *Gods Call*, p. 15.

endeavored to show that "Justification of a Sinner before God, flows not from his own legal righteousness, but from the Righteousness of Christ, freely imputed by God, and received by Faith."[61]

Benefits of Salvation

In addition to exhorting their congregations concerning the necessity of salvation, the clergy eagerly extolled the benefits of experiencing God's saving grace. One result of salvation, they maintained, was a dramatic transformation of the convert's old sinful nature, though not to sinless perfection. Here internalized Christian belief as opposed to mere externalized form was emphasized. Man was renewed from the inside out by the power of God. Thomas Shepard preached that by salvation "a man is morally made a new man, another man; All things are become new . . . he hath new thoughts, new opinions of things, new desires, new prayers and praises, new dispositions. . . ."[62] New attitudes were created, according to John Cotton, which included meekness, modesty, diligence, deadness to the world, and love for one's enemies. Furthermore, the saint experienced "a certain kind of inward joy, and comfort in the Lord" that the unconverted soul did not know.[63] Nathaniel Gookin was enthusiastic about the benefits he derived from his salvation; he enjoyed having his "understanding opened," "a sanctified heart," "pardon of sin," "reconciliation with God," "favour of the Lord," and "a state of immortality."[64] Urian Oakes was grateful that the saints were recipients of "the special love of God in his Son Jesus Christ. . . ."[65] Salvation brought "peace with God," the "inward peace of a good conscience," and peace with men—"especially the saints."[66] It was Jonathan Mitchel's belief that God's salvation enabled the saints to possess "full Joy . . . the Lord would have us not only sip, but take full draughts of the water of life."[67]

The Eternal Security of the Believer

One of the greatest benefits of salvation was the comfort and assurance of knowing that once true saving faith had been experienced, the

61. Samuel Willard, *Fig Trees Doom*, p. 49; *A Brief Discourse of Justification* (Boston, 1686), p. 6.

62. Shepard, *Sound Believer*, p. 235.

63. Cotton, *Christ the Fountaine*, pp. 111–20.

64. Nathaniel Gookin, sermon of May, 1687, *Sermon Notes, 1687*, Harvard University MS, p. 67.

65. Oakes, *Unconquerable Souldier*, p. 3.

66. Allin, *Legacy of Peace*, in Burgess, ed., *Dedham Pulpit*, pp. 17–18.

67. Mitchel, *Discourse of the Glory*, p. 208.

saint was eternally secure. Salvation did not come and go in Puritan theology; if once truly present, it remained forever. While this doctrine provided inner peace and security in an insecure and often hostile world, it did not cure nagging doubts experienced by some Puritans concerning the validity of their religious experience in the first place. At the same time, this doctrine tended to lessen the importance of Christian behavior and conformity among the community of saints.

The converted Puritan was eternally secure in his salvation because God had elected him for salvation. References to the sovereign selection by God of some for salvation (election) and some for damnation (reprobation) are scarce in seventeenth-century sermons. An initial reaction to this lack of references might be to doubt the strength of the Puritans' commitment to the Calvinist view of election—that only those predestined to enjoy salvation through Christ would be saved. However, it becomes clear upon closer examination of the sermons that election was an underlying assumption so basic that it did not require much attention. Furthermore, it would have been a discouragement to godly living and a destroyer of hope if the clergy had continually harped on the theme that if one were not of the elect, one's situation was hopeless regardless of the life one led. Nobody knew if those who had not yet undergone a conversion experience were among the elect, so the best approach was to urge them on to salvation in the hope that God had indeed chosen them "before the foundation of the world." This doctrine of election again points out that Puritan theology included elements that were accepted from the Bible by faith and were not clearly understandable to human reason.

Concerning the security of the believer, Thomas Shepard preached that "true saving Grace in the Hearts of Believers can never fail. John 4.14, Rom. 11.1." It was Shepard's opinion that those who did fall away and denounce the faith "never had Oyl in their Vessel, never had a dram of Grace in their heart, Thus, I John 2.19."[68] Josiah Flynt encouraged his flock with the message that "the Lord Jesus Christ will not disowne, nor desert, the lowest and weakest degrees of true faith, but will preserve and perfect them."[69] Richard Mather assured his hearers that "justification once obteyned, can not be lost. A man once justified shall never lose his justified estate, nor fall from it."[70] "Nothing can separate a Christian from the Love of God in Christ," preached Urian Oakes.[71] Nathaniel Gookin promised his congregation

68. Shepard, *Parable of Ten Virgins*, pp. 228, 232.
69. Flynt, sermon [1670s], Harvard University MS, p. 239.
70. Richard Mather, *Certain Sermons*, p. 7.
71. Oakes, *Unconquerable Souldier*, p. 2.

that "those that believe on him [Christ] shall never perish, why? because none is able to pluck them out of his hands."[72] John Cotton also left some very clear statements concerning his view of the security of the believer. In 1641 he wrote that "this spirit of Grace within thee will never leave till it hath brought thee to an estate of Glory." In a sermon published in 1645 Cotton promised the saints that God "will pardon us freely, he will heal us throughly; so that wee shall not perish, notwithstanding our corruption." In a volume published in 1650, he attacked those who doubted the security of the saints by emphasizing that true saints do not ultimately fall away into apostasy. Finally, in a sermon published posthumously in 1658, Cotton asserted that "if we have once given God the heart, in time hee will have all, and though hee meete with many skirmishes, yet hee will prevaile in the end." The conversion experience is validated when we confess faith in Christ with "heart and mouth" and once that is done, "Christ will never depart from you."[73]

Assurance of Salvation

Edmund S. Morgan has stated that when it came to being certain of one's salvation in Puritan New England, "in order to be sure one must be unsure."[74] However, a study of numerous sermons dealing with salvation indicates that the populace did not wish to be in doubt about a matter as important as their eternal destiny, and that the ministry repeatedly gave instructions to them on how to discern if one had truly experienced saving faith and conversion. By the time the clergy had finished, relatively little mystery remained concerning one's status with the Lord. To feel a sense of assurance about one's salvation "without the Word" to support it, however, was mere "false Comfort."[75] Furthermore, "true assurance can't be without Faith. . . ."[76] One of the many charges John Cotton leveled at Roman Catholics was their inability to be certain of salvation. It was a "Popish Doctrine" that said it was "impossible for a man to know

72. Gookin, sermon of 1687, *Sermon Notes, 1687*, Harvard University MS, p. 11.

73. Cotton, *Way of Life*, p. 26; *Covenant of Grace*, p. 17; *Holiness of Church Members*, p. 50; *Saints Support & Comfort*, pp. 6, 22.

74. Edmund S. Morgan, *Visible Saints: The History of a Puritan Idea* (Ithaca, N.Y., 1963), p. 70.

75. Cotton, *Several Questions of Serious and Necessary Consequence, Propounded by the Teaching Elders, Unto M. John Cotton of Boston in New England with His respective Answer to each Question* (London, 1647), p. 2.

76. Increase Mather, sermon of May 23, 1686, *Substance of Sermons*, Huntington Library MS, p. 213.

that he is in an estate of grace."[77] "It is the lazy Christian that usually lives without assurance," commented Jonathan Mitchel.[78]

One could know whether one possessed personal salvation, according to the clergy, from both negative and positive evidence. There were certain clear signs, stated Nathaniel Gookin, that if habitually evident demonstrated rather convincingly that one was not a recipient of salvation. These included disobedience, no fear or love of God, no desire to pray, and using "the name of God irreverently." In another sermon Gookin maintained "that for any person to be wholly without chastisements, is a sad sign, that whatsoever their profession is, yet they are not indeed ye sons of God."[79] According to Thomas Shepard, "When a man's affections grow out of the world, and there is no fear or sorrow . . . no Christ is there."[80]

Positive signs of the presence of salvation in one's life were more numerous. "Growth in grace" was a sign, according to Increase Mather, whereby one may "know his interest in Christ." Such spiritual growth involved "becoming more mortified to ye world" and being able to "bear Afflictions with Thankfulness."[81] In *Christ the Fountaine of Life*, John Cotton devoted a section to "signs of life"— the presence of salvation. Among these signs were "inward refreshment and satisfaction" because one's sins were forgiven, love for God, pliableness of spirit, being easy to please, acknowledging when one is wrong, and possessing "sweetness of life and speech." Cotton also stated that it was a sign of regeneration "when we love and respect those Christians whom we previously despised and who have wounded us." He went on to say that

> you shall not finde a more comfortable evidence of your good estate before God, than when you keepe afresh within you the love of your brethren, and find your hearts inwardly cleaving to every good duty, and be ready to doe and suffer anything for God; keepe this frame in you, and then feare not, you will have comfort in your way in the end.

The ultimate and yet simplest key to assurance of salvation was, according to Cotton, merely to answer the question, "do you receive him [Christ]?" in the affirmative. Cotton rejected an emotional expe-

77. Cotton, *Christ the Fountaine*, pp. 190, 235.
78. Mitchel, *Discourse of the Glory*, p. 207.
79. Gookin, sermons of Apr., 1687, *Sermon Notes, 1687*, Harvard University MS, pp. 27, 44.
80. Shepard, *Parable of Ten Virgins*, p. 208.
81. Increase Mather, sermon of Apr. 4, 1686, *Substance of Sermons*, Huntington Library MS, p. 118.

rience as necessary for salvation, but instead trusted the Bible's promise that if "your hearts have thus embraced Christ . . . then you have Christ, whether you see him, or feel him or no. . . ." Cotton even insisted that assurance of a saint's salvation "may be maintained to him, when the frame and course of his spirit is growne much degenerate, Isai. 63.16."[82] Josiah Flynt saw a love for the Word as a proof of regeneration[83] and Nathaniel Gookin believed that it was evidence of salvation if Christ was "precious unto your souls," and if "we find the working of his spirit in us . . . Leading us on & quickening us in the wayes of god. . . ."[84] Assurance of salvation was given further credence by the idea of the covenant of grace. God in his Word had made promises which he had committed himself to fulfill for those who truly had faith. Thomas Hooker warned against excessive reliance on emotion when it came to certainty of salvation. "A man's faith may be somewhat strong when his feeling is nothing at all," Hooker asserted. "Therefore away with your sense and feeling, and go to the promise."[85]

The Pursuit of Holiness

While salvation was the most critical theological concern in Puritan New England, the responsibilities of the faithful following conversion were emphasized as well. The Puritans recognized that the life of a saint was not an easy one; sin lurked in every shadow, and the old nature of the best of saints could easily be revived and run amuck. The ministry reminded believers that a successful Christian life did not come without effort; indeed, it was "hard to believe in Christ . . . hard to desire Christ, and nothing but Christ; hard to follow Christ all the day long."[86] The Puritan saint was expected to live life in the pursuit of holiness.

Since believers were, as the Word expressed it, the "temple of God,"[87] the clergy frequently exhorted them to behave accordingly. The duties of a saintly life were ideally to be performed out of love

82. Cotton, *Christ the Fountaine*, pp. 101, 158–59, 39, 45; *Several Questions*, p. 3.

83. Flynt, sermon [1670s], Harvard University MS, p. 109.

84. Gookin, sermon of Mar. 6, 1687, *Sermon Notes, 1687*, Harvard University MS, pp. 7, 9.

85. Quoted in Norman Pettit, "Hooker's Doctrine of Assurance: A Critical Phase in New England Spiritual Thought," *New England Quarterly* (Dec. 1974): 519. This article also contains a good analysis of the differences between Cotton and Hooker over the order in the process of salvation.

86. Shepard, *Sincere Convert*, p. 117.

87. Cotton, *Holiness of Church Members* [quoted from 2 Cor. 6:16], p. 48.

and gratitude to God, rather than in fear, although the chastisement of the Lord could be expected in the lives of his erring people. The standard for Christian behavior and attitudes was, of course, the Bible, or more specifically the Bible as interpreted by the clergy within their cultural context. Through a knowledge of the Bible and personal discipline, New England's saints were expected to live "the life of sanctification" which Thomas Shepard defined as a life renewed "unto the image of God, or of God in Christ"—a life exercising "the habits of holiness."[88] Puritan Christians were urged to "give up our selves" to Christ and to realize that they were made by and for Christ.[89] To live in a holy manner, John Norton preached to his flock, "you must denie your selves, and you must doe it dayly & take up your cross."[90] "Faith and Love will make a Christian deny himself," preached Increase Mather in 1697, "that so he may promote the Interest of Christ, and the good of his People."[91]

Self-denial actually resulted in self-fulfillment, giving the Puritans a meaning and identity as long as they were in harmony with God's program.

Love for and Submission to God

Puritan saints were expected to deny themselves, focus their highest affections on God, and be in submission to him. They were told to "walk in Christ Col. 2. 6,7."[92] "We ought to walk, even as he [Christ] walked," admonished Cotton Mather, for such submission to God the Father was the duty of "Holy and Happy Men."[93] Submission to God was to be further demonstrated by an attitude of satisfaction with the circumstances in which God placed his children. "Be content with such things as you have," urged Cotton Mather. "Learn Paul's Lesson, In whatever state to be content."[94] While the unconverted were urged to come to Christ out of mixed motives of fear and God's love, the saints were encouraged to please God with obedience spurred on by their love for him. "The keeping of the commandments . . . from a slavish fear, and not from love, is no pleasing," maintained Increase Mather.[95] The saints' responsibility to love God was eloquently urged

88. Shepard, *Sincere Convert*, p. 117.

89. Cotton, *Christ the Fountaine*, p. 33; Jonathan Mitchel, sermon of Sept., 1651, Harvard University MS, p. 38.

90. John Norton, sermon of Apr. 4, 1657, Boston Public Library MS, n.p.

91. Increase Mather, *David Serving*, p. 9.

92. Cotton, *Christ the Fountaine*, p. 176.

93. Cotton Mather, *Early Piety*, pp. 3, 18.

94. Cotton Mather, *Service of the Tabernacle*, pp. 27–28.

95. Increase Mather, *David Serving*, p. 7.

on the Dedham congregation by their pastor, John Allin, who exhorted them to "show our love to him, and let our love be inflamed to him; let us be willing to die for him that died for us; let us love him with all our hearts and souls, and all our might, that hath so greatly loved us."[96] In the eyes of Thomas Shepard, God was "merciful" and "gracious," a "most Patient and Longsuffering Being" and the saints should "Labour for increase of love and familiarity with Jesus Christ, by taking notice of him, by coming often to him, by musing daily on his love. . . ."[97] John Cotton, in describing the "Holinesse of Church Members," stated that true saints ought to "joyne themselves to the Lord, to serve him, to love his Name, to be his servants."[98] "Love God with a filial affection," urged Samuel Willard. "He deserves your best love, who hath shown you such love. . . ."[99]

Obedience and Faithfulness

A proof of one's love for God was faithful obedience to the will of God as expressed "sometimes by his Word, and sometimes by his Providence [God at work in circumstances]."[100] Because they had been exposed to the spiritual light of God and His Word, the saints were urged to "walk therefore as children of light."[101] Josiah Flynt contended that believers enjoyed "libertye," but it was "not a freedome to live as they list [desire], & yet trust in Christ for salvation, as Libertines would have it: but it is a holy spirituall libertye, a libertye from servitude [to sin]."[102]

Only the saints had the resources needed to live lives of obedience to God—God's Spirit, faith, and the Word—and they were urged to strive to that end. Using Paul's metaphor, Cotton Mather urged his congregation to believe that "it is ye duty of every christian to run with patience ye race that is set before him."[103] The Christian life was elsewhere referred to as a battle, with "every true Believer" being "a Souldier, engaged in a Warfare." These saintly warriors were highly motivated to obey their Commander because they had a "Banner to fight under: even the love of Christ. . . ."[104] Cotton Mather reminded

96. John Allin, *The Spouse of Christ*, in Burgess, ed., *Dedham Pulpit*, p. 15.

97. Shepard, *Short Catechism*, p. 4; *Three Valuable Pieces*, p. 26.

98. Cotton, *Holiness of Church Members*, p. 22.

99. Willard, *Child's Portion*, p. 42.

100. Cotton, *Christ the Fountaine*, p. 36.

101. Eph. 5:14 quoted by Jonathan Mitchel in sermon of Oct., 1651, Harvard University MS, p. 85.

102. Flynt, sermon [1670s], Harvard University MS, p. 320.

103. Cotton Mather, sermon [ca. 1682], Huntington Library MS, n.p.

104. Oakes, *Unconquerable Souldier*, p. 5.

his congregation from Romans 12:1 that they were to present their bodies to God as living sacrifices, and that such "Obedience which we render unto God, is to be a continued Expression of Gratitude unto Him."[105] The saints were not to be mere men-pleasers, but their ultimate motivation for obedience was to be love and awe for the Almighty. It was the Puritan saints' responsibility to God to make "religion their business, studying to keep all God's commandments and ordinances blameless, and to do all those things that are pleasing in his sight."[106] Consequently, the saints were instructed to eliminate everything "superfluous and wicked" in their lives and to avoid breaking their peace with God.[107] Nathaniel Gookin preached to his flock that "it is the work of a christian to consider what it is that god calls him to, in every case, and condition, and to obey that call."[108] The clergy made it clear that the beliefs of the saints, based on the statements of the Word, should permeate every area of life, inwardly as well as outwardly, and the saints were exhorted to "do all you do, humbly & valiantly in the name of the Son of God."[109] Since God was faithful to his Word, it was a "great and momentous Duty, incumbent on the People of God, to be true and faithful in their promises." Samuel Willard implored his hearers to "maintain an entire and constant respect to ye commandments of god,"[110] while John Cotton, a generation earlier, urged the saints throughout New England to be "circumspect, pure, faithful, and zealous."[111]

The clergy emphasized that the saintly life was to be a life which brought forth "fruit," a biblical term referring to various manifestations of sainthood. Samuel Willard preached a series of sermons on the subject, later published under the title *The Barren Fig Trees Doom*, in which the barren fig tree was a figure of one professing sainthood but bearing no Christian fruit. Willard emphasized that God expects that believers "should bear pleasant fruit, the works of Righteousness, and true Holiness" and that "the fruits that God looks for in his Church are good works, acts of true Obedience to his revealed will [the Word]." Furthermore, Willard maintained, God

105. Cotton Mather, *Christian Thank-Offering*, pp. 1, 13.

106. William Adams, sermon of Sept. 21, 1678, *Sermon Notes, 1672–1675*, Boston Public Library MS, p. 52.

107. Cotton, *Christ the Fountaine*, pp. 141, 104.

108. Nathaniel Gookin, sermon of May, 1690, *Sermon Notes, Apr. 24–Aug. 13, 1690*, Harvard University MS.

109. Danforth, *Parting with Friends*, p. 62.

110. Samuel Willard, *Promise Keeping a Great Duty* (Boston, 1691), p. 4; sermon of July 8, 1686, *Substance of Sermons*, Huntington Library MS, p. 293.

111. John Cotton, *Seven Vials*, p. 23.

examines everyone living under grace to see if they are bearing fruit.[112] John Cotton pointed out some specific "fruits" of the faith which the saints should possess: they should delight in God's Sabbath days, "be helpful to children and servants," be concerned for "the brethren" and "counsell them, and stir them up to good wayes," and they should grow in patience. A further Christian fruit, according to Cotton, was a change in demeanor. After undergoing conversion, he asserted, "life is much altered, you are not so light and wanton as you were; but you take a farre more grave, and wise, and stayed course, and to much better purpose both for Church and Commonwealth. . . ."[113] Nathaniel Gookin urged his congregation to maintain moral purity since "it is the duty of every believer to glorify god with his body for you are not your own but you are bought with a price." The saints were given general encouragement to strive to produce fruit in order "to be such as that your light may shine before men, that others may be brought to glorify god"[114] and to realize that fruitful Christians themselves glorified God.[115]

The conduct of the saints was supposed to imitate Christ's as a result of their being "filled with the spirit," "walking before God in both your particular and general calling," fasting as the occasion demanded, devoting "a good Proportion of their Estates to Pious Uses," and in general seeking happiness through service to God.[116] According to Samuel Willard, "man's greatest business,which he hath in this life . . . is happiness: it is that which every life ought to aim at. . . . The only way for us to improve the favours of God unto the enjoyment of happiness, is in the service of God."[117] The saints were to "be espoused to Christ" and "divorced from all other things" so that their hearts would "be taken off from all worldly contentments."[118] They were to keep spiritual values foremost among their concerns, and "live as strangers in this world . . . for fast we are passing to another world, here we have no continuing place."[119]

112. Willard, *Fig Trees Doom*, pp. 21, 76, 56.
113. Cotton, *Christ the Fountaine*, pp. 149, 100; *Way of Life*, p. 108.
114. Nathaniel Gookin, sermon of Oct., 1687, *Sermon Notes, 1687*, Harvard University MS, p. 61; sermon of May, 1690, *Sermon Notes, Apr. 24–Aug. 13, 1690*, Harvard University MS, p. 81.
115. Increase Mather, *Greatest Sinners*, p. 85.
116. John Norton, sermon of Dec. 18, 1657, Boston Public Library MS, n.p.; Cotton, *Saints Support & Comfort*, p. 68; Cotton Mather, *Humiliations*, p. 17; *Durable Riches* (Boston, 1695), p. 4; Willard, *Mercy Magnified*, p. 87.
117. Willard, *Mercy Magnified*, pp. 86–87.
118. Shepard, *Parable of Ten Virgins*, pp. 10, 12.
119. Flynt, sermon [1670s], Harvard University MS, p. 79.

The Saints' Response to Adversity

For people who claimed God's special favor and blessings, the adversities of life in New England posed a knotty theological problem. It was the lot of the clergy to explain the ways in which the Lord dealt with New England's saints so as to give meaning to the events of life within the worldview framed by the Word. Affliction and adversity, if infused with theological purpose, could be a tool for righteousness and faith rather than doubt and despair.

The assumption underlying the whole issue of adversity was that it served a divine purpose and that if God's people responded properly they would emerge from the experience stronger than before. "God is to be seen and adored in all the Tribulations that come upon his Church at any time," explained Samuel Willard.[120] Cotton Mather insisted that "we are to consider the hand of God in all our losses. . . . consider every loss as ordered, not by Chance, but by God. . . ." It was further believed that the saints should expect adversity, and that "the Christian that promises himself an Immunity from Afflictions in the Evil World, is indeed . . . a Fool." Before the saints could "put a-shore on the Land flowing with Milk and Honey . . . we must Sail through a turbid Ocean full of horrible Tempest."[121] There was "no distresse so grievous but may befall the best of Gods servants."[122] Being chastised by God, Nathaniel Gookin insisted, was the "common lot" of his children. "A suffering condition is no sure mark of an unregenerate condition," he asserted, "for a child of god may be under the chastenings of ye Lord, & so be under adversity." A month later, in May of 1687, Gookin again stressed that the "people of god while in this world may be, yea oftentimes are in a low and necessitous condition. . . . they are oftentimes encompassed with many dangers, they dwell in ye world which hates them. . . ." In 1690 he again preached that "a christian may be called unto suffering in his course of christianity: the troubles of ye righteous are many."[123] According to Samuel Willard, however, "There is a vast difference between suffering for sin, and for christ."[124] The former was seen as a natural consequence of the violation of God's laws, the result of the internal enmity of the saints'

120. Willard, *Fig Trees Doom*, p. 15.

121. Cotton Mather, *Durable Riches*, pp. 4, 6; *Right Thoughts in Sad Hours* (London, 1695), pp. 7–8.

122. Cotton, *Saints Support & Comfort*, p. 37.

123. Gookin, sermons of Apr. 14 and May, 1687, *Sermon Notes, 1687*, Harvard University MS, pp. 42–43, 80–81; sermon of May, 1690, *Sermon Notes, Apr. 24–Aug. 13, 1690*, Harvard University MS, p. 99.

124. Samuel Willard, sermon of July 8, 1686, *Substance of Sermons*, Huntington Library MS, p. 296.

"own sinful nature," while the latter was a saintly privilege and blessing in disguise.[125] Joshua Moodey gave his flock further clues as to the types of adversity they could expect to encounter: "1. Fatherly chastisement from god ... 2. Troubles from within; through ye canaanite [the Indians] Left in ye Land. 3. Sorrows from Satan. His wiles and methods. 4. Evils from men; persecutions."[126] The saints could profit from all types of adversity, however, if they kept in mind Joseph Belcher's observation that the saintly life was not easy. To the contrary, "the life of a Believer ... is that of a warfare, which is not a life of ease and idleness, but attended with many hazzards, and hardships, which every Christian must endeavour to endure as a good Souldier of Jesus Christ."[127]

Once their congregations were convinced that adversity was a normal part of God's program for his people, the clergy elaborated upon the benefits of adversity in the pursuit of holiness. Cotton Mather preached that "all your Afflictions are indeed your Advantages. Tis a sweet Promise that you have to feed upon, in Rom. 8.28, All things shall work together for good, unto them that love God."[128] Through the experience of affliction, the saints would be purified. They could rest in the presence of the "great design of God in all, even the severest Afflictions which his children suffer." According to Samuel Willard,

It becomes not the people of God to look upon the fiery tryal which befals the Church of Christ in the world, as a strange thing.

[T]hey [trials] are designed by God himself, who is the Soveraign and Supream disposer of all things, to be probationary, and used as a Refiners fire to purge out the dross, and not waste the good mettal which is cast into it. . . .

Willard went on to enumerate the positive results of adversity, providing that the saints responded properly:

by sore afflictions the people of God are made more humble, and made pliable to any command of God: they are sometimes stiffe and inflexible in days of prosperity, but now [in adversity] they subject

---

125. Oakes, *Unconquerable Souldier,* p. 6.

126. Moodey, sermon of Mar. 4, 1686, *Substance of Sermons,* Huntington Library MS, pp. 1–2.

127. Belcher, *Worst Enemy Conquered,* p. 5.

128. Cotton Mather, *Batteries,* p. 136.

themselves to the framing hand of God, and are ready to receive his stamp and impression. . . .[129]

Adversity might come as a result of disobedience to God, who rightly was angered by sin, "yet this anger is managed by love, and shall work accordingly. God's displeasure at his Children shall do nothing but what love directs," assured Samuel Willard.[130] In 1651 John Cotton summed up well the clergy's view of adversity in the lives of true believers: "When we feel the Lords hand in all the punishments and Judgments that befall us, and we bear it willingly, this is solemnly to worship him, and to be wrought upon as clay in the hand of the Potter. . . .[131] Cotton comforted his congregation with the fact that although "the tribulations of Gods people are sometimes great and deepe" they are nonetheless "always safe and passable."[132] Nathaniel Gookin steadfastly maintained that in periods of adversity God "is faithful and if you trust in him he will deliver you."[133] Those thus delivered had a special responsibility, however, to pursue holiness all the more, because "sins after great and eminent Salvations, Deliverances, and mercies, they pull down greater Judgments."[134] Saints who remained faithful to God during adversity could say with Cotton Mather as he quoted Job 23:10, "When He hath Tryed me, I shall come forth as Gold."[135]

The Coming Kingdom

The American Puritans' eschatological expectation is a significant aspect of their theology oftentimes overlooked by historians. While it is true that English Puritanism was on the whole more enthralled with apocalyptic radicalism than was the case in New England, it would be a grievous error to deny the impact of millennial expectations in the American experience. Millennial ideas have, in fact, in the last few years come to be viewed in "both England and America as central to Puritan faith and indispensable to its proper historical in-

129. Willard, *Fiery Tryal*, pp. 3–4, 9.
130. Willard, *Spiritual Desertions*, p. 32.
131. Cotton, *Christ the Fountaine*, p. 14.
132. Cotton, *Saints Support & Comfort*, p. 30.
133. Nathaniel Gookin, sermon of June, 1687, *Sermon Notes, 1687*, Harvard University MS, p. 135.
134. Allen, *Serious Advice*, p. 2.
135. Cotton Mather, *Service of the Tabernacle*, p. 86.

terpretation."[136] Many Puritans of New England, especially those of the founding generation, looked with keen anticipation for the millennium, the establishment of Christ's righteous kingdom on earth.

The religious struggles faced by Puritans in seventeenth-century England were seen as but one part of a cosmic battle heralding the approach of the kingdom of Christ. Other signs were the activities of the Roman Catholic Church, seen as the embodiment of the Antichrist, and the infidel Turks, both of which were soon to be judged. The gathering of the elect in New England was in itself seen as an indication of the last days. The Puritans, in their typical fashion, were not interested in merely formulating theological ideas about the end of the age; they wanted to be active participants in this real life-and-death struggle.

Indeed, New England was born in an atmosphere of crisis and cosmic struggle, to which the preaching of John Cotton was a major contributor. Cotton had engaged in apocalyptic preaching before ever coming to America. In the late 1630s Cotton began a series of lectures in the new Boston based on the Book of Revelation, which touched a responsive chord in his hearers and attracted even other ministers to his church for these meetings.[137] Cotton's eschatological scheme of things predictably identified the seven-headed beast of Revelation 13 as the Roman Catholic Church, weakened through the growth of evangelical preaching since the time of John Wycliffe. The second beast described in Revelation 13:11 was the pope himself. According to Cotton, the powers of Antichrist and Satan would be placed in bondage for a thousand years by means of powerful gospel preaching. Thus the millennium would be experienced not through Christ's bodily presence on earth but through faithful preaching and revivals of unprecedented dimensions. In fulfillment of biblical prophecy, Satan would be released after a thousand years, resulting in a resurgence of evil, the revival of Roman Catholicism, and the persecution of the saints. This situation would not be long endured, however, for soon Christ himself would return, deal with the forces of wickedness,

---

136. J. F. Maclear, "New England and the Fifth Monarchy: The Quest for the Millennium in Early American Puritanism," *William and Mary Quarterly* 32 (Apr. 1975): p. 224.

137. Ibid., p. 233. Three known printed works resulted from these lectures: *An Exposition upon the Thirteenth Chapter of the Revelation* (London, 1655); *The Powring Out of the Seven Vials: or an Exposition of the 16. Chapter of the Revelation, with an Application of it to our Times* (London, 1642); and *The Churches Resurrection, or the Opening of the Fift and Sixt verses of the 20th Chap. of the Revelation* (London, 1642).

bring forth the resurrection of the dead, and proceed with the last judgment.[138]

What made Cotton's preaching all the more compelling was his constant reference to things presently experienced. He had calculated the period of beastly activity, that is, the tyranny of the papacy, beginning with A.D. 395 and concluded through his study of biblical prophecy that the beast would be active 1,260 years. In 1640, he cautiously announced his theory: "I will not be two [sic] confident, because I am not a Prophet, nor the Son of a Prophet to foretell things to come, but so far as God helps by Scripture light, about the time 1655 there will be then such a blow given to this beast . . . as that we shall see a further gradual accomplishment and fulfilling of this Prophecy here."[139] Dying in 1652, Cotton did not live to see the collapse of the imminent millennial hope he so ardently championed.

Cotton became known in both Old and New England as a prophet of the millennium, although he was by no means the only such voice. While precise details and dates varied, several New England divines saw the dawning of the millennial age at hand. John Wheelwright urged that the forces of Antichrist be attacked by "a Spirituall burning, . . . by the fire of the Gospell" rather than by an "externall burning of Rome."[140] Anne Bradstreet, on the other hand, took a much more militant stance in her ambitious poem, "A Dialog between Old England and New," composed in 1642. In this work, which is both historical and apocalyptic, she envisions the armies of Christian England making short work not only of Rome but also of the Turks, and in the process bringing salvation to the Jews:

> This done, with brandished swords to Turkey go,
> For then what is't but English blades dare do,
> And lay her waste for so's the sacred doom,
> And do to Gog as thou hast done to Rome.
> Oh Abraham's seed, lift up your heads on high,
> For sure the day of your redemption's nigh;
> The scales shall fall from your long blinded eyes,
> And Him you shall adore who now despise.
> Then fullness of the nations in shall flow,
> And Jew and Gentile to one worship go;
> Then follows days of happiness and rest;
> Whose lot doth fall to live therein is blest.[141]

138. See Cotton Mather, *Exposition upon the Thirteenth Chapter*, passim; *Churches Resurrection*, pp. 3–21.

139. Quoted in Maclear, "New England and the Fifth Monarchy," p. 233.

140. Quoted in ibid., p. 240.

141. Quoted in ibid., p. 236.

So preoccupied were some New England Puritans with these concerns that Thomas Lechford, a Boston lawyer and sometime critic of the authorities, complained in 1640 that some people "cry out of nothing but Antichrist and the Man of Sin." He even found his reputation tarnished because he dared to suggest in an unpublished treatise that perhaps the pope was not the Antichrist after all.[142] Yet all devout Puritans looked forward to the culmination of history and their vindication as faithful saints: "then will Christ appear to be the greatest and most glorious Monarch that ever was . . . the Lord shall be King over all the earth" and "the honour due to God shall be given to him."[143] While this millennial hope remained strong, the sense of urgency diminished with the progression of the seventeenth century and especially with the collapse of the Puritan government of England (see chapter 13). New Englanders came to see that they were perhaps not so much standing at the end of an age as they were themselves in the process of building a new age in a new world.

142. *Note-Book Kept By Thomas Lechford, Esq., Lawyer, In Boston, Massachusetts Bay, From June 27, 1638 to July 29, 1641.* American Antiquarian Society, *Transactions and Collections,* 7 (Cambridge, 1885), pp. 276, 50.
143. Increase Mather, *Greatest Sinners,* pp. 82, 84–85.

6

The Churches and the Ministry

If there was one institution the Puritans of New England wanted to establish with great care and correctness, it was the church. Ecclesiastical concerns were at the root of the Puritan movement in Old England, and the frustrations of nonreform there made New Englanders all the more hopeful for genuine reform in their Zion in the wilderness. As we have seen, the Puritans, unlike the Pilgrims of Plymouth, never repudiated their ties with the Church of England. It was no secret, however, that Puritan churches in New England differed from the Anglican establishment. Strongly held beliefs, resolute Puritan wills, and three thousand miles of ocean made this deviation from the Anglican norm possible. In the environment of the New World, basic Puritan beliefs were retained while at the same time certain innovations were made in church polity. American Puritanism thus fostered a new attitude toward the church, while attempting to deal with the age-old religious problem of human corruption.

The Nature of the Church

Biblicists that they were, the New England Puritans desired to establish churches that were built upon the solid foundation of the Word. The true church was not an institution of mere human origin, but was divinely established and headed by Jesus Christ. "It is the Lord Jesus Christ, as GOD-MAN, who is The Head of the Church; and in that capacity we have our Union with Him," proclaimed Cotton Mather.[1] The church was "first initiated by Christ himself, and after-

1. Cotton Mather, *Blessed Unions*, p. 6.

99

ward put in practice by the Apostles." Christ had told Peter, "Thou art Peter, and upon this Rock I will build my Church." Rejecting the Roman Catholic interpretation that Peter was the "Rock," a justification for papal authority, John Eliot asserted that "the Rock confessed is CHRIST: Christ Confessed, is the Foundation of the Visible Church. . . ."[2] It was John Cotton's contention that "all things, and all Governments in the world, should serve to Christ's ends, for the welfare of the Church whereof he is the Head."[3] Christ's role as head of the church was by no means the least of his functions. He was "above Principalities and powers, but above all the rest, there's this Dignity conferred upon him, that he is made Head of the Church."[4] Puritan saints were taught to see Christ as having an active role in this headship of the church. To Christ were ascribed "all the blessings that befall the Church" and the saints' response should be to maintain scrupulousness in church membership standards in order to please Christ, "the foundation,"[5] who was also "the author and the maintainer of the peace of his church."[6] The church, John Cotton maintained, was "Christ's kingdom" whose authority and power were "rec'd. from the Scripture."[7] The church was also portrayed in both Scripture and Puritan sermons as the bride of Christ and the "mystical body of the Lord Jesus."[8] The social nature of the church implied by the body analogy was noted by Nathaniel Gookin:

> All that fear god are the members of this misticall body of Christ: and christians cannot be without one another, no more than one member can say unto another member of ye body, I have no need of thee: Every member of this body of Christ is beneficiall, therefore we should have fellowship with all those members of Christ. . . .[9]

It is interesting to note that Richard Mather, a generation earlier, used the same biblical concept of the church as the body of Christ not to show church members' dependence on one another but rather to show

---

2. Eliot, *Communion of Churches*, p. 2.

3. John Cotton, *A Discourse About Civil Government In a New Plantation Whose Design is Religion* (Cambridge, 1663), p. 15.

4. Increase Mather, *Mystery of Christ*, p. 197.

5. Cotton, *Book of Canticles*, p. 74; *Holiness of Church Members*, p. 57.

6. James Allen, sermon of May 1, 1690, *Sermon Notes, Apr. 24–Aug. 13, 1690*, Harvard University MS, p. 36.

7. Cotton, *Doctrine of the Church*, p. 10.

8. Cotton Mather, *Companion for Communicants*, p. 58.

9. Nathaniel Gookin, sermon of May, 1690, *Sermon Notes, Apr. 24–Aug. 13, 1690*, Harvard University MS, p. 75.

that "the whole body is not an eye" and that therefore "all the body of the Church are not endewed with Power of Church Government."[10]

The church over which Christ presided consisted ultimately of all true believers in all places throughout the ages. But this universal aspect had to be lived out in local congregations. A true local church, according to John Eliot, "is a company of visible saints combined together, with one heart, to hold Communion in all the instituted Gospel-worship, Ordinances and Discipline, which Christ hath fitted for, and given unto a particular church."[11] Another mark of a true church was that it consisted of "a company of called ones, not by men only, whose call may be altogether rejected; but of God, who by calling maketh such impression upon the hearts of men, as convinceth them of the voice of God in the Word, and subdueth them to yeeld subjection to the Word. . . ."[12]

To John Cotton, the preaching of the gospel was a sign of a true church, if it were accompanied by a profession of faith according to the Word. However, "the preaching of the word alone, without some professed subjection to it, will not be a mark of a true Church. The preaching of the pure word of God purely (as done by Paul at Athens, Acts 17) was no certain mark of a pure Church there." Another sign of a true church, in Cotton's opinion, was that members were "regenerate and sanctified in Christ. . . . If a society of men should have the word of God truly taught unto them," he maintained, ". . . and yet be never wrought upon to submit themselves to the call of God . . . I durst not account such a society for a Spouse and Church of God." However, Cotton conceded that "hipocrites, and false brethren may creep into the Church, yea into the purest Churches . . . such hipocrites, and false brethren may afterwards break forth into open notorious scandals, yea and may (at least for a time) be tolerated in them, and yet not take away the nature and essence of a true visible Church."[13] Some impurity was inevitable in a fallen world.

The importance of membership in a New England church in the early seventeenth century can scarcely be overstated, for such membership was a passport to full participation as a citizen of the earthly Promised Land. Only church members could participate in the Lord's Supper and present their children for baptism. Early in the New England experience it was determined by Governor Winthrop and other leaders that the vote should be expanded in Massachusetts to include freemen who were also church members. Church membership

10. Richard Mather, *Answer to Two Questions*, p. 12.
11. Eliot, *Communion of Churches*, pp. 1–2.
12. Cotton, *Holiness of Church Members*, p. 5.
13. Ibid., pp. 9–10, 1, 4, 17.

was also a screening device to keep the churches as pure as a sin-infected world would allow. New England Puritans tended to shun theological innovation, desiring instead to base their lives and doctrines on their interpretation of the Bible. In the area of church membership, the New England Puritans made a significant contribution to ecclesiastical practice, but even then it was not so much an innovation as it was a return to the practice of the New Testament.

What the Puritans did was to return to the concept that saving faith was a basic criterion for membership in a truly God-pleasing local church. Puritans in England had argued for some time that faith was an essential part of a true church, but they stopped short of demanding a convincing conversion narrative from each member of the congregation. Membership in England's national church was open to all, and even the restless Puritans believed that God could work through that church to bring about the salvation of his elect. Even the Separatists, who were responsible for the founding of Plymouth Colony, did not require proof of conversion for church membership. However, Plymouth later copied the policy of Puritan Massachusetts for a "pure" regenerate church membership.[14]

Francis J. Bremer has traced the origins of this policy in New England to the preaching of John Cotton which resulted in a revival of religious fervor in Boston in 1634. Governor Winthrop remarked about the large numbers of conversions and additions to the church at that time. These new converts were given the opportunity to testify of their religious experiences, in order to encourage the congregation. According to Bremer, "what started as an edifying exercise very soon came to be recognized as an essential step in one's admission to the church."[15] In a sermon to his congregation in 1636, John Cotton admonished them to "let no member come in but he that knoweth Christ, and that knoweth he is a Child of Wrath; and let him go on, not in his own strength, but in a depending frame upon Jesus Christ."[16] This practice shortly went beyond what Cotton had perhaps intended, and came to involve more than a statement of belief on the part of the applicant for church membership. Would-be communicants were required to describe the working of God's grace in their lives in terms of the steps that had brought them to a final realization that they were indeed chosen of God for salvation. Their lives were expected to back up their profession as well, with some allowances made for human frailty. Church leaders had the opportunity to cross-

14. Morgan, *Visible Saints*, pp. 65–66.
15. Francis J. Bremer, *The Puritan Experiment* (New York, 1976), p. 98.
16. John Cotton, *A Sermon Preached by the Reverend, Mr. John Cotton, Teacher of the First Church in Boston in New England* (Boston, 1713), p. 27.

examine and probe applicants for membership, to be as certain as possible that they were truly among the elect.

The "Half-Way Covenant"

It was clear in the first generation that not all those arriving on New England's shores were as yet converted to Christ. It was hoped that many were of the elect, with the time of their conversions yet in the future. The tightening of church membership requirements in the 1630s demonstrates the extent to which the population was as yet unconverted. Between 1637 and 1639 more than 1,000 newcomers arrived in Boston, yet only 79 were added to church membership rolls. Of the 362 families living in Boston in 1639, 197 of them had no family member belonging to a church. Of a total Boston population in 1650 of about 3,000, fewer than 500 were church members.[17] While it is theoretically possible that some people who had experienced conversion could have chosen not to become church members, it seems unlikely that many (or even any) would choose this path.

This growing unconverted population increased in the second generation after the founding of Massachusetts. The failure of many children of the first generation to undergo a conversion experience led to a compromise of the recently developed policy of a church membership comprised of only the elect. Anabaptist views, which opposed the administration of the rite of baptism to infants, were making inroads in a few scattered areas by the 1660s and the magistrates of the Bay Colony were concerned. The need to clarify the meaning of baptism, coupled with declining membership roles, helped spawn what eventually came to be known as the Half-Way Covenant. Basically, the idea was to permit the baptism of children of baptized individuals who were not yet full communicants in the church. Although their children could be baptized, neither they nor their children could partake of the Lord's Supper until full church membership had been granted, preceded by the relating of a convincing conversion experience. Variations of this were practiced by a few congregations in the 1650s and the issue was discussed by an assembly of ministers in 1657, which supported the general concept. Implementation, however, rested with each individual congregation.

A much larger synod met in 1662 to deal again with the question of baptism, conversion, and church membership. When it was over, the nearly eighty assembled ministers and lay representatives had in effect recommended two kinds of church membership. Full communicant members were those who could attest to a conversion experience.

17. Rutman, *Winthrop's Boston*, pp. 141, 144, 147.

They could have their children baptized, participate in the Lord's Supper, and, if they were adult males, they could be involved in the church's government.

A more restricted membership was suggested for baptized children who had not yet undergone a conversion experience. They were subject to the church's government, but could not receive the Lord's Supper, vote on church matters, or have their children baptized. However, such individuals could, by meeting certain standards of knowledge and conduct as adults, become "half-way" members by voluntarily submitting to the authority of God and his church, thus acknowledging (or "owning") the covenant made by their parents at the time of their baptism. They were then eligible to offer their children for baptism, although they were still excluded from the Lord's Supper without a demonstration of saving faith. The Half-Way Covenant proved to be a pragmatic compromise dealing with the dilemma created by the Puritans' insistence on both infant baptism and a church membership composed of true believers.

Reaction to the Half-Way Covenant was mixed, with the greatest opposition coming not from the clergy but from the laity. Even churches that did accept the new policy in principle were often hesitant to make use of it. It has been suggested by Edmund S. Morgan that rather than entering a period of religious decline after the first generation, there was instead "the rise of an extraordinary religious scrupulosity." Morgan believes that an understanding of the conversion experience had been refined to the point where the second generation "rejected, as inconclusive, religious experiences that would have driven their parents unhesitatingly into church membership."[18] Robert G. Pope has determined that by 1692 about 80 percent of New England's churches were utilizing the Half-Way Covenant. Some churches, such as the one at Dorchester, were frightened into accepting the new policy after the devastating Indian uprising known as King Philip's (Metacom's) War was interpreted as a possible manifestation of God's wrath for neglecting the church's children.[19] This argument against leaving out the children was often used by the clergy to push for adoption of the Half-Way Covenant. One can only speculate how fearful the clergy may have been that a "pure" church would continue to dwindle in impact and numbers.

18. Edmund S. Morgan, "New England Puritanism: Another Approach," *William and Mary Quarterly*, 18 (Apr. 1961): 241–42. Robert G. Pope, *The Half-Way Covenant* (Princeton, 1969) also puts forth the theory of greater scrupulosity on the part of the second generation.

19. Pope, *Half-Way Covenant*, pp. 187–88.

Church Polity

New England Puritan churches not only differed from the Church of England in their criteria for membership, but they differed considerably in issues of governance as well. Viewing many of their problems in England as stemming from an episcopal form of church government that was unresponsive to the needs of local congregations, the New England leadership eliminated ecclesiastical hierarchy. The clergy's belief in the active headship of Christ over his church, their rejection of papal authority, and their disappointment with royal reforms in England made Congregationalism an attractive alternative to government by bishops. The clergy viewed themselves as a preaching ministry, not a sacerdotal one, under the same authority of Christ as their congregations. The New England churches were given to local communities to control, partly for theological reasons, but also as a response to the unpopular centralism which shaped English religious and political life during the Stuart monarchy.[20]

Theoretically, Congregationalism meant that each local congregation was free to establish its own covenant, secure (and dismiss) its own pastors, and run its own affairs without outside interference. This was largely carried out in practice, although the opinions of other clergymen, neighboring congregations, and the civil magistrates did not generally go unnoticed. As new towns were created in the wilderness, small groups of men would come together and examine each other for worthiness as "pillars" of a new church. Once the pillars were in place (often seven godly men formed this group), they proceeded to draw up a church covenant, setting forth their mission, commitments, and ideals. Other townsfolk were then invited to seek membership, and were examined for worthiness by the "founding fathers." Once a membership was created, church officers were chosen and a pastor was called by vote of the members. Some twenty churches were thus "gathered" in New England during the 1630s by use of a covenant, the congregational election of a minister and his ordination by the congregation's leadership, and the voting in of additional church members.

The Cambridge Platform, drafted by a committee of clergymen between 1646 and 1648, codified this procedure of gathering churches and also set forth other details of church polity. This document recognized five church officers: pastors, teachers, ruling elders, deacons, and "ancient widows." The pastor preached the Word and administered the sacraments. The teacher was essentially an associate, whose

20. See Timothy H. Breen, "Persistent Localism: English Social Change and the Shaping of New England Institutions," *William and Mary Quarterly* 32 (Jan. 1975): 3–28.

preaching often emphasized doctrinal exposition. Both of these individuals were ordained into the ministry. The other officers were of the laity. Ruling elders were elected to oversee the admission of new members, preside over church business meetings, pray over the sick, and in general do what was necessary to keep the congregation living in a harmonious, scandal-free way. Some congregations found it difficult to fill this office and abandoned it, leaving the ministry with more work on its hands. The financial affairs of the church were placed under the supervision of the deacons. They were responsible for collecting the offerings and disbursing them as needed. The "ancient widows" were elderly women so designated out of appreciation for their service to the congregation.

Once a church was established, candidates for membership appeared before the congregation following an initial screening by the church officers, gave testimony concerning their salvation experiences, and were voted into membership. New members indicated their intention to uphold the church covenant, which in effect made all members their brothers' (and sisters') keepers. Church members scrutinized each other's behavior, and did not hesitate to publicly censure erring brethren. Congregations also voted to recommend their members to other churches when a move necessitated a parting. Excommunication of recalcitrant members was within the power of the congregation, but was generally used only in extreme situations.

The Goal of Church Unity

The Puritan clergy of seventeenth-century New England were concerned about schism from the very start of their experiment. They took pride in the fact that their churches could claim to be nonschismatic since there had been no formal separation from the Church of England. Their principle of uniformity at least technically had not been violated.[21] This strong desire of the Puritans for both unity and purity posed what Edmund S. Morgan perceived to be the "Puritan dilemma."[22] John Cotton was but one of many who warned against Separatism and urged the saints "not to separate from the Church for corruption sake" and "not to looke only at her corruptions, but to see her comliness also."[23]

When a division did occur between John Cotton and other Massachusetts Bay ministers during the antinomian controversy (see

---

21. See Perry Miller, *Orthodoxy in Massachusetts* (Cambridge, Mass., 1933), p. 139.
22. Morgan, *Puritan Dilemma.*
23. Cotton, *Book of Canticles*, p. 32.

chapter 13), every effort was made to reconcile the apparent differences of opinion. In their reply to Cotton's answers to their "sixteen questions" designed to test his orthodoxy, the investigating ministers concluded:

> Now we bow our knees to the Father of Lights, to clear up all our judgments in one truth, that we may all think and speak and preach the very same thing, which will advance the glory of his blessed truth, and the comfort of many a Soul who else will not be a little disheartened and unsettled in their holy course and frame by the apparent difference that may be between us.[24]

"It is the delight of Hell," wrote Thomas Shepard, a great champion of Puritan unity,

> to set & see Churches at variance among themselves. . . . It is a wonderful thing to see what a small occasion of offence will do; a word, a gesture, a garment, a matter of indifferency, 'tis strange to see, how much small matters will gore, if Satan's head be in them. . . .[25]

Fortunately, "although Satan hath been oft busie to make breaches among us, yet the ministers of Christ have been hitherto generally (if not all) of one heart and mind in the maine and principall things of his Kingdome amongst us," wrote pastors Allin and Shepard.[26] Accusing Christianity in Old England of being racked with "schismes and divisions," Thomas Shepard was pleased to report (somewhat optimistically) to New England's detractors in 1645 that "the reports of the divisions in New England are fables; The Churches are here in peace; the common wealth in peace; The Ministry in most sweet peace."[27]

Cotton Mather preached in 1692 that "there is a Blessed Union, which Believers on the Lord Jesus Christ, are Through Him, to have with One Another." Using as his text a verse from Christ's prayer for unity (John 17:21), Mather urged that "as far as we can, we should be of the same Opinion, and hold the same Doctrine of Christianity; be oure we must concur in all the Fundamental Ones, or else we cut off

24. Quoted in David D. Hall, ed., *The Antinomian Controversy, 1636–1638* (Middleton, Conn., 1968), p. 77.

25. Shepard, *Parable of Ten Virgins*, p. 8.

26. Allin and Shepard, *Defence of the Answer made unto the Nine Questions or Positions Sent from New-England, Against the Reply Thereto by that Reverend Servant of Christ, Mr. John Ball; Entitled, A Tryall of the New Church-way in New England and in Old* (London, 1648), p. 28.

27. Thomas Shepard, *New Englands Lamentation for Old Englands present errours, and divisions, and their feared future desolations if not timely prevented* (London, 1645), p. 5.

our selves from the Communion of Saints."[28] Pastor John Oxenbridge saw unity as imperative for the effectiveness of the church in the community. Even the "appearance of disagreement" would "hinder the order of Churches . . . and hinder the conversion of Youth which we would promote, and promote prophaness, superstition and popery. . . ."[29] Concerned about conditions in England, Thomas Shepard preached that "a spirit of rage and division . . . a spirit of wrangling and contention . . . goes before the calamity of a people." Such a lack of unity "is a forerunner of all misery."[30] The saints were encouraged by Samuel Willard to remember that they "are all of one Household, called the Household of Faith."[31]

The family of God maintained its cohesiveness and peaceful existence, according to John Cotton, because of the success of the leadership in "the establishment of pure Religion, in doctrine, worship, and government, according to the word of God." If New England lost its grip on the Word, and "if Religion be corrupted," then, predicted Cotton, "there will be warre in the gates . . . and no peace to him that cometh in, or goeth out."[32] A remarkable degree of theological unity did seem to exist during most of the seventeenth century. According to historians Timothy H. Breen and Stephen Foster, orthodox Puritan faith, coupled as it was with the Congregationalist system of church government, proved "flexible enough to accommodate moderate differences of opinion" while at the same time providing a standard useful "for detecting and expelling extremists, thereby precluding any prolonged clash over religious fundamentals."[33]

The Church's Mission and Indian Missions

The Puritan churches of New England were created because devout men and women believed that God had created the institution of the church, Christ was the head of it, and society needed it. The church's most basic and essential mission was to bring glory to God. Believers were to do this, as Puritan John Field declared from his English prison cell in 1572, by preaching the gospel, embracing true religion, strengthening and comforting one another, daily growing and increasing in true faith, and framing their lives, government, and ceremonies

28. Cotton Mather, *Blessed Unions*, pp. 40, 42.
29. Oxenbridge, *New England Freemen Warned and Warmed*, p. 44.
30. Shepard, *Wine for Gospel Wantons* (Cambridge, 1668), pp. 6, 8.
31. Willard, *Child's Portion*, p. 15.
32. Cotton, *Doctrine of the Church*, p. 50.
33. Timothy H. Breen and Stephen Foster, "The Puritans' Greatest Achievement: A Study of Social Cohesion in Seventeenth-Century Massachusetts," *Journal of American History* 60 (June 1973): 10.

according to the Word of God.[34] Society needed to hear and heed the Word of God as preached from New England's pulpits. For the converted, it was refreshment to the soul and a challenge to greater Christian maturity; for the as yet unconverted, it was likely the means that God would use to bring them to salvation. Evangelism was much on the minds of the clergy, but it was generally focused on those within the Puritan camp.

While a major professed goal of the whole Puritan undertaking in the New World was the evangelization of the Indians, the Puritans were, on the whole, found wanting in missionary zeal. Considerable historiographical debate has occurred over just how well or how shabbily the Puritans treated the native inhabitants. The Indians of New England, divided into various tribes of the Algonquian family, were not numerous when Europeans began arriving in the seventeenth century. They most certainly did not flourish after the white man's arrival. While the Indians saw economic advantage in dealing with the white man, most of them had little use for the white man's society, culture, or religion. Puritan attitudes toward the Indians were complex, ranging from pity to hostility. In general, it can be said that the Puritans regarded the Indians as human, but inferior in all ways to Europeans. In most areas of Puritan-Indian interaction, the Puritans responded with attitudes and actions that were often harsh and almost always ethnocentrically biased. The Puritan demanded that the Indian conform to the Puritan way or else be counted as the enemy. Antagonism was based on more than racial differences, but G. E. Thomas has pointed out that "no matter how hard the Puritan tried to transform the Indian or how completely the Indian conformed, the cause was ultimately hopeless because the Indian could never become white."[35]

It would perhaps be expecting too much for the early years of the Puritan experiment in America to yield much evangelistic work among the Indians. The colonists were faced with difficulties of survival, and preoccupied with their own needs. The Congregational system that developed in New England really took no thought for the spiritual needs of the Indians, and it was only the dedication of a few remarkable souls, such as John Eliot, that produced any spiritual impact at all among the natives. The Puritan reverence for the Word of God demanded that any missionary activity include a translation of the Scriptures into the Indians' own language—an exceedingly difficult job, but one that was carried out by John Eliot. Eliot's zeal was

34. Morgan, *Visible Saints*, p. 14.
35. G. E. Thomas, "Puritans, Indians, and the Concept of Race," *New England Quarterly* 48 (Mar. 1975): 27.

enhanced by his conviction, not widely shared by others, that the New England natives were actually Hebrews—long-scattered descendants of the ten tribes of Israel.[36] Cultural and linguistic differences aside, perhaps a greater barrier to widespread Indian acceptance of Puritan Christianity was the fact, as Bremer has pointed out, that Puritan theology is inherently complicated: "Puritanism was one of the most subtle and intellectually demanding variants of the Christian faith. Englishmen found mastery of the Puritan theology exceedingly difficult; American Indians must have found it more so."[37]

In spite of the obstacles, the missionary work of John Eliot, Thomas Mayhew, Jr., Thomas Mayhew, Sr., John Cotton, Jr., Abraham Pierson, Thomas James, and others resulted in the creation of fourteen "praying towns"—villages of Christianized Indians who were taught to live as Englishmen. About 1,100 Indians were involved in such communities prior to the Indian uprisings of the 1670s, but it is impossible to ascertain how many of them underwent a genuine religious conversion. With Metacom's (King Philip's) War, the feelings of many Puritans toward the Indians turned ugly. Herded onto an island in Boston Harbor for their own protection, the "praying Indians" were not immune from the fear and hostility caused by the war, and missionary zeal greatly diminished. Eliot's desire to turn all of New England's Indians into pious Englishmen was doomed to failure, probably before he even started.

The Puritan Ministry

Given the Puritans' emphasis on believing and living according to the written Word of God, it is not surprising to find that a ministry well-prepared in the study of the Scriptures was deemed essential for the maintenance of the true faith. Formal higher education was a virtual requirement for any young man aspiring to the pastorate, and the founding of Harvard College in 1636 to accommodate such a need in America is so well known as to require but brief mention. In *New England's First Fruits*, John Eliot recalled that "One of the next things we longed for, and looked after, was to advance Learning, and perpetuate it to Posterity; dreading to leave an illiterate Ministry to the Churches, when our present Ministers shall lie in the dust."[38]

The ministers themselves occasionally suggested which positive traits should be cultivated by those of their calling. John Cotton mentioned that the responsibilities of the ministry included getting along

36. Maclear, "New England and the Fifth Monarchy," p. 245.
37. Bremer, *Puritan Experiment*, p. 201.
38. John Eliot, *New England's First Fruits* (London, 1643), p. 12.

amicably with the saints, maintaining lives of personal holiness, being faithful to their calling, having a fruitful ministry, and being selfless and hospitable.[39] One of Increase Mather's criteria for evaluating Jonathan Mitchel as a successful preacher was the fact that "oft times there were more weepers than sleepers in the Congregation, under his awakening Ministry."[40] Upon the death of the Reverend Thomas Shepard, neighboring pastor Urian Oakes delivered an elegy in which he outlined further desirable ministerial traits. Said Oakes of his departed brother,

> His Look commanded Reverence and Awe,
> Though Mild and Amiable, not Austere:
> Well Humour'd was He (as I ever saw)
> And rul'd by Love and Wisdome, more than Fear.[41]

But above all, the Puritan minister was expected to know the Word and to communicate it effectively.

While it is likely that Puritan theology, a Congregational form of church government, and a restrictive policy of church membership with an emphasis on purity limited the power of the clergy, the Puritan ministers of New England were nonetheless the region's most distinguished and respected professional group in the seventeenth century. Certainly more ministers were attracted to New England than to Virginia, which was founded earlier. John Eliot listed thirty-seven practicing ministers in Massachusetts in 1650—one for every 415 English inhabitants. By contrast, in Virginia in 1649 there were but six ministers, or one for every 3,239 persons.[42] Some ninety ministers came to New England in the 1630s, although some were never called to a church and others stayed but briefly.[43]

The clergy attempted to retain an influence over their communities, which was moral rather than legal, by reminding the laity of ministerial importance from time to time. These reminders increased with the passage of the seventeenth century as the clergy perceived that their status was slipping in an increasingly secularized society. It was absolutely necessary to have men capable of preaching the Word, John Cotton stated rather strongly, for "God's people are in an unsafe condition without God, while they are without a teaching priest."[44] Ministers portrayed themselves as ambassadors for Christ, speaking

---

39. Cotton, *Book of Canticles*, p. 112; *Holiness of Church Members*, p. 56.
40. Mitchell, *Discourse of the Glory*, p. viii.
41. Oakes, *Elegie*, p. 10.
42. Darrett B. Rutman, *American Puritanism* (Philadelphia, 1970), pp. 31, 51.
43. David D. Hall, *The Faithful Shepherd* (Chapel Hill, N.C., 1972), p. 72.
44. Cotton, *Christ the Fountaine*, p. 184.

what God would have them utter and at times having to say things against the apostacy of their times which did not make them popular. New Englanders were warned by Josiah Flynt that "if thou despisest these messages, thou despisest not man, but God; they are his words we speake, & his errand we deliver. . . . We ministers stand before you in Christs stead, & shall hee have a refusal from you?" Flynt went on to implore his congregation to "be not angry with God's ministers for declaring the truth, thinke not they speake as they would have it; no, their soules travail in pain to see Christ formed in you. . . ."[45] Whenever a prominent minister died, it was interpreted as a sign of judgment and an indication that God was removing his faithful servants before the full measure of his wrath descended on his erring people. As leading clergymen died with the progression of the seventeenth century, it was feared that the end result might be "a Famine of the Word, the Scattering of the Flock."[46]

Although the clergy were aware of their great responsibility "to be careful how they apply . . . the truths of the word of god"[47] to the people of God, they were likewise very aware of their own human frailty. Their theology of sin and human depravity prohibited the Puritans from being perfectionists or utopians. No saint on earth, including the ministry, could possibly arrive at sinless perfection, although one should nonetheless strive for it. "There is none on this side of the Grave so holy, but to have in him some defilement, none so clean but there may be some spots and blemishes found in him," pronounced Samuel Willard.[48] Thomas Shepard warned his flock that they should "not trust men too far, nor boast of any man too much. . . ."[49] Joseph Belcher explained to his hearers that "a Christian must not expect to experience a state of perfection here in this life: No, that estate is reserved till he comes to experience a state of Glory. The best of men in this life have a double nature in them."[50] James Allen maintained that even God's choicest servants are "but men of like infirmity with other good men in this world, therefore expect not too much. . . ."[51] Thomas Shepard put to rest any idea of ministerial infallibility by exhorting his congregation to distinguish the voice of God and the voice of the preacher: "Draw near to God in the Word, by looking on it as God speaking to thee," he stated, but then went on to add, "I do not speak

45. Flynt, sermon [1670s], Harvard University MS, pp. 152, 160, 8.

46. Danforth, *New England's Errand*, p. 19.

47. Flynt, sermon [1670s], Harvard University MS, p. 7.

48. Samuel Willard, *The High Esteem Which God hath of the Death of his Saints* (Boston, 1683), p. 4.

49. Shepard, *Parable of Ten Virgins*, p. 65.

50. Belcher, *Worst Enemy Conquered*, p. 16.

51. Allen, *New England's choicest Blessing*, p. 8.

that the soule should take every thing that Ministers speak as the Word of God, but that which is the Word of God, take it as God speaking."[52]

Three distinct generations of clergy were evident in New England during the seventeenth century. The first generation were born in England, generally before 1610, and were educated at Cambridge or Oxford. The second generation were for the most part born in England between 1620 and 1640, and educated at Harvard. The third generation were American-born after 1640 and educated at Harvard. While all three generations displayed an orthodox Puritan theological orientation, a growing movement toward clerical professionalism can be discerned with each successive generation as society became increasingly secularized and pluralistic, thus weakening clerical influence.

During the early years of the first generation, one's standing as an ordained minister of the gospel was entirely dependent upon one's relationship to a group of believers covenanted together as a local church. Standards of scholarship and piety for the ministry existed, but they were not formalized or standardized from one congregation to the next. The congregation selected their own minister and laymen participated in his ordination ceremony while the candidate himself generally preached the ordination sermon. This initiation into the ministry reinforced the idea that the pastor was one of the body of believers, not above them. By the middle of the seventeenth century a tension existed, as David D. Hall points out, between the prophetic and priestly roles of the ministry.[53] The ordination ceremony of new pastors came to be handled not by the congregation, but by other ministers. This was a significant change, for it symbolized that the candidate was credentialed by joining a professional order rather than by action of a local congregation. By the end of the century, laymen were often excluded from the ordination service altogether. Eventually, the ministry "began to suggest that they themselves constituted a peculiarly holy group of men—as if in a society gone wrong they alone embodied the religious life of the community."[54]

It appears that a move toward a professional order of ministry developed due to a perceived decline in the ministry's status and influence. The more secular and pluralistic New England became, the more the ministry clamored for mandatory support and stricter laws

52. Shepard, *Subjection to Christ*, p. 189.

53. See Hall, *Faithful Shepherd*; see also James W. Schmotter, "The Irony of Clerical Professionalism: New England's Congregational Ministers and the Great Awakening," *American Quarterly* (1979): 148–68.

54. J. William T. Young, Jr., "Congregational Clericalism: New England Ordinations before the Great Awakening," *William and Mary Quarterly* 31 (July 1974): 483, 487.

regarding heresy, blasphemy and church attendance requirements. Lay preaching increased in the 1650s, indicating a growing dissatisfaction with the ministry's increased formalism. Congregations began entering into formal contracts with ministers of the second generation, somewhat undermining the image of the pastor as the self-sacrificing shepherd of the flock. In spite of growing problems, waning influence, and the dismissal of an occasional pastor by a local congregation, it is surprising to note the many years that some pastors stayed on and were loved, or at least tolerated, by their congregations. John Wilson, first pastor in Boston, remained in his pulpit from 1630 until his death in 1667. James Allen pastored at Boston's First Church from 1668 until his death in 1710. Increase Mather preached from Boston's Second Church pulpit in the years 1664 to 1723, assisted and followed by his son Cotton Mather between 1685 and 1727. Samuel Willard pastored the Third Church in Boston between 1678 and 1707. John Allin's tenure in the Dedham pulpit lasted from 1639 to 1671, while John Danforth held the same pulpit between 1682 and 1730. John Eliot faithfully served the Roxbury church in various capacities, including missionary work with the Indians, between 1632 and 1690. These and others like them truly were "faithful shepherds" whose lives affected nearly all seventeenth-century New Englanders to at least some degree.

7

Public Worship, Preaching, and Private Piety

While the essence of Puritanism lay in an individual, internalized faith, the public expression of that faith through a corporate worship experience was an integral part of the Puritan way. Public worship was also deemed essential for those in the community who had not yet had a conversion experience. In addition to corporate worship, the true saint, and even the would-be saint, was expected to maintain a personal devotional life that was rigorous by nearly any standard.

The Pattern of Public Worship

New England Congregational services in the seventeenth century were held in the plainly decorated town meetinghouse. Public worship generally adhered to the following pattern: Sunday morning, about nine o'clock, the service would be opened by the pastor with a prayer lasting about fifteen minutes. A psalm might then be sung, without instrumental accompaniment. The teacher, if present as a second member of the ministerial team, would then read and briefly expound upon a chapter from the Bible. At this point, a psalm might again be sung, usually led by the ruling elder. Then came the most vital element of the meeting, the preaching of a Bible-based sermon by the pastor. Following the sermon, which could easily run an hour in

Some of the material in this chapter was first published in "Biblical Texts and Themes in American Puritan Preaching, 1630–1700," *Andrews University Seminary Studies* 21 (Summer 1983): 113–28.

duration, a lengthy prayer was offered, psalms were sung, and opportunity was sometimes given for two or three of the elders to speak briefly if they so desired. Periodically the Lord's Supper was observed. The offering preceded the benediction and blessing, given by the teacher. By two o'clock Sunday afternoon the meetinghouse was again a place of worship. The pastor began with a prayer, a psalm was sung, the teacher read a Scripture passage, prayed, and preached, the rite of baptism was performed as needed, and the pastor concluded with the benediction. All together, the average Puritan spent about six hours in church on Sunday. A weekly "lecture" virtually identical in structure and style to a Sunday sermon was given, often on Thursday, with the pastor and teacher frequently alternating weeks. The distinction between pastor and teacher became blurred early in the New England experience, however, as smaller congregations found they could get along more economically with just one minister.[1]

The forms of public worship were given legitimacy by the Word of God, and anything not found in the Scriptures was suspect. John Cotton carried on a dialogue with himself in a volume published in 1650 in which he asked, "May not the Church, in the Celebration of the Sacraments, use other Rites . . . than those expressed in the Scriptures, or add to them of her own authority?" He answered vehemently in the negative, stating that those who "teach or decree any thing, either in matters of Faith or Ceremonies, contrary to the Word"[2] were guilty of heresy. John Norton warned that "great care must be had in matters of Divine Worship that all things proceed according to the Prescript Word of God."[3] Increase Mather stated that "nothing should be admitted into the worship of God but what there is Scripture warrant for, nor any thing neglected which the Lord hath instituted."[4]

Preaching and acts of worship were not limited to Sunday services and weekday lectures. Since the pulpit provided the means whereby all that concerned the individual and community could be proclaimed, nearly every event of major significance called for a sermon. Natural and man-made disasters, Indian attacks, funerals, crimes, election days, executions, days of thanksgiving, humiliation, and fast-

---

1. See Cotton, *Doctrine of the Church,* pp. 5–8; Henry Martyn Dexter, *The Congregationalism of the Last Three Hundred Years as Seen in its Literature,* vol. 1 (New York, 1880; repr. 1970), pp. 452–53; Ralph G. Turnbull, *A History of Preaching,* vol. 3 (Grand Rapids, 1974), p. 22; Charles E. Hambrick-Stowe, *The Practice of Piety* (Chapel Hill, N.C., 1982), pp. 99, 103–4.

2. Cotton, *Some Treasure Fetched Out of Rubbish* (London, 1650), pp. 9, 15.

3. Norton, *Three Sermons,* p. 30.

4. Increase Mather, *A Call From Heaven* (Boston, 1679), p. 90.

ing were all suitable occasions for worship through a discourse from the Word.[5]

Puritan theology did not allow for ritualistic sacraments whereby grace was dispensed through outward forms without a response from the heart. It was, however, anticipated that God would act on hearts through various ordinances, including the sacraments of baptism and the Lord's Supper. No official list of ordinances was ever drawn up, and some variations occurred between local congregations, but prayer, singing of psalms, giving of offerings, fasting, renewing the covenant, and Sabbath worship itself were often included. Most of all, there was preaching from the Bible—the Word of God.[6]

The Importance of Biblical Preaching

The preaching of the Word was the original and foremost ordinance of New England Puritanism.[7] As a public display of the importance of the Word and its preaching, the pulpit was generally placed in the center position at the front of the meetinghouse.[8] It was beneficial for the Puritan community to receive as much exposure to the preached Word as possible, inasmuch as the elect were "Born again by the Word of God, which Liveth and Abideth Forever."[9] Apart from the Scriptures there was little if any chance of finding the path to eternal life. Samuel Willard asserted that "wee had never known christ & ye way to salvation, had it not been for this Blessed Book."[10] In the opinion of John Cotton, if the Bible were taken away, the principal means of man's knowledge of salvation would be gone. Although Cotton conceded that "the Scriptures are mighty through God, whether preached or read, or heard, or conferred upon, or meditated upon,"[11] the ministry agreed that their preaching was an especially effective

5. A typical example is a sermon by Increase Mather "occasioned by that awfull Providence which hapned in Boston . . . when part of a Vessel was blown up in the Harbour, and nine men hurt, and three mortally wounded. . . ." (*Times of Men*, title page).

6. Hambrick-Stowe, *Practice of Piety*, pp. 93–94.

7. See John Cotton, *The Keyes of the Kingdom of Heaven, and Power thereof, according to the Word of God* (London, 1644), p. 2. In discussing what the "keyes" are, first and foremost on Cotton's list is "the preaching of the Word which is the opening and applying of it." The Puritans' top priority is defined as "godly preaching" in J. Sears McGee, *The Godly Man in Stuart England* (New Haven, 1976), p. 9.

8. Hall, *Faithful Shepherd*, p. 16.

9. Cotton Mather, *Unum Necessarium*, p. 46.

10. Samuel Willard, sermon [1686], *Substance of Sermons*, Huntington Library MS, p. 282.

11. Cotton, *Christ the Fountaine*, p. 198.

way to make the Word known. Jonathan Mitchel asked the question, "how is faith wrought?" and answered that this was accomplished "by openinge & applyinge ye word by ye ministry."[12] John Davenport proclaimed from his pulpit that "Gods usuall way which he will bless for the converting or turning of elect sinners to himself, is by sending his Ministers with a Message from himself to them, in their Preaching Gods Word unto them."[13] Josiah Flynt succinctly stated the case when he informed his congregation that "the only ordinary way to obtein faith, is by a diligent attention to the preaching of the word of God."[14]

The biblical sermon was of great importance to the theological life of the community. It was also the principal outlet for public expression of society's disappointments, conflicts, and aspirations, and provided an explanation of the events comprising daily life. To a society that was keenly interested in the wherefore of God's wrath and the means of retaining his favor, the Bible-based Puritan sermon "possessed powerful appeal for a generation of listeners and readers who made the sermon the most popular literature of the period."[15]

Attendance at public worship where the Word was preached was urged upon the populace by the ministry and further encouraged by mandatory attendance laws. It was considered a great privilege and responsibility, at least by the Puritan leadership, to attend worship services. "To enjoy the word and Ordinances of God publickly dispensed is a great mercy," Increase Mather reminded his congregation. The preaching of the Word in public worship was "such a blessing as is enough to make amends for many sorrows and afflictions."[16] It was the desire of Josiah Flynt's heart that "all persons come to the house of God, and bring their bodily presence thither where the Gospell is preached. . . ."[17] It was clear to the true saint that "time spent in God's House is better than that spent about any secular Business or Worldly Concerns."[18]

It is apparent that not everyone in New England took every possible opportunity to listen to Puritan sermons. While the novelty and clarity of Puritan evangelical preaching was a drawing card for many of the first generation of Englishmen in America, the excitement tended to wear off with time. Several ministers became distraught

12. Jonathan Mitchell, sermon of Jan., 1652, Harvard University MS, p. 140.

13. Davenport, *Gods Call*, p. 6.

14. Flynt, sermon [1670s], Harvard University MS, p. 59.

15. Emory Elliott, *Power and the Pulpit in Puritan New England* (Princeton, 1975), p. 11.

16. Increase Mather, *Call From Heaven*, p. 15.

17. Flynt, sermon [1670s], Harvard University MS, p. 268.

18. Joshua Moodey, *A Practical Discourse Concerning the Choice Benefit of Communion with God in His House* (Boston, 1685), p. 13.

with the falling off of church attendance in the 1670s. Increase Mather asked, "What are the Evils that have provoked the Lord to bring his Judgments on New England?" and the first item on his list of sins was the neglect of public worship. In another sermon, Mather bemoaned that "publick attendance upon the worship of God is omitted by many: some seldome hear a sermon on the Lords day much less on Lecture dayes."[19] Josiah Flynt was perturbed by "a generation in the world, & those not a few, who account preaching to be foolishnesse." He was particularly troubled by "those who cast off the ordinances as needlesse, & useless things" and those "who turn their backs upon the preaching of the word."[20] Joshua Moodey condemned those who attended worship services with "such coldness, formality . . . and with so little heart and hungring after Fellowship. . . ." Moodey went on to offer "sharp Reproof" to those who fell asleep during his sermons. The very fact that he had to publicly ask, "Is there not more refreshment and Sweetness in a Sermon than in a Napp?"[21] probably indicates that there were those in his congregation who did not think so.

The ministry saw their preaching as important partly because it was designed to be so practical for daily living. The clergy were not interested merely in intellectual or philosophical exercises; they desired to preach as simply and effectively as possible the great doctrines they found in the Word. The ministry wanted to see saintly living in action, not mere contemplation; they wanted behavior based on internalized beliefs and motivated out of love for God, not mere outward assent to a creed.

The Structure of Puritan Sermons

The effective communication of the Word required a sermon structure that emphasized clarity of thought and development, and permitted a wide range of ages and intellects in the congregation to follow with interest what was being said. The basic structure of Puritan sermons aided in the communication process, and remained essentially constant throughout the seventeenth century and even beyond. Sermons were based on biblical texts of usually one verse, but occasionally longer biblical passages were employed. Most sermons were complete by themselves, but series of sermons based on either a short but meaty text or a longer text were also fairly common.[22] Most pub-

19. [Increase Mather], *The Necessity of Reformation* (Boston, 1679), pp. 1–2; Increase Mather, *Divine Providence*, p. 99.

20. Flynt, sermon [1670s], Harvard University MS, p. 264.

21. Moodey, *Practical Discourse*, pp. 3, 83, 75.

22. Samuel Willard, e.g., in his *Mercy Magnified* published a series of twenty-eight sermons he had preached on the story of the prodigal son (Luke 15).

lished sermons were given titles, some elaborate at times, but there is no evidence that sermons were given titles at the time they were preached.

The text for the sermon came first. The scriptural passage under consideration was read in context. Several minutes were generally spent placing the text into its historical context. Care was taken to explain by whom and to whom the passage was written or spoken and also what circumstances surrounded its writing. Words within the text were carefully defined and frequently the passage was exegeted from the Greek or Hebrew so that every possible shade of meaning was exposed to scrutiny.

Following this introductory section a formal statement of the principal teaching to be expounded in the sermon was set forth. This doctrine was nearly always related very closely to the biblical text and was often merely a restatement of it. The stating of a doctrine served to give a focus to the entire sermon and informed the congregation of just what the main point of the homily was. From time to time a sermon was preached with more than one doctrine, but this was the exception rather than the rule. The relevance of the text for the contemporary audience was always set forth. Since it was believed that God's message was timeless, biblical texts were never without their lessons for the present. When a sermon was deemed worthy of publication, the doctrine was clearly marked with a large "D," or "DOCT:" or "DOCTRINE" so that the reader could not miss it (a boon for the modern researcher as well as the Puritan saint). Published sermons or other theological treatises generally included a preface, "To the Christian Reader," in which the merits of the volume and the qualifications of the author were extolled by a fellow clergyman.

In an intellectual climate in which reason was not the least of virtues, the clergy took great care in their sermons not only to state a doctrine, but also to make clear the reasons why the doctrine should be accepted as truth. This section of the sermon was generally headed "Reasons" or "Proofs" and made up a substantial portion of the homily. An attempt was made to support the doctrine with logic, human experience, the pronouncements of noted theologicans and church fathers, common sense, and most of all with as many biblical passages as could be construed to have any bearing on the matter at hand. Sometimes the "Reasons" portion of the sermon was put in a mock dialogue format with a "skeptic" asking questions or raising objections which the minister would then answer.

The concluding section of the sermon, again quite lengthy, was generally entitled "Application" or "Use" and served a number of functions. An attempt was made to show why the doctrine being preached was important. Often a comparison was made between the biblical ideal and the New England reality, and congregations were exhorted to take specific steps to bring their attitudes and behavior into line with the biblical model as interpreted by the clergy. Puritan sermons were by no means merely intellectual exercises, but were calls to action, almost always demanding a response from the members of the congregation. It was hoped that with the aid of the "breath of the Spirit" the preacher's biblical message would "sinke deeply."[23] A doctrine preached by William Brattle in 1686 summed up well the purpose of Puritan preaching: "We should reckon practice ye End of Hearing, & reckon that wee have not done with a sermon, till wee come to that."[24]

The way in which Puritan sermons were organized shows the influence of Petrus Ramus, a sixteenth-century French philosopher and follower of the Reformation whose ideas became widely accepted among Protestant thinkers. Ramus advocated clarity, precision, and a method of argument that began with the familiar and led to the unfamiliar. The way the Puritan clergy "opened" their texts and stated and proved their doctrines is illustrative of the Ramist theory of reliance upon axiomatic truth rather than syllogistic reasoning. The Ramist concept that the theory developed in arriving at a conclusion mattered less than the practical application of the conclusion can also be seen in the sermons of seventeenth-century New England.

The Style of Puritan Preaching

The preaching of the clergy in seventeenth-century New England was characterized by an intensity of spirit and a seriousness of purpose stimulated by strong doctrinal convictions growing out of the ministry's absolute belief in the Word. Their desire to do nothing to obscure or detract from God's message as recorded in the Bible fostered an emphasis on the "plain style" of preaching which shunned undue eloquence or the use of Latin or other foreign phrases, even though the clergy were certainly able to use them. Henry Dunster, an early president of Harvard College, wrote to ministerial students that "In handling the Doctrine be as plain as may be, only look what concerns the understanding of the Doctrine. . . . From the Doctrine come to Application to the soul wherein consists the life of preaching."[25]

The sermons of Puritan New England were devoid of humor and contained relatively few anecdotes and illustrations not drawn di-

23. Cotton, *Way of Life*, p. 163.
24. William Brattle, sermon of May 9, 1686, *Substance of Sermons*, Huntington Library MS, p. 183.
25. Quoted in Eugene E. White, "Puritan Preaching and the Authority of God," in De Witte Holland, ed., *Preaching in American History* (Nashville, 1969), p. 57.

rectly from Scripture. The urgency of the message can be sensed from the passionate and, at times, pleading language of the minister as he expounded the Word. Plainness, persuasion, and practical application were hallmarks of the preaching of the era, as the clergy opened the Word of God to their hearers.

The jeremiad, a sermon genre denouncing corporate sin and warning of judgment in the style of the Old Testament prophet Jeremiah, was a useful weapon in urging conformity to the Word of God. In reciting New England's "spiritual failures and moral deficiencies" the jeremiad became, in Miller's estimation, "the one literary type which the first native-born Americans inevitably developed, [and] into which they poured their energy and passion. . . ." Miller is probably correct in explaining that the jeremiad did not really develop until the second generation because "the founding clergy had many other topics to occupy their minds."[26]

Sermon Texts

Some scholars have made assumptions about the content of Puritan preaching based on an analysis of Old and New Testament texts used by the clergy. But do sermons based on New Testament texts necessarily stress, as Emory Elliott suggests, "mercy and grace" and a "gentle, loving, and protective Christ" while sermons with Old Testament texts give us "the image of the angry and wrathful God the Father"?[27] Is it valid to assume that the Puritan ministry used one Testament or the other to emphasize a certain view of God and his dealings with men, or to assume that one Testament or the other was preferred by the clergy as a whole? A comparison of sermon texts with the actual doctrinal themes of the sermons indicates that clear-cut differences between Old and New Testament preaching are hard to find. A sample of nearly 500 sermons preached in 5 Massachusetts communities between 1630 and 1700 indicates that 42.1 percent were based on Old Testament texts, whereas 57.9 percent were based on New Testament texts.[28] Puritan preaching was not oriented more toward the Old Testament than the New. Since the clergy viewed both Testaments as the unified Word of God and without error or defect of any kind, sermon texts were drawn from all parts of the Bible.

---

26. Miller, *New England Mind: Colony to Province*, pp. 28–29.
27. Elliott, *Power and the Pulpit*, pp. 13–14, concludes that such is the case.
28. Carden, "Biblical Texts and Themes," p. 114.

Typology

Utilization of typology as a method of biblical interpretation by the Puritan clergy helps in understanding their belief in the unity of both Testaments. The use of "types" was in itself a biblical concept whereby Old Testament characters, rituals, places, and the like had a reality of their own but were also viewed as symbols or foreshadowings of New Testament realities. Thus many Old Testament passages were interpreted with a dual meaning—a past reality or symbol which served as the type and pointed to the antitype, a later or still future reality, which was always "something more glorious than the type." Samuel Willard explained that "as to the Histories of the Old Testament, besides that they are Exemplary and Written for our Admonition, there are many persons and things recorded in them, which are also Typical, referring to Christ and to spiritual things."[29]

Biblical typology was not a novel idea to the Puritan divines of New England. In actuality, while the Puritans may not have realized it or cared to admit it, the use of typology was a major feature of medieval Catholic literature which was carried on through the Reformation. This system of interpreting the Scriptures served as a basic system of linking the Old Testament with the New Testament. In recent years, historians have finally come to realize that "an understanding of typology is central to reading Puritan texts and to identifying the references of Puritan imagery," and that "to be unaware of typological traditions is to distort basic Puritan beliefs."[30]

Some of the types expounded in the sermon literature included God's ordering of the details of the Jewish tabernacle as a type of the "Gospel Church," Noah's ark as a "Type of Gods Church" (with Christ as the door), the Promised Land of Canaan as a type of heaven, and the dark-skinned woman of the Song of Solomon as a type of a sinful church. Israel's deliverance from Egypt was interpreted as "a type of God's people coming out of sin, and passing through the red sea of Christ's blood, and going through the wilderness of temptations." Baptism was given typological meaning as symbolic of affliction and cleansing in the blood of Christ, the Babylonian captivity of Israel was viewed as "a type of that great captivity, partly of sin, which God's people are subject to be drawn to," and Israel's wars to drive out the pagan Canaanites were paralleled with the believers'

29. Willard, *Child's Portion*, p. 7; *The Man of War* (Boston, 1699), p. 4.

30. Thomas M. Davis, "The Traditions of Puritan Typology," in Sacvan Bercovitch, ed., *Typology and Early American Literature* (Amherst, Mass., 1972), p. 11. For a survey of the development of a typological view of the Bible, see Jean Danielou, *From Shadows to Reality: Studies in the Typology of the Fathers*, trans. Wulstan Hibberd (London, 1960).

wars to drive sin out of their lives. The destruction of Jerusalem and the dissolution of the Jewish state were interpreted as "a type of the great day of Judgment." Most of ancient Israel's recorded experiences were believed to have meaning for the saints of New England; Urian Oakes referred to "New-England-Israel" in one of his sermons.[31]

The greatest and most frequent antitype in Puritan sermons was Christ, who was seen as the principal subject of both Testaments. Some of the Old Testament types viewed as prefigures of Christ included Samson, the Mosaic tabernacle and the later temple, the tree of life in the garden of Eden, as well as Adam, Moses, Joseph, and Solomon. David was viewed as typifying Christ as the head of the church, the high priest was seen as a type of Christ's making intercession to God for the saints, and the penitential sacrifices of the Mosaic law were considered as prefiguring Christ's atoning death.[32]

To the Puritans, the primary subject of the Bible was Christ and the plan of salvation available through him. With this shared belief, various interpreters could reach general agreement concerning the meaning of many scriptural passages. John Cotton asked, "What were the [Old Testament] ceremonies but shadows of Christ . . . ? All the understanding Israelites did see that these things did point at Christ."[33] Cotton Mather displayed his enthusiasm for typological interpretations as he proclaimed,

> Among all the many Subjects which a Preacher of the Gospel has to insist upon, I know not whether any would carry a greater mixture of pleasure and profit, than that of the Types which exhibited Evangelical Mysteries unto Israel of old. . . . In every Chapter of the

31. Willard, *Sinfulness of Worshipping,* p. 15; Cotton Mather, *Work Upon the Ark,* p. 4; Samuel Willard, sermon of Mar. 10, 1686, *Substance of Sermons,* Huntington Library MS by Cotton Mather; Increase Mather, *Mystery of Israel's Salvation,* p. 54; Mitchel, *Discourse,* p. 197; Shepard, *Church Membership of Children,* p. 6; Cotton, *Book of Canticles,* pp. 23–24, 31; *Way of Life,* p. 157; *Saints Support & Comfort,* pp. 32, 34; Urian Oakes, *Unconquerable Souldier,* p. 12; *New England Pleaded with, And pressed to consider the things which concern her Peace at least in this her Day* (Cambridge, 1673), pp. 17, 23.

32. Thomas Shepard, *The Saints Jewel* (Boston, 1708), p. 46; Norton, *Three Sermons,* pp. 121, 136; Cotton, *Christ the Fountaine,* pp. 2, 78; Cotton Mather, *Batteries,* p. 48; Willard, *Sinfulness of Worshipping,* p. 15; Cotton, *Bloudy Tenent,* p. 72; *Book of Canticles,* p. 21; Increase Mather, *Mystery of Israel's Salvation,* p. 125; Willard, *Covenant of Redemption,* pp. 9–10, 43; Eliot, *Harmony of the Gospels,* p. 53; Willard, *Covenant-Keeping,* p. 78; *Good Ruler,* p. 6; Cotton Mather, *Present from a Farr Countrey,* pp. 36, 40; Norton, *Three Sermons,* pp. 33–34.

33. Cotton, *Sermon Preached by the Reverend, Mr. John Cotton, Teacher of the First Church in Boston in New England* (Boston, 1713), p. 23.

Bible, there is to be found something of our Blessed Jesus . . . every paragraph of the Bible is a spot of Ground where before we dig far, we shall find the Pearl of Great Price [Christ]. . . . And not only the Person of the Messiah, but His Conditions, and the Miseries, and the Enemies, from which we are by Him delivered: All of these were Preached in and by those Types of old.[34]

Increase Mather stated that when it came to the Mosaic law, "All the Ceremonies did one way or another point at Christ."[35] John Norton concurred, preaching that "truths of Christ are laid up under the types of the Ceremonial Law, [so that] if you understood it, you would see Christ through it. . . ."[36] John Cotton, in referring to the psalms, stated that they were "full of Christ, as [are] other Scriptures."[37] Cotton Mather concisely summarized Puritan biblical interpretation when he stated, "In short, Jesus Christ is the key that unlocks all the Scriptures. We have searched the Scriptures, and know them to good purpose, when we have dug so far into them, as to find them all testifying of the Lord Jesus Christ."[38]

Principles of Biblical Interpretation

In addition to the use of typology as a method of interpreting the Bible in their preaching, the clergy followed other general principles in explaining the Word. Samuel Willard indicated that a compound meaning was acceptable in Scripture passages where a type was involved, but otherwise "it would undermine the Authority of Holy Writ to allow two distinct senses to one Text."[39] Thomas Shepard set forth the principle that "one Scripture gives light unto another," that is, the meaning of a given text should be clarified by comparison with other biblical passages since the Bible, being without error, could not contradict itself.[40] The Puritan clergy were biblical literalists in the sense that they believed that all statements in Scripture had literal truths behind them. However, the clergy could not be accused of ignoring the presence of literary devices and taking every biblical phrase in a literal sense. Parables, for example, were seen as "Allegorical comparisons, where, under the title of persons or actions, some other

34. Cotton Mather, *Work Upon the Ark*, pp. i–ii, 2.
35. Increase Mather, *Power of Godliness*, p. 95.
36. Norton, *Three Sermons*, p. 33.
37. Cotton, *Singing of Psalmes*, p. 4.
38. Cotton Mather, *Addresses*, p. 10.
39. Willard, *Man of War*, p. 4.
40. Shepard, *Church Membership of Children*, p. 12.

thing is represented."[41] The divine purpose in the use of biblical parables was to clothe "Spiritual Things with Earthly Language, to accomodate them the more to Human Understandings, and to shew the rationality of them. . . ."[42] John Cotton certainly did not take the Book of Revelation in a literal sense, but bent the symbolism and allegory of the book to fit recent religious events and to attack the Church of Rome. On one occasion, Cotton described Revelation's "bottomless pit of ignorance & darknesse" as "a lively description of the Friers & Priests of the Church of Rome."[43] Samuel Willard did not hesitate to describe much of Revelation as "Allegorical."[44] Not even hell's lake of fire and brimstone was taken in a strictly literal sense by Increase Mather. He stated that "The Scripture expresseth the Punishment of sinners in the World to come by such Metaphors because it will be more intolerable than those things really and literally done would be." However, in another sermon he set forth the hermeneutical principle that "a literal interpretation of Scripture ought never to be rejected for an allegorical one, except necessity compel thereunto. . . ."[45] John Norton realized that not every passage in the Bible was intended to be taken in a literal sense and that to preach nothing but a completely literal interpretation "exposeth Scripture to the imputation of nonsense."[46]

No doubt Puritan biblical interpretation reveals much about Puritan values; passages of Scripture were often interpreted very parochially as reflections of contemporary concerns and perspectives. For example, the Book of Canticles, or Song of Solomon, is a rather sensual love song but this aspect of the book was completely overlooked. The Puritan clergy, who were protective of the privacy of sexual relations within marriage, chose to emphasize the allegorical aspect of the book as a type of Christ's love for the church.[47] Although this approach to Canticles was by no means original to the Puritans, they may have reached new heights in spiritualizing the details of female anatomy described therein. John Cotton, in his lengthy exposition of the book, interpreted "lips" as "utterance of doctrine," "neck"

41. Flynt, sermon [1670s], Harvard University MS, p. 249.
42. Willard, *Fig Trees Doom*, p. 3.
43. Cotton, *Seven Vials*, p. 150.
44. Willard, *Child's Portion*, p. 133.
45. Increase Mather, *Solemn Advice*, p. 40; *Mystery of Israel's Salvation*, p. 8.
46. John Norton, *The Heart of New England rent at the Blasphemies of the Present Generation* (Cambridge, 1659), p. 9.
47. Cotton, *Way of Life*, p. 19; Mitchel, *Discourse of the Glory*, p. 32; Cotton, *Book of Canticles* .

as "faith," and "breasts" as the ministry "giving the sincere milk of the word."[48]

It was believed that the Spirit of God (or Spirit of Christ) was essential in preparing the heart of the well-studied minister to properly interpret the Word to his congregation. Samuel Willard voiced his concern that in expounding the Scriptures to his hearers he "not go beyond the mind of the Spirit of God. . . ."[49] Thomas Shepard said of the faithful clergy that "They cannot think a thought; Christ furnished them with thoughts; the Minister knows not what to say, yet his thoughts are from him [Christ]. They cannot speak . . . the Lord opens their mouth."[50] In spite of divine guidance in interpreting the Scriptures, much study was required and, owing to human frailty, proper results could not be guaranteed. Although the Word of God plainly set forth truths necessary for salvation, it was acknowledged that there were also difficult passages where "the words are somewhat darke, and there is much variety in the interpretation of them."[51]

Sermon Themes

In New England Puritan preaching, certain themes appeared with considerable frequency during the course of the seventeenth century. My analysis of sermons preached by twenty-four clergymen spanning three generations between 1630 and 1700 indicates that nearly 80 percent of the sermons can be categorized into five general thematic areas (based on the doctrinal teaching stated for each sermon): (1) the problem of sin, (2) the call to holy living, (3) the call to salvation, (4) the person and work of Christ, and (5) family relations in the church and home.[52] The thematic emphases within each generation should give us a glimpse into the clergy's perspectives of what was important for the people of seventeenth-century New England to hear and heed.

In all three generations of seventeenth-century clergy, the theme most frequently preached was a condemnation of sin. Such sermons took several approaches. Some dealt with specific sins, some with the general concept of sin and its impact on society and the individual; many sermons on this topic dealt with the spiritual consequences of sin and the availability of forgiveness through true repentance. The percentage of sermons dealing primarily with sin was lowest for the first generation of clergy and highest for the second generation, while

48. Cotton, *Book of Canticles*, p. 112.
49. Willard, *Man of War*, p. 19.
50. Shepard, *Parable of Ten Virgins*, p. 97.
51. Cotton, *Seven Vials*, p. 2.
52. Carden, "Texts and Themes in Puritan Preaching," p. 120. The sample includes 466 sermons.

the third generation preached on this theme nearly as frequently as
the second. It is interesting to note that while the second generation
preached against sin primarily from the Old Testament, the third generation turned more often to the New Testament for a discussion of
sin. This further demonstrates the interchangeability of both
Testaments in Puritan preaching.

The second most frequent theme in the sermons under consideration was that of holiness. Although the Puritan clergy denounced the
idea that good works obtained merit toward salvation, it was agreed
that the saints had definite responsibilities to God following conversion. Believers were, as the Bible expressed it, the "temple of God,"[53]
and they should conduct themselves accordingly. The as-yet-
unregenerate members of the congregation were also urged to live
lives of holiness, not to earn their salvation, but rather to promote the
good of the covenanted community. It was, of course, the Bible—or
more accurately the Puritan interpretation of the Bible—that provided
clergy and laity alike with guidelines for saintly behavior and
attitudes. The emphasis given to the theme of holiness was more
constant for the three generations of clergy than was the case with the
other sermon themes. Little difference is noted among the generations
of clergy concerning choice of Old Testament or New Testament texts
for this theme in their preaching.

Sermons preached on the theme of the need for salvation were third
in frequency. The ministry, devoting nearly 20 percent of their
sermons to this theme, clearly recognized that by no means had their
entire congregations undergone conversion experiences. This was true
as much for the first generation of ministers—in fact, their sermons
dealing with a call to salvation made up the largest single percentage
among the five main sermon themes (26.7 percent). The second generation of clergy in the sample showed a greatly reduced emphasis on
this theme (8.5 percent of the sermons), while a renewed surge of interest in the topic of salvation appeared in the sermons of the third
generation (22.9 percent), who preached during a time of perceived declension and tapering off of conversion experiences. A large percentage
of sermon texts were drawn from the New Testament, although the
Old Testament was also used frequently.

The fourth sermon theme, in order of frequency, was that of the
person and work of Christ. Sermons with this as the primary theme
account for 10 percent of the sermons for all three generations. It is of
interest to note that over one-fourth of these sermons were based on
Old Testament texts. This should not be surprising, however, in light
of the Puritans' typological interpretation of the Old Testament and

53. 2 Cor. 6:16 quoted in Cotton Mather, *Holiness of Church Members*, p. 48.

their understanding that Christ was the focal point of the whole Bible. A marked decline in frequency for each successive generation can be noted. In fact, sermons focusing on the person and work of Christ were preached four times more frequently by the first generation of clergy than by the third. It was perhaps this lack of preaching about Christ in the latter years of the seventeenth century that caused Increase Mather to lament, "It is marvellous to consider what Ignorance is in many that call themselves Christians; . . . if they are examined about Christ, they are found exceeding ignorant."[54]

A fifth thematic categorization is based on sermons dealing with the concept of the family of God in its various aspects. When it came to explaining God's relationship to man as well as man's relationship to his fellow man, the biblical authors frequently used the human family as an analogy. This approach was deemed important by the Puritan ministry, who placed a strong emphasis on human relationships and who viewed church and community in familial terms. The saints were conceptualized as being members of the family of God, and a good deal of Puritan theology was pictured in domestic terms. Several of the sermons preached on this theme called for a strengthening of domestic life. Increase Mather, for example, stressed the importance of families in a sermon in 1679 in which he bemoaned their decline: "Families are the Nurceryes for Church and Commonwealth, ruine Families, and ruine all. Order them well and the public State will fare the better; the great wound and misery of New England is that Families are out of order."[55] It is noteworthy that the third generation of ministers provided more than their share of sermons on the family theme, going freely to both Testaments for their texts. In the closing years of the seventeenth century, many of the clergy perceived a growing apostasy on the part of New England's young people. Increase Mather sadly observed that "there is a doleful degeneracy appearing in the face of this generation [of youth], and no man can say, but that the body of the present generation will perish both temporally and eternally. . . ."[56]

An examination of the doctrinal themes of seventeenth-century Puritan sermons leads to the conclusion that certain broad themes recurred in the ministry's preaching. It can be concluded, furthermore, that sermon material was drawn freely from all parts of the Bible and that it is inappropriate to make generalizations about the nature of Puritan preaching based on a differentiation in the clergy's use of the Old and New Testaments. It can also be concluded that among the

54. Increase Mather, *Mystery of Christ*, p. 38.
55. Increase Mather, *Call from Heaven*, p. 91.
56. Ibid., p. 19.

ministerial fellowship of the seventeenth century there was flexibility
and freedom in the selection of sermon material (and even in its interpretation on nonessential points), yet at the same time there existed a
set of limits within which one could expect most sermons to fall.
These limits were the themes with which the Bible dealt extensively
and to which the ministry were attracted because of events and trends
which were perceived by each generation as having importance for
New England's "errand into the wilderness."

The Practice of Piety

The clergy in their sermons emphasized obedience and faithfulness
to God in general terms, and also admonished their flocks to carry out
specific religious duties. One activity heartily urged was that of
prayer. In a published sermon entitled *The Godly Man is a Praying
Man*, Increase Mather's main point was that "it is the duty of every
man, and especially godly men, to be much in prayer." It was also incumbent upon the "true Fearers of God" to be "constant in the practice of that duty of Family Prayer." Mather went on to define prayer as
"a making known the desires of our hearts before God, in the name of
Jesus Christ, concerning things agreeable unto his will." The prayers
of the saints did not go unheeded, according to Mather, for such
prayers would "do much towards the averting of wrathful judgements
and desolations."[57] For the saint to disregard prayer was "wicked
Folly" and was equivalent to living "as if there were no Soul, no Hell,
no God." In light of the biblical admonition to pray, the saints should
do nothing less than offer up "Dayly and Serious Prayers." Cotton
Mather prodded his congregation to their knees by emphasizing the
duty of prayer, especially in the "fearful times" in which they were
living.[58]

John Cotton was convinced that "God is very sensible of prayer:
men doe not think there is such force in prayer, as there is." Cotton
cautioned against the exercise of prayer as a mere mindless ritual,
however. Believers could be "certaine of the hearing and granting of
their petitions" as long as their prayers were asked humbly, in faith
and in Christ's name. Those desiring results must believe in God's
ability to answer, live lives of obedience to God, and pray "according
to God's will." Furthermore, praying saints were encouraged to be

---

57. Increase Mather, *Power of Godliness*, pp. 56, 4; *Heaven's Alarm to the
World* (Boston, 1681), p. 15.
58. Cotton Mather, *Batteries*, pp. 47, 51–52, 58, 48; *The Day*, p. 22.

persistent in their requests, and to use the Word as a guide for appropriate prayer topics.[59]

Prayer was a Christian duty for the individual believer, but it also played a major role in family devotional time. As an aid to family devotional practice, manuals with appropriate prayers were published and were apparently followed quite closely by Puritan families. Morning prayers emphasized confession of sin, a request for forgiveness, and thanksgiving to God for his beneficence. Prayers were also offered before and after meals, with thanksgiving and humility the themes. It was God's goodness that made the meal possible; it was a sign of human weakness and dependence that food was required. Such mealtime prayers often asked the Lord to grant the same intensity of hunger for spiritual truth that was experienced in the desire for physical nourishment. Prayers following the meal were a type of benediction, focusing attention on the kingdom of God "as the family moved away from the table and back into the world. . . ."[60] Prayers in the evening before retiring often focused on the analogy of laying down in death and awakening to new life, with requests made for safety throughout the night.

Another approach frequently used in the quest for pious living was the conference—a meeting, or series of meetings, with another believer with whom one might share spiritual burdens and from whom one might receive spiritual insight and advice. Private counseling of this nature was not an exclusive prerogative of the clergy, although it frequently involved them and became a major part of a pastoral ministry. Such conferences were often held between parents and children, as mothers and fathers agonized to be used of God to lead their offspring into his kingdom.

Private piety was also encouraged through pastoral admonitions to read, study and meditate upon the Word of God as well as sound devotional books. Also commonly encouraged and practiced were spiritual self-examination and diary-keeping. John White's *Way to the Tree of Life* was perhaps the most complete manual on how to study the Bible available in the seventeenth century. According to White, "Spirituall Raptures seize on a man, even while he is reading the Scriptures" and God will work in three stages as His Word is studied: "First, the wounding and terrifying. Secondly, the converting and renuing. Thirdly, the comforting and reviving of the heart."[61]

---

59. Cotton, *Saints Support & Comfort*, p. 89; *Christ the Fountaine*, pp. 192, 210–11, 214, 220, 235.

60. Hambrick-Stowe, *Practice of Piety*, pp. 145–50.

61. Quoted in ibid., p. 159.

Self-examination was a periodic, if not daily, ritual for the Puritan saint who took stock of his spiritual progress, or lack thereof, while reflecting on recent events in his or her life. Even the most trivial events of the day could be seen in light of divine providence at work in one's life, and spiritual applications were constantly plucked from the joys and frustrations of everyday life. Samuel Sewall, for example, "spiritualized" his spilling of a can of water by remarking "that our Lives would shortly be spilt."[62] Often a Puritan's self-examination took the form of a diary. Many of these volumes would overwhelm the modern reader with the authors' sense of guilt and anguish in their quest for spirituality, although spiritual ecstacies were also recorded. What is sometimes disconcerting is the range and frequency of mood swings to be found in such diaries, most of which were never intended to be read by others.

Conclusion

Through public worship and private acts of piety, the Puritans of seventeenth-century New England were encouraged forward in their pilgrimage. The prize was salvation, a gift of God and yet something to be striven for with an intensity that most modern minds find incomprehensible. While the Puritans' pilgrimage involved the spirit and the intellect, it also required a sojourn in the world and a practical working out of the practice of piety as they lived with themselves and their fellow pilgrims.

---

62. Quoted in Robert Middlekauf, "Piety and Intellect in Puritanism," *William and Mary Quarterly* 22 (July 1965): 469.

8

Social Ethics
The Communal Ideal
and the Practice of Inequality

The Puritan experience in America was a serious attempt to bring biblical precepts to bear on the realities of life. From the beginning of the American experiment, the Puritan leadership had reminded those going to the New World of their Christian social responsibility. A sense of community and common purpose for the glory of God was an essential ingredient of early American Puritanism. Puritan society cannot be rightly understood without the recognition that it was group-oriented, especially in the earlier decades of New England's settlement. A truly Christian society, in Puritan thinking, consisted of individuals voluntarily sacrificing their own concerns for the good of the whole. In a very real sense for the Puritans, society was an organism, something larger and grander than the sum of its parts.

A Public Spirit, Christian Love, and Self-denial

Preaching a farewell sermon to the Winthrop expedition just before their departure for the wilds of America, the Reverend John Cotton of Boston, England, admonished the group to "go forth, every man that goeth, with a publick Spirit, looking not on your own things only, but

Some of the material in this chapter was previously published in "The Communal Ideal in Puritan New England, 1630–1700," *Fides et Historia* 17 (Fall–Winter 1984): 25–38.

also on the things of others: Phil. 2,4."[1] This "public spirit," or communal outlook, was seen as the best means, if not the only means, to achieve "the same last End" of both church and state, "viz., the Glory of God. . . ."[2] A communal spirit was also a practical means of expressing Christian love one to another while at the same time aiding in the attainment and preservation of order. This was given practical application in the opening clauses of the town covenant of Dedham. A handful of settlers established that town when they were granted a large tract of wilderness southwest of Boston in 1636. As they commenced this undertaking, they covenanted together "in the fear and reverence of our Almighty God" to "profess and practice one truth according to that most perfect rule, the foundation whereof is everlasting love." The quest for unity, peace, and love in the community is apparent in the Dedham covenant's second clause, which calls for the cooperation of like-minded settlers eager to edify each other "in the knowledge and faith of the Lord Jesus," who would also seek the encouragement and good of each other, "out of which may be derived true peace."[3] This desire for a communal orientation applied to the churches as well as to towns. Joining a local church, John Cotton wrote, involved the members "submitting of themselves to him [God], and one to another in his feare; and their walking in professed subjection to all his holy Ordinances; their cleaving one to another, as fellow members of the same body, in brotherly love and holy watchfulnesse unto mutual edification in Christ Jesus."[4]

Thomas Hooker, who wanted to leave Cambridge, Massachusetts, with part of his congregation for Connecticut, was dissuaded at least temporarily by Massachusetts Bay officials who argued "that, in point of conscience, they ought not to depart from us, being knit to us in one body, and bound by oath to seek the welfare of this commonwealth."[5] Hooker and company did leave a year later in 1635 but on friendly terms. Thirteen years later this same divine set forth an eloquent statement of the Puritan communal ideal—the need for mutual submission of all for the common good:

1. John Cotton, *God's Promise to His Plantations* (London, 1634; repr. Boston, 1686), p. 18.
2. Cotton, *Civil Government*, p. 7.
3. Excerpts from the Dedham covenant, quoted in Kenneth Lockridge, *A New England Town: The First Hundred Years* (New York, 1970), pp. 4–5.
4. John Cotton, *The Way of the Churches of Christ in New England* (London, 1645), p. 2.
5. John Winthrop, *The History of New England from 1630 to 1649*, ed. James Savage (Boston, 1825), 1:140.

For if each man may do what is good in his owne eyes, proceed according to his own pleasure, so that none may crosse him or controll him by any power; there must of necessity follow the distraction and desolation of the whole, when each man hath liberty to follow his owne imagination and humorous devices, and seek his particular, but oppose one another, and all prejudice the publike good. In the building, if the parts be neither mortified nor braced, as there will be little beauty, so there can be no strength. Its so in setting up the frames of societies among men, when their mindes and hearts are not mortified by mutuall consent of subjection one to another, there is no expectation of any successful proceeding with the advantage to the publike. To this appertains that of the Apostle, Every one submit unto another.

Mutuall subjection is as it were the sinewes of society, by which it is sustained and supported. . . . Hence every part is subject to the whole, and must be serviceable to the good thereof, and must be ordered by the power thereof. It is the highest law in all Policy Civill or Spirituall to preserve the good of the whole, at this all must aime, and unto this all must be subordinate.[6]

The prolific Cotton Mather (who produced fourteen children and four hundred books) penned an enlightening treatise, published in 1690, subtitled "A Discourse on the Necessities and Advantages of a Public Spirit in every Man." In this work he enumerates the things all must be willing to sacrifice for the common good of the people of God—in short, everything they are and everything they have: (1) "the Pleasures of our own Repose" when the service of God and his people shall beckon; (2) "our Estate," that is, all personal possessions; (3) "our Honour . . . We are swoln with the vainest Air, if we count our sevles too Bigg to do what is bespoke for the Interest of those that we should be Benefactors unto. . . ." [Mather exemplified this in the personal care he gave his parishoners]; and (4) "our Lives" if need be. "If we have a call to ride into the very Bowels of the Earth, for the Service of the Public, we should as He of old, with all Spur and Speed be there." Mather continued his admonition: "Tis said, Eat and Drink unto the Glory of God; every Bit of Meat, every Drop of Drink, that we have; and whatever is reckoned in our All, may be devoted unto the Glory of God, if so, it must go to the Service of His People too."[7]

Puritan saints and would-be saints were exhorted to submit themselves completely to God and to one another. "The Earth is the Lords and the fulness thereof," reminded John Cotton. "His are our

6. Thomas Hooker, *A Survey of the Summe of Church-Discipline* (London, 1648), p. 188.

7. Cotton Mather, *The Present State of New England* (Boston, 1690), pp. 11–15, 19.

Countries, our Towns, our Houses, and therefore let us acknowledge Him in them all." To labor for "wisdome, wealth, honour, and pleasure" for oneself alone and to make these things "the top of our hopes and desires" would surely result in the ultimate loss of "our labour and happinesse both."[8] To seek such self-aggrandizement was to manifest what Cotton Mather called "a private Spirit . . . an evil much to be Rebuked." "Alas, For this Private Spirit!" bemoaned Mather in 1690. "It is this that has a more Dismal Aspect upon our own Land, than all the other things that Bode ill unto us."[9] What Mather referred to as "a private Spirit" Thomas Hooker called "that traiterous sin of Self-love." Such an attitude was "the Devills . . . Masterpiece, that Grand Fundamental Designe, on which he has built his Kingdome ever since." Contrasted with self-love, according to Hooker, is the ideal of "Self-denyall" which is the "very Foundation of Christianity, yea the Grand Designe of all Theologie."[10]

In short, the good of the whole Puritan society depended on subjection and subordination. When any man followed his individual desires, in some sense every man would ultimately suffer for it. What was needed was an attitude of voluntarism and service, essential ingredients in the communal ideal. Voluntarism, Miller has rightly insisted, "did not mean license, it meant knitting the whole body together as one man to achieve God's design."[11] Cotton Mather admonished that "We ought Every one of us to Serve our Generation, before we fall asleep [in death], or it will be but an uncomfortable Sleep that we shall fall into."[12] "To Exalt, we must abase our selves: To be the First, we must become last of all," Thomas Hooker reminded his congregation.[13]

Service for the public good definitely included an individual's vocation or "calling." William Perkins, whose writings were probably the most widely read of any English Puritan preacher, defined a vocation or calling as "a certain kinde of life, ordained and imposed on man by God, for the common good . . . he abuseth his calling whosoever he be that . . . implys it for himselfe, seeking wholly his own, & not the common good. And that common saying, Every man for himselfe, and God for us all, is wicked, as it is directly against the end of every

---

8. Cotton, *God's Promise*, p. 12; *A Briefe Exposition with Practical Observations Upon the Whole Book of Ecclesiastes* (London, 1657), pp. 42–43.

9. Cotton Mather, *Present State of New England*, pp. 20–23.

10. [Thomas Hooker], *Heautononaparnumenos: Or a Treatise of Self-Denyall* (London, 1646), pp. 4–6.

11. Miller, *New England Mind*, p. 427.

12. Cotton Mather, *The Serviceable Man* (Boston, 1690), p. 55.

13. [Hooker], *Treatise of Self-Denyall*, p. 7.

calling or honest kinde of life."[14] Anything less than a public spirit was an unacceptable violation of the Puritan ideal in New England.

Inequality and the Common Good

The Puritan communal ideal demanded total obedience to God and commitment of all of life to his service, a self-sacrificing public spirit motivated out of Christian love, and a spirit of mutual subjection and edification for the good of the whole, even to the point of one's vocation. One thing the communal ideal did *not* involve was the idea of social equality. Indeed, few concepts could have been further from the minds of American Puritans than the idea that human beings are equal or should be treated as such. Inequality was necessary to hold society together—a part of the divine order of things. "Nothing therefore can be imagined more remote either from right reason or true religion," stated William Hubbard in 1676, "than to think that because we were all once equal at our birth, and shall be again at our death, therefore we should be so in the whole course of our lives."[15] Christian love and self-denial for the public good did not intend to imply human equality, and in fact the communal ideal was very far from advocating Christian communism in the towns of New England. Kenneth Lockridge, who in his detailed study of early Dedham, Massachusetts, calls it a "Christian Utopian Closed Corporate Community" and a "commune," explains that "as long as within the levels of society the gap between the high and the low was not too extreme, as long as men of rank acquitted themselves responsibly and with a proper modesty, and as long as the lower ranks freely respected the upper, hierarchy was expected to add to collectivism yet another source of harmony, not to detract from it."[16]

The Puritans believed in God's appreciation of variety, hence all men were not created alike or with equal stations or abilities. When each functioned as God intended, he was contributing to the well-being of all. John Winthrop made this clear in his speech on board the *Arbella:*

14. William Perkins, *A Treatise of the Vocations, or Callings of men,* repr. in Darrett B. Rutman, *John Winthrop's Decision for America: 1629* (Philadelphia, 1975), pp. 57, 59.

15. William Hubbard, *The Happiness of a People in the Wisdome of their Rulers Directing And in the Obedience of their Brethren Attending Unto what Israel ought to do* (Boston, 1676), p. 10.

16. Lockridge, *New England Town,* pp. 10–11, 16.

God almightie in his most holy and wise providence hath soe disposed of the condicion of mankinde, as in all times some must be rich some poore, some highe and eminent in power and dignitie; others meane and in subjeccion to hold conformity with the rest of his workes, being delighted to shewe forthe the glory of his wisdome in the variety and difference of the Creatures and the glory of his power, in ordering all these differences for the preservacion and good of the whole and the glory of his greatness. . . .[17]

According to Winthrop, God created inequality as an inducement for men to love one another. By not being equal, men would "have need of [each] other, and from hence they might be all knitt more nearly together in the Bond of brotherly affeccion."[18]

Puritan Racial Attitudes

Puritan racial attitudes were consistent with their nonegalitarian views. While influenced to some degree by theological considerations, these attitudes do not seem to have differed significantly from those held by other contemporary Englishmen. The number of blacks in Massachusetts was small in the seventeenth century—perhaps two hundred in 1680 and close to five hundred by the turn of the century—but their presence did create some controversy. Some Puritans held slaves while a few seemed to have qualms about it. There was no serious question, however, that blacks were human beings with souls, descended from the common parents of all mankind. The prevailing view in Western Christendom that bondage was for non-Christians only was challenged in the American colonies. In Massachusetts, Cotton Mather attempted to persuade any doubters that baptism did not wash away slavery. Mather went so far as to indicate that Christianized slaves were more docile and productive than their heathen counterparts.[19]

On the other hand, attempts were made in both Massachusetts and Rhode Island to limit slavery to a certain term of years, and some Puritans, such as Samuel Sewall, advocated the complete abolition of slavery.[20] While some white New Englanders held derogatory attitudes toward blacks and considered them strange and exotic, the Puritans' commitment to law and due process gave New England blacks far

17. Quoted in Foster, *Their Solitary Way*, p. 12.
18. Quoted in ibid., p. 41.
19. See Bernard Rosenthal, "Puritan Conscience and New England Slavery," *New England Quarterly* (Mar. 1973): 62–81; also Cotton Mather, *The Negro Christianized* (Boston, 1706).
20. See Samuel Sewall, *The Selling of Joseph, a Memorial* (Boston, 1700).

greater opportunity for justice than was the case in some of the other English colonies. Blacks in Massachusetts had access to legal counsel, and they could testify in court against whites. Charges could not be brought against blacks with less evidence than would be required for whites, and blacks could appeal legal decisions that went against them. It is also significant to note that punishment for fornication between the races was no different than that meted out for fornication between members of the same race. Some New England blacks in the seventeenth century were free; a few were even prosperous. Those who were slaves were generally house servants rather than field hands. They usually lived in their masters' homes, had considerable time to themselves, and their mobility was not generally restricted. More restrictive legislation began to appear in the eighteenth century, such as a ban on interracial marriage in 1705, as the number of blacks in Massachusetts increased and fears grew that social disorder would result if their activities remained unchecked.[21]

The Puritans' treatment of the Indians was on the whole less noble than their treatment of the black population. Those who were converted through serious evangelistic efforts invited the suspicion of their own people while at the same time they were not likely to receive full acceptance into Puritan society. The Indians really had no legal property rights in Puritan eyes since they had not subdued the land to English standards. Winthrop expressed the English view that since "they [the Indians] inclose noe land, neither have any settled habytation, nor any tame cattle to improve the Land by and soe have noe other but a Naturall Right to those Countries, so as if we leave them sufficient for their use, we may lawfully take the rest. . . ." [22]

Indian complaints against white injustices were often met with violent retaliation on the part of white New Englanders. The Pequot War of 1637 was an overzealous Puritan response to the killing of a troublesome Puritan exile. Major John Mason, sent to deal with the Pequots for their misdeeds, set fire to one of their villages. As a result "many of them were broiled unto death in the revenging flames" and "in a little more than one hour, five or six hundred of these barbarians were dismissed from a world that was burdened with them; not more than seven or eight persons escaping of all that multitude."[23] The Puritans viewed such "successes" as coming from the hand of God. Mason's analysis of the situation was that "thus the Lord was pleased

21. Robert C. Twombly and Robert H. Moore, "Black Puritan: The Negro in Seventeenth-Century Massachusetts," *William and Mary Quarterly* 24 (Apr. 1967): 224–42.

22. Quoted in Thomas, "Puritans, Indians, and the Concept of Race," p. 11.

23. Cotton Mather, *Magnalia Christi Americana* (London, 1702; repr. Hartford, 1852), 2:555.

to smite our enemies in the hinder parts and to give us their land for an inheritance."[24] While the Indians rarely killed women and children during intertribal warfare, they learned that Englishmen were not so discriminating. John Underhill, a Puritan captain involved in the Pequot War, explained that "when a people is grown to such a height of blood, and sin against God and man . . . sometimes the scriptures declareth Women and Children must perish with their parents . . . we had sufficient light from the word of God for our proceedings."[25] The ethnocentricity and harshness with which the Puritans often treated the Native Americans were exacerbated by the Puritans' view of themselves as a New Israel in the Promised Land according to God's covenant with them. When the analogy between Old Testament Israel and the Puritan experience was pushed far enough, the Indians became the pagan Canaanites whom the Lord ordered destroyed for standing in the way of his program for his people. An opposing view held by some earlier in the century was that the Indians were the lost tribes of Israel who had been darkened by exposure to the sun and ceremonial paint. However, as the seventeenth century wore on, the hapless Indians came to be seen increasingly as a separate heathen race, more worthy of contempt than anything else.

Further Manifestations of Inequality

The inequality of men was not limited to those of other races. The Puritans saw themselves as anything but egalitarian. One way in which this was manifested was the way in which land was distributed to town inhabitants. In the Massachusetts town of Sudbury, land was granted according to financial standing, with the wealthier receiving more and better land. Land grants in Dedham and most other seventeenth-century New England communities were likewise given on an unequal basis to town residents. In the case of Boston, contention arose over land grants and a board of seven men was elected to oversee future grants. They generally followed a policy of limited distribution of town land based on family size, but saw to it that the largest grants were for "the better sort" whose financial position and status in the community warranted this kind of recognition. By 1637 land grants in Boston evidenced a great disparity in size, from a high of seven hundred acres to a low of eight acres.[26]

That New England Puritan society took inequality seriously is evident in various ways, including the use of honorifics ranging upwards

24. Quoted in Thomas, "Puritans, Indians, and the Concept of Race," p. 15.
25. Quoted in ibid., p. 15.
26. Rutman, *Winthrop's Boston*, pp. 77, 79.

from "goodman" to "esquire." The order of names appearing on school class lists as well as the seating arrangements in most churches had meaning in terms of social ranking. In summary, knowing and accepting one's place on the social scale was deemed vital for the harmonious functioning of society as a whole. Clearly, all men were *not* created equal in Puritan New England and this was seen as a help, not a hindrance, to a sense of community.

A Sense of Community: Covenants and Consensus

The communal ideal was formalized for New England's Puritans by means of the covenant concept whose theological roots have been discussed earlier. The necessity of covenants in society was articulated by Puritan leaders including John Cotton and John Winthrop. According to Cotton, "all civil Relations are founded in Covenant. . . . There is no other way given whereby a people . . . free from naturall and compulsory engagements, can be united or combined together into one visible body . . . but only by mutual Covenant; as appeareth between husband and wife in the family, Magistrates and subjects in the Commonwealth, fellow Citizens in the same Citie."[27] Winthrop expressed the view that "it is the nature and essence of every society to be knitt together by some Covenant, either expressed or implyed."[28] The Dedham church, a covenanted body of "persons knitt firmly in ye band of love," began its covenant with the assertion that "no union of many persons into one body can be made without mutuall consent or some kind of covenant." The church covenant went on to promise that those who signed it would "through ye help of ye lord . . . live together in this our holy fellowship according to ye rule of love in all holy watchfulness ov'r each other & faithfull mutuall helpfullness in ye waies of god for ye spirituall and temporall comfort & good of one an other in ye lord."[29]

Once one was accepted as a member of a local church, the communal bond was so strong that it was difficult to disassociate oneself from the body. Excommunications were relatively rare, and occurred only when every means to encourage the errant party to repent had failed. When Anne Hutchinson was finally excommunicated from the Boston church during the antinomian controversy of 1637, several other church members, who had not been so disciplined, followed her

27. Quoted in Foster, *Their Solitary Way*, p. 156.
28. Quoted in Rutman, *Winthrop's Boston*, p. 50.
29. Don G. Hill, ed., *The Record of Baptism, Marriages and Deaths, and Admissions to the Church and Dismissals Therefrom, Transcribed from the Church Records in the Town of Dedham, Massachusetts, 1638–1845* (Dedham, Mass., 1888), pp. 3, 12.

to Rhode Island, that "cesspool of heresy" established by Roger Williams (see chapter 13). The church in Boston sent letters, and even messengers, to Rhode Island not to harass the recalcitrant Bostonians but to demonstrate Christian love by encouraging them back into the community of believers they had left. So strong was the communal bond of the church covenant that the Boston church could not let go of its members as long as there was the slightest chance they could be restored to fellowship.[30]

The covenant fostered a communal spirit by convincing New Englanders that they were on a special mission, and by emphasizing that each one was personally responsible for the success or failure of that mission. The covenant, by its appeal to a common mission and shared values, also committed men to conformity and consensus, both highly valued in Puritan New England. Such unity was necessary, most Puritans believed, in order to survive in the wilderness, adequately reform the church, and experience a decent quality of life. In fact, community leaders were obsessed with consensus, according to Benjamin Labaree, because "disunity, dissension, disorder were but different names for what Puritans feared most—the disintegration and ultimate collapse of their endeavor to establish a New Zion in the wilderness."[31] As Roger Williams, Anne Hutchinson, John Wheelwright, and others learned, one could comfortably remain in Massachusetts only as long as one's behavior and expressed ideas coincided with the community consensus. In town and church meetings, as well as in relationships among neighbors, continuing dissent was not generally tolerated. In fact, emphasis was placed on unanimity as part of the communal ideal. The ideal vote in a town meeting was a unanimous vote, and most ministers would not consider a call to a church in which the congregation had not voted unanimously to extend the call. The importance of unity was evident in the following century as well; it is interesting to note that the view of heaven held by Jonathan Edwards was of a place where "you shall be united in the same interest, and shall be of one mind and one heart and one soule forever."[32] When disputes did arise, every effort was made to reach "a full and amicable agreement" in which all parties "were in peace and fully satisfied."[33] This striving for harmony and consensus was a source of social tranquility in Puritan New England. Rebellions and

30. See Larzer Ziff, "The Social Bond of Church Covenant," *American Quarterly* 10/4 (1958): 454–62.

31. Benjamin Labaree, *Colonial Massachusetts. A History* (Millwood, N.Y., 1979), pp. 47, 63.

32. Quoted in Michael Zuckerman, *Peaceable Kingdoms—New England Towns in the Eighteenth Century* (New York, 1970), pp. 57–58.

33. Quoted in ibid., pp. 57–58.

factions were rampant in other colonies in the seventeenth century, while Massachusetts was impressive for its "absence of internal, organized violence." "The Bay Colony's most startling accomplishment," maintain Timothy H. Breen and Stephen Foster, was "fifty years of relative social peace." Because of the Puritans' commitment to God and the communal ideal, "it was incumbent upon all men to work out their disputes as peacefully as possible thinking always of their greater obligation to the commonwealth as a whole and ultimately to God himself."[34]

The Communal Ideal Applied

Serious attempts were made to put the communal ideal into practice in a number of ways. The actual physical layout of towns and land allotments in early Massachusetts was designed to foster a communal spirit. Physical proximity of people was part of the plan—there was no place in the Puritan system for the solitary frontiersman or farmer. It was expected, rather, that all would live in towns; in fact the initial plans of the Massachusetts Bay Company indicate an intention for the immigrants of 1630 to settle together in one large town surrounded by farmlands.[35] John Cotton made it clear that "society in all sorts of human affairs is better than solitariness" and he was quick to condemn "popish anchorites and hermits who think solitary life a state of perfection."[36]

While the ideal of life together in one large Puritan town did not materialize, the various towns that were established carried out the communal ideal on a local level. The meetinghouse in the center of town, used for both worship and community business, became a physical embodiment of the inhabitants' commitment to their community. As Timothy H. Breen has pointed out, "the very act of meeting together became in itself a ritual act that reinforced the sense of community."[37] The symbol of the meetinghouse and the act of meeting together were so important to the communal ideal that on September 8, 1636, the General Court of Massachusetts issued an order prohibiting the building of a residence more than one-half mile from the meetinghouse in each town.[38] What went on in the town

---

34. Breen and Foster, "Puritans' Greatest Achievement," pp. 5–7, 12.
35. See Rutman, *Winthrop's Boston*, pp. 96–97, 280–83. See also Nathaniel B. Shurtleff, ed., *Records of the Governor and company of the Massachusetts Bay in New England* (Boston, 1853–1854), esp. 1:43.
36. Cotton, *Book of Ecclesiastes*, pp. 44–45.
37. Timothy H. Breen, *Puritans and Adventurers* (New York, 1980), p. 79.
38. Shurtleff, *Records of Massachusetts Bay*, 1:181.

meetinghouses of New England was designed to contribute to the communal spirit as well. When the community met for worship and religious instruction on Sundays and Thursdays, they heard homilies urging Christian love and conformity to the laws of God. The congregational polity of the churches can itself be seen as a form of communalism, with authority over each church being shared by the members of the congregation alone and residing in no higher body or individual. The various local churches themselves experienced complete equality and autonomy in their relationship to each other.[39]

Local government through the town meeting was another vital source of communal identity. The town meeting, as the source of local power and authority, was itself the government which then granted limited amounts of authority to individuals or committees for a limited duration, usually no more than a year at a time. In the case of the town of Sudbury, "every major issue was discussed in open town meetings, and over 132 meetings were held in the first fifteen years after settlement. More than 650 orders, 'agreed by the town,' were passed in this period. . . ."[40]

One of the more important duties of local government was to determine land policies. Here again the communal ideal was put into practice in many communities. A basic decision immediately facing newly created towns was whether to have an "open field," "enclosed" land system, or possibly some combination of the two. The town meeting usually decided in favor of the system to which the majority of original settlers had been accustomed in England. While some towns such as Watertown felt that individual farms were not detrimental to the spirit of community, many towns, such as Sudbury and Dedham, opted for the open field system. There were certain advantages to this system: "Open fields meant that scarce equipment could be shared, labor pooled, and the cohesiveness of the community preserved because some of the land was set aside for all to cultivate cooperatively."[41] In the case of Sudbury, many farmers did not have their own plowshares and oxen; twenty years after Sudbury was settled, only one-third of the town's families possessed these items and shared them with the rest.[42]

In spite of nearly limitless acreage available to the first generation of settlers, very conservative land distribution policies were followed by the towns. This was done partly to provide for future needs, but

---

39. See Cotton, *Churches of Christ in New England.*
40. Sumner Chilton Powell, *Puritan Village* (Middletown, Conn., 1963), p. 93.
41. Labaree, *Colonial Massachusetts,* p. 51.
42. Powell, *Puritan Village,* p. 81.

also to preserve close physical proximity and a sense of community. In the case of Plymouth, a mere acre of land was given to each person to be held as private property until the colony was seven years old, and that one acre was to be "as near the town as might be."[43] In the case of Dedham, which received a grant of two hundred square miles from the General Court, new admissions to the town were halted temporarily in 1637 after only forty-six house lots had been assigned.[44] After the initial grants were made to the inhabitants of Sudbury, the remaining 19,200 acres (89 percent of the town's area) were declared to be "the commons"—"a sort of town bank account in land."[45] Stiff fines were levied by the town meeting in Sudbury for those who would selfishly enclose parts of the vast common area for private use, thus demonstrating the townsmen's strong opposition to fellow citizens who cared more about personal interests than the good of the whole community. Beginning in 1640, citizens of Sudbury had to receive permission from officials appointed by the town meeting to do so much as fell a tree on common land; thus was communal property jealously guarded from private exploitation.[46] In Boston, no one was able to sell real property without the approval of town-appointed supervisors.[47]

In addition to their conservative land policies the towns had other means of fostering a communal spirit. Michael Zuckerman suggests that Puritan leaders used public education in Massachusetts as a means "to suppress self-expression and promote uniformity" among the younger generation.[48] That this was the Puritans' primary motive for public education is questionable, but certain community values were no doubt inculcated by means of the schools, as is the case today. A more obvious method of instilling a communal spirit was the way in which all men were obligated to devote a certain share of time to the community. In Dedham, as in most other towns, each man labored on community roads or fences and took his turn at filling necessary but often tedious duties such as clerk, surveyor, assessor, fence-viewer, poundkeeper, and so on. He who refused to serve was assessed the cash equivalent of his labor.[49] The government of the Massachusetts Bay Colony and the towns themselves had a further very

43. William Bradford, *Of Plymouth Plantation,* ed. Samuel Eliot Morison, (New York, 1952), p. 145.

44. Lockridge, *New England Town,* p. 8.

45. Powell, *Puritan Village,* pp. 93–94.

46. Ibid.

47. Rutman, *Winthrop's Boston,* p. 78.

48. Zuckerman, *Peaceable Kingdoms,* p. 76.

49. Lockridge, *New England Town,* p. 16.

practical means of fostering a communal spirit through the regulation of wages and prices.[50] This prevented exploitation and hindered economic individualism in the best interests of society.

The Communal Ideal Compromised

Despite godly intentions, practical applications, and considerable success, the communal ideal was never fully achieved, nor did it endure as the shared belief of most Americans. Indeed, the Puritans' communal ideal suffered from conceptual flaws and paradoxes, and even from the beginning was not necessarily shared by all settlers. A number of settlers demonstrated that they did not always care to seek after the ways of God with all their hearts and that they would not necessarily subordinate their interests to the greater good of their communities.[51] Winthrop and other leaders did not seem to recognize the impossibility of creating a society founded on Christian love when only a portion of the persons involved in the enterprise were truly regenerate Christians. New England was planned as a communal Christian society, composed of saints and sinners, but held together by qualities available only to the saints. The Puritans were too conscious of sin and human depravity to believe in an actual earthly utopia, yet they continued to seek perfection in what they knew to be an imperfect world. Even the idea of the covenant, a key part of the communal ideal, was paradoxical to the Puritan concept of human nature. The covenant ideal, as Miller has pointed out, builds on human choice—on the rational decision of men to do the right thing. It assumes that man is naturally good, intelligent, and capable. "By inference," Miller states, "it denied original sin, [and] proclaimed the competence of human reason. . ."[52] The communal ideal was also compromised by the fact that the Puritans were too devoted to unity to ever succeed in fully achieving it. Either Puritans got along harmoniously, or they separated so they would not have to get along at all. New towns proliferated because people in the old towns could not always agree.

From Governor Winthrop's perspective, the communal ideal was first compromised when the immigrants of 1630 dispersed and established several towns instead of all flocking to Boston. Governor Bradford of nearby Plymouth Plantation viewed a similar dispersion

---

50. See, e.g., Shurtleff, *Records of Massachusetts Bay*, 1:76, 91.

51. One need only briefly peruse Shurtleff, *Records of Massachusetts Bay*, vol. 1, to find numerous examples of "criminal individualism" beginning as early as Sept., 1630 (see pp. 76–80).

52. Miller, *New England Mind*, pp. 413–14.

from the town of Plymouth to individual farms in the countryside as the "ruine of New England."[53] As years passed and the population grew, it became increasingly impractical for all Puritan farmers to live in the original towns and spend much of their day walking to and from their increasingly far-flung fields. Peripheral villages appeared in remote areas of the town lands and demanded autonomy, and then, even more subversive of the system, some individuals built homes on their lands apart from the peripheral villages and ceased to be an active part of any community.[54] This situation posed a fundamental threat to the communal ideal. The land itself with its economic opportunities was proving disruptive of the communal spirit which Winthrop, Cotton, and others had so strongly advocated.

"Success" was beginning to mean "failure" for the communal ideal and the Puritan ministry was quick to point out that economic success was a root cause of New England's declension. These "Jeremiahs" of the later seventeenth century frequently reminded the populace of the divergence between the dream and the reality of New England. There no doubt existed a craving for individualism on the part of enough persons to warrant the sermonic literature condemning such a spirit. Herein lay another paradox—stress was put on social communalism, while individualism was emphasized when it came to one's spiritual relationship to God. To the detriment of the communal ideal, acquisitive instincts and the values of individualism and liberty made inroads and ultimately prevailed in New England and the rest of America. The conflicting ideas and ideals of an increasingly pluralistic society overwhelmed the spirit of unity which Winthrop so much desired.

While the Puritan communal ideal was never fully realized, it did exercise a great influence on New England for a number of years. Kenneth Lockridge sees Dedham as a genuine "utopian commune" lasting at least fifty years, while Michael Zuckerman sees communal values surviving in Massachusetts to the eve of the Revolution.[55] While Puritanism has been influential in the cultural development of America in many respects, the Puritan communal ideal has long since been replaced by other more characteristic American values. If individualism, tolerance, equality, and liberty are great American virtues of our day, we must go elsewhere other than Puritan New England for

53. Bradford, *Plymouth Plantation*, 2:152–53.

54. See Lockridge, *New England Town*, p. 82; see also Richard L. Bushman, *From Puritan to Yankee* (New York, 1967), chap. 4, "Outlivers," pp. 54–72.

55. Lockridge, *New England Town*, p. 53; Zuckerman, *Peaceable Kingdoms*, p. 70.

their origins. What our Puritan forebears valued was far different: a communal ideal consisting of unity by means of exclusiveness, intolerance for ungodliness and dissent, self-denial, subordination, and a public spirit for the common good, and all motivated, at least theoretically, by Christian love one for another. As noble in its context as that vision may have been, it was not to endure.

9

Social Ethics
Work, Wealth, and Welfare

The Puritan worldview served to take some of the drudgery out of work, some of the pride out of wealth, and some of the shame out of poverty. By providing a theological foundation for all facets of life, the Puritans attempted to see work, wealth, and human want from a biblical perspective, but it was a perspective neither unaffected by their general cultural milieu nor static. In their understanding of work, wealth, and welfare, the Puritans were largely ideological borrowers, drawing on the fairly recent and radical Reformation heritage. To a large extent, Puritan views on these subjects were quite similar to those held by their Anglican brethren.[1] But, true to form, the Puritans seem to have held their positions with greater intensity.

Labor and Calling

Puritan views of work must begin with the Reformation's rejection of the bifurcation of human endeavor into things sacred and things secular. All work was to be undertaken for the glory of God; it made no difference if it was "washing of dishes" or the "preaching of the word of God."[2] To Puritan descendants of the Reformation, faithfulness to the tasks God placed before them was more important than

1. See Timothy Breen, "The Non-Existent Controversy: Puritan and Anglican Attitudes on Work and Wealth," *Church History* 35 (1966): 273–87.
2. William Tyndale, quoted in Leland Ryken, *Worldly Saints* (Grand Rapids, 1986), p. 25.

the specific functions involved. All of life was under God's direction
and it was the saint's obligation to bring the parts of life into a harmonious whole for God's glory. One's spirituality and one's vocation
were to be thoroughly integrated. All legitimate work (legitimacy
being defined as "what is useful unto human society"[3]) was assumed
to carry divine approval and served as a means whereby God could be
honored through diligent application to the task at hand. One's choice
of work was dependent on a calling given by God. In the Puritan view
of things, God called his saints with both a general calling and a
specific calling. The general calling was God's prompting to accept the
covenant of grace—a call to salvation through faith in Christ. A proper
response to this call or covenant, that is, a conversion experience, was
the one and only prerequisite for Puritan sainthood. But beyond this,
God called his people to specific vocations "ordained and imposed on
man by God, for the common good. . . . Every person of every degree,
state, sex, or condition without exception must have some personal
and particular calling to walk in."[4] One should approach this calling
with a diligence born of the realization that every action was under
the watchful eye of God.

The widely esteemed writings of English Puritan Richard Baxter
helped establish American Puritan attitudes toward one's work and
calling. To Baxter, hard physical or mental labor was a meaningful
ascetic technique which helped one resist temptation. Unwillingness
to work, on the other hand, could well be a symptom of an unregenerate heart.[5] But it was not labor in and of itself that was pleasing to
God. What was of greatest importance was the rational, systematic,
methodical, disciplined labor of a specific calling, without which "the
accomplishments of a man are only casual and irregular . . . he spends
more time in idleness than at work."[6]

It was possible to participate in more than one calling at a time,
provided that the combination was useful, proved detrimental to no
one, and did not lead to unfaithfulness in any one specific calling.
While one should not lightly shift from one calling to another, the
changing of one's vocation was certainly possible if it meant pursuing
something useful for the glory of God.[7] Puritans were warned, however, against a spirit of discontent when it came to their work. "A
Christian should not be too ready to fall out with his calling," cau-

3. See Morgan, *Puritan Family*, p. 71.

4. Quoted in Ryken, *Wordly Saints*, p. 27.

5. See Max Weber, *The Protestant Ethic and the Spirit of Capitalism* (New
York, 1958), pp. 158–59.

6. Quoted in ibid., p. 161.

7. Ibid., p. 162.

tioned Cotton Mather. "Many a man, merely from covetousness and from discontent throws up his business."[8]

To view work primarily as a means to personal wealth or status would be to miss the early Puritans' perspective entirely. Labor was elevated nearly to the rank of a sacrament, not as a means of earning salvation but as a means of glorifying God and serving the public good. Labor became an individualized form of worship for the Puritans, but even great diligence in it carried no divine guarantee of material prosperity. Any success that one enjoyed in the world of work was due to the goodness of God and for one to boast of being a "self-made man" would be to invite ridicule if not charges of heresy. Conversely, lack of material prosperity, even in the face of diligent effort, was not to be viewed as God's judgment on sin or as an indication of moral or spiritual deficiency. However, these views, while true for the first generation, became less widely shared as the seventeenth century drew to a close.[9]

Wealth

New England's first-generation Puritans were wary of wealth. Governor John Winthrop saw sufficient importance in the case of an emigrant to Massachusetts named Mansfield, who grew rich and then "lost his godliness, and his wealth soon after," to include it in his *History of New England from 1630–1649.*[10] Economic success did not necessitate spiritual calamity, but it did seem to make it more likely. Roger Williams wrote:

> The neerer Christs followers have approached to worldly wealth, ease, liberty, honour, pleasure, etc. the nearer they have approached to Impatience, Pride, Anger, and Violence. . . . And the further and further they have departed from God, from his truth, from the Simplicitie, power, and Puritie of Christ Jesus and true Christianitie.[11]

Yet it was required that some men be wealthy and some poor, since a hierarchy of wealth and status was at the heart of God's plan for mak-

8. Quoted in Ryken, *Worldly Saints*, p. 29.

9. See Christine Leigh Heyrman, "A Model of Christian Charity: The Rich and the Poor in New England, 1630–1700" unpublished Ph.D. diss., Yale University, 1977, p. 12.

10. John Winthrop, *The History of New England from 1630–1649*, ed. James Savage (Boston, 1853), 2:141.

11. Roger Williams, *The Complete Writings* (New York, 1963), 7:224.

ing his people interdependent.[12] Money was not inherently evil; in fact the Puritans clearly viewed money and private property as legitimate. Wealth, however, was seen more often as a temptation than a blessing, even though it was acknowledged as coming from the hand of God. While it was possible to be godly and rich at the same time, the seeking of riches through one's own efforts and the use of wealth for one's own gratification were roundly condemned.

Affluence could be dangerous because it made one feel self-sufficient and in need of neither God nor one's fellow man. The acquisition of material things could cause a man to "deny God, and to say in pride, and contempt of him . . . who is the Lord?"[13] When one replaced God with wealth as the object of one's greatest satisfaction, one was guilty of idolatry in Puritan eyes. A further Puritan concern about wealth included the fear that it would consume so much time and energy that service to God and others would be hampered. It was also realized that wealth tended to be habit-forming; its acquisition often created an insatiable appetite for more.

New England was not advertised as a place where one might settle for the purpose of accumulating wealth, although that very thing did happen in some cases. Actually, the founders of New England were more fearful of emigrants in pursuit of wealth than they were of those stricken with poverty. The experiences of early Virginia had proven to the Puritans what could happen when the love of riches infested the founding generation, and New Englanders wanted no part of it. Robert Cushman, who handled the business affairs of Plymouth Colony for a time, noted how obnoxious and worldly the settlers of Virginia had become in their search for wealth.[14]

Puritan Material Culture

The concern that Puritans expressed about the accumulation of wealth and its adverse effects on the things of the spirit should not be misconstrued, however, to mean that early New Englanders had no appreciation for possessions of high-quality craftsmanship and beauty. In actuality, the Puritans of seventeenth-century New England brought with them, and produced in America, furniture, china, glassware, clothing, art, and artifacts of all kinds that display refined taste, and at times even elegance. While "luxury" was condemned as a wasteful extravagance and depicted as "a knife in the hands of a child,

---

12. Heyrman, "Model of Christian Charity," pp. 6–7.
13. John Robinson, quoted in Ryken, *Worldly Saints*, p. 62.
14. Robert Cushman, *The Sin and Danger of Self-Love Described* (Boston, 1724), p. 24.

likely to hurt, if not taken away,"[15] shoddiness was certainly no virtue. In short, the Puritans were not ascetics.

By 1650, New England was described as a land of "orderly, fair, and well-built houses, well furnished many of them, together with orchards filled with goodly fruit trees and gardens with variety of flowers."[16] As for the furnishings, the dominant style in seventeenth-century New England was mannerism, which was characterized by heavy ornamentation and exaggerated proportion. The "plain style" of Puritan preaching did not apply to New England home furnishings. Robert F. Trent has insightfully noted that

> one of the supreme paradoxes of New England history is that the Puritan settlers, so often caricatured as doughty fanatics and anti-art philistines, were, in fact, advanced, literate, and aesthetically aware people whose religious scruples did not preclude the enjoyment of material prosperity and visual delight. Even more paradoxically, the Mannerist style they enjoyed had its origins in the hedonistic Roman Catholic courts of Italy, which Puritans deplored as the vanguard of the Antichrist.[17]

Objects owned and used by New England Puritans of the seventeenth century included much silver, some of it heavily ornamented. Occasionally an exotic object, such as a coconut shell, was "tipped" or mounted in silver. Finely crafted wine glasses, mugs, and pitchers were common possessions. Bowls, dishes, and cups were often decorated in bright colors. Brightly colored "turkey work" upholstery, embroidery, and bed hangings were sufficiently abundant to lay to rest the stereotypical black-and-white Puritan world. Colorful attire for men and women is evidenced in Puritan portraits as well as in extant articles of clothing. Joined and often highly ornate chests, cabinets, and chairs were frequently found in Puritan households.[18]

It is clear that Puritan material culture was hardly utilitarian. Fine craftsmanship was admired and sought by early New Englanders. Possession of "nice things" was no vice, provided, of course, that devotion to God and service to his people were not supplanted or dimin-

---

15. William Perkins, quoted in Ryken, *Worldly Saints*, p. 65.

16. Edward Johnson, quoted in Robert Blair St. George, "Set Thine House in Order: The Domestication of the Yeomanry in Seventeenth-Century New England," *New England Begins: The Seventeenth Century* (Boston, 1982), 2:165.

17. Robert F. Trent, "The Concept of Mannerism," *New England Begins: The Seventeenth Century* (Boston, 1982), 3:368.

18. See the catalog of a superb 1982 exhibit at the Museum of Fine Arts, Boston, *New England Begins: The Seventeenth Century*, 3 vols. (Boston, 1982).

ished by one's material possessions. For the devout Puritan, the soul continued to be the greatest possession of all.

Puritan Views of Poverty

The first generation of New England Puritans was of the opinion that piety did not guarantee success, and success was not necessarily an indication of piety. Poverty, therefore, was not to be viewed as punishment from the hand of God. It was quite possible for godly individuals to experience dire poverty, but this did not happen by chance. A loving heavenly Father had the ultimate good of the afflicted always in mind, and could well use poverty to teach spiritual lessons, lessen interest in worldly concerns, or drive the believer to closer dependence on him. Poverty was not virtuous in itself, however, and was not something to be sought after as certain Catholic orders advocated.[19] The poor were not regarded as parasites, but as full members of society who had valuable contributions to make. However, the growing numbers of poor during the seventeenth century, coupled with the growing prosperity of the merchant class, brought significant changes in social attitudes toward the poor that were quite apparent by the 1690s.

Winthrop and others of the first generation saw no paradox in expecting poverty to be the experience of some folks in the new Zion in the wilderness. After all, Christ had told his followers that they would always have the poor with them. Economic differences, rather than ruining the Puritan experiment in America, were expected to aid the social order by encouraging social interdependence. Poverty was not regarded as inherently evil or to be equated with depravity, nor were the poor seen as second-class citizens or saints. John Cotton explained that "no man can certainly discern the love or hatred of God to himself or others, by their outward events or estates." Thomas Hooker concurred, asserting that poverty was "no argument of Gods displeasure."[20] One's economic condition was ultimately determined by a sovereign God, not individual merit or shortcomings. Poverty that could be avoided, however, should be avoided. Thomas Hooker made it plain that

we must not bring misery on our selves, there is no credit or comfort in this. . . . It is folly for a traveller to goe through a slough when hee may escape it. . . . one man must not take every mans potion . . . so

19. Ryken, *Worldly Saints*, pp. 60–61.
20. Quoted in Heyrman, "Model of Christian Charity," p. 12.

afflictions are potions, one hath disgrace, another poverty, every man must take his own potion.[21]

A shift in attitudes toward the poor late in the seventeenth century can be partially explained by the fact that the number of indigent persons in New England was sharply on the rise, most noticeably in Boston.[22] This growth of poverty can be attributed to the influx of refugees, including widows, orphans, and disabled soldiers, coming from interior areas devastated by Indian raids. As a port of entry, Boston attracted increasing numbers of European immigrants, some of whom had few financial resources upon arrival. Furthermore, the maritime trade, which employed many Bostonians, was often seasonal in nature and left men and families inadequately supported in slow times.[23]

Sermons of the late seventeenth century indicate that the clergy made a significant distinction between the "worthy" poor and the "idle" poor whose plight was essentially their own doing and who could, if so inclined, exert themselves to better their positions. By this time poverty was less likely to be blamed on divine planning and more likely to be seen as caused by weaknesses of human character. The poor were often portrayed as vicious, as the association between sin and poverty became increasingly clear in clerical eyes. This repeated connection between vice and impoverishment undermined the first generation's assertion that poverty was acceptable and even to be expected. By the end of the seventeenth century, poverty was viewed as despicable instead.

The third-generation ministry perceived that the poor were, more so than others, victimized by their own weaknesses and vices. Drunkenness was a chief moral lapse which made men poor and kept them in that state, according to Cotton Mather. In fact, Mather had grave reservations about a dole for the idle poor, whom he assumed would buy strong drink with their alms.[24] Ministerial railings against the drinking habits of the poor principally emphasized economic loss. But excessive drinking was by no means the only vice charged to the poor, and economic considerations were not the only concerns. Swearing, whoring, theft, covetousness, slothfulness and general spiritual deficiencies were seen during the third generation as characteristic problems of those in poverty. Added to the catalog of sins of the poor was the fact that they displayed an unholy pride and were often

---

21. Quoted in ibid., p. 50.
22. Carl Bridenbaugh, *Cities in the Wilderness* (New York, 1955), p. 233.
23. Heyrman, "Model of Christian Charity," pp. 105–6.
24. Cotton Mather, *The True Way of Thriving* (Boston, 1695), p. 20.

ungrateful for charity offered, sometimes even refusing to accept it.[25] The poor were clearly bad for Puritan public relations; Christine Heyrman has noted that "their slothfulness and vicious habits undermined New England's reputation as a prosperous, godly, disciplined community."[26]

Charity

Given changing attitudes toward poverty between the first and third generations, it is not surprising to find varying views of the role of charity as the seventeenth century unfolded. The strong community bond advocated by the leadership of the first generation called for Christian love and generosity of the highest order. The proper extent of charity depended less upon an individual's capacity to give than upon the need at hand. In fact, Governor Winthrop argued that Christians must at times "give beyond theire ability" to aid those in need.[27] The poor had a right to relief from those of means; they deserved support as fellow Christians since differences in economic status were the result of God's sovereign decree. In fact, God gave wealth to some in order that they might meet the needs of the poor. It was more than money that was owed to the poor, however; it was also a "bond of brotherhood" that made the work of charity "perfect," according to Winthrop.[28] True Christian charity, for the first generation, involved high motives on the part of donors. Those who were generous for selfish reasons were denounced by Cushman: "with a secret aim at themselves, they will take pains to do a man good, provided that he will take twice so much for them, they will give a penny so as it may advantage them a pound. . . ."[29] It is also important to recognize that Puritan charity was not seen as the sole responsibility of the rich. All men had responsibility to do good as the occasion presented itself.[30]

Sermons of the late seventeenth century indicate that the clergy were concerned not only about the behavior of the poor but also about the behavior of the rich. The ministry was well aware of the power and influence of the wealthy merchant class, and sought to attract and at the same time control this segment of society. In essence, the

25. Heyrman, "Model of Christian Charity," pp. 130–33, 136–37, 140.
26. Ibid., p. 155.
27. John Winthrop, "A Model of Christian Charitie," in *Puritan Political Ideas*, ed. Edmund S. Morgan (New York, 1965), p. 78.
28. Ibid., p. 84.
29. Robert Cushman, *The Sin and Danger of Self-Love Described* (London, 1622; 2d ed. Boston, 1724), pp. 11–12.
30. Winthrop, *Model of Christian Charitie*, p. 76.

clergy urged the wealthy to do works of charity which would then make them feel good about themselves. When it came to acts of charity, the third generation of clergy focused their attention less on the poor than on the rich. Charity was seen as more for the benefit of the well-to-do than the needy; it was a sound investment that would pay not only eternal dividends but was likely to increase one's estate in this life.[31] According to Heyrman, by the turn of the century charity had become

> the ultimate act of calculated, economic rationality, performed with the understanding that a tangible return would be forthcoming. The practice of charity evinced not Christian love, but instead the donor's complete mastery of the skills of secular, economic individualism.[32]

This attitude provides further evidence that by the end of the seventeenth century the original social ethic—the Puritan communal ideal—had evolved into something quite different. Economic individualism had become legitimized and even sanctified by the clergy, and the "city on a hill" would never be quite the same.

31. For a prime example of this approach to charity by a third-generation clergyman, see Cotton Mather, *Bonafacius* (Boston, 1710).
32. Heyrman, "Model of Christian Charity," p. 214.

10

In Pursuit of Godly Government

The tension between freedom and responsibility is an age-old human problem. Responsibility for the American Puritans meant building and maintaining a society according to a biblical paradigm, and using whatever authority was necessary to curtail deviation from that paradigm. Since the human race was by nature in a sinful state and prone to do evil, government was viewed as a necessary restraining influence which kept society from tearing itself apart. In the Puritan scheme of things, a vigorous government, if godly, was to be desired, not feared. Such a government served primarily to preserve the societal organism and was only secondarily concerned with the protection of individual rights.

The exact form that political authority was to take was open to debate and change, however, nearly from the beginning of New England's settlement. Perhaps this was due in part to the fact that although matters of doctrine and church polity were spelled out with some detail and clarity in the Bible, civil government, at least in the New Testament, was not. And the Puritans did not assume the presence of a Moses in their midst, communicating direct divine revelations to the people apart from the written Word. The Puritan concept of government instead relied on the heritage of the past—most specifically the English past. If New Englanders consciously and deliberately followed a model of civil government, it was an eclectic children of Israel-England concept, blending the English parliamentary and peasant traditions with the idea of a special "chosenness" embodied in the idea of the covenant.

New England Puritans shared basic assumptions about the nature of government with most Western Europeans. Life was seen as a more unified, organic whole than our compartmentalized, specialized worldviews allow today. The idea that life could be divided into separate and mutually exclusive political and religious spheres was beyond comprehension. Purity of doctrine and right conduct did not always come easily, and civil government was to be in partnership with the church in the preservation and furtherance of truth and justice. Puritan political philosophy and theology reflect a belief in an absolute standard, a fundamental law of right and wrong as spelled out in the Bible, a belief in the paramount importance of right conduct, and a high degree of awareness of the existence of evil and human failure. Because of these views, two things were unthinkable: toleration of heresy and absolute authority wielded by anyone less than God himself.

The Establishment of Government in Massachusetts

Political legitimacy for the Puritan experiment in New England rested initially with the charter of the Massachusetts Bay Company, granted by the English monarchy. The company was chartered ostensibly to turn a profit in the New World for the sake of investors, but to most Puritans the significance of an American plantation was to be measured not monetarily, but spiritually. Yet, the structure and function of a government for a civil society had to be forged from what was essentially a commercial trading company. This meant that innovation, experimentation, and adaptation were necessary on the part of the Puritan leadership to develop a suitable government that would be reasonable enough to attract settlers, strict enough to preserve Puritan orthodoxy, and sufficiently in conformity with English law to prevent the intervention of the Crown. It was a difficult assignment, but one that was carried out with remarkable success for several decades.

Initially, the governance of the Puritan experiment in Massachusetts rested with the governor and eight magistrates who were required by the charter to meet quarterly in a session known as the General Court. Between meetings of the General Court, the governor and magistrates (also known as assistants) met regularly to carry out the routine affairs of government as they saw fit. Having arrived in Massachusetts in June of 1630, the first official meeting of the General Court was held in October, although Governor Winthrop and the magistrates had held earlier meetings to deal with several issues, including the setting of maximum wages in a new settlement where skilled labor was in great demand. Winthrop and his associates made a significant decision, not required by the charter, to expand the franchise to include the colony's freemen, who were then granted the power to elect the assistants. Residents of the colony were thus given a substantial voice in the colony's affairs, at least in terms of deciding who their magistrates would be. Initially the governor was chosen by the assistants, but within two years even the governor was being elected by the colony's freemen, although their choice was limited to the assistants. A further development took place in the government of Massachusetts in the early 1630s whereby individual towns were permitted to select representatives, known as deputies, to join with the assistants in the meetings of the General Court. The assistants and deputies met together, although not always in agreement, until 1644 when the two bodies began to meet separately. The assistants continued to hold veto power, however, over the legislative activities of the deputies despite their periodic objections.

The extent of the power and responsibilities of civil rulers was one of the hotter political issues in early New England. At the heart of the matter were the conflicting concepts of discretionary authority, that is, the magistrate's right to exercise any power he deemed appropriate, and delegated authority, which allowed a more active role for the electorate and reduced the limits of authority possessed by the magistrate. This struggle was most visible in conflicts between the upper and lower houses of the Massachusetts General Court, although Governor Winthrop himself entered the fray on occasion.

Democracy and Political Leadership

Over the years there has been considerable historiographical debate as to whether Puritan New England was theocratic or democratic. Current interpretations reject the earlier notion that theocracy was prevalent,[1] but it is not appropriate to think of New England government as democratic in the modern sense either. "Democracy" was a term rarely used in the seventeenth century except derisively; it had the same connotations to most Puritans that the term "anarchy" has in our day. Popular rule was not seen as a legitimate form of government, although limited popular participation in the selection of the officers of government was appropriate. While the percentage of adult males who participated in electing leaders was fairly impressive in some Puritan communities, it must be understood that a great deal of

1. For some examples of this theocratic interpretation, see Herbert L. Osgood, *The American Colonies in the Seventeenth Century* (New York, 1904); James Truslow Adams, *The Founding of New England* (Boston, 1921); Thomas Jefferson Wertenbaker, *The First Americans, 1607–1690* (New York, 1927) and *The Puritan Oligarchy* (New York, 1947); Vernon L. Parrington, *Main Currents in American Thought* (New York, 1927).

deference was paid to an aristocratic leadership who found themselves repeatedly reelected to positions of authority. Rarely did an election provide a clear-cut choice between different political philosophies; rather it served chiefly as an opportunity to validate the status quo. Only a few were suited by God to rule, and John Winthrop's view of the masses was widely shared: "the best part [of the people] is always the least, and of that best part the wiser is always the lesser."[2] On the local level, selectmen ran town affairs, but the legendary New England town meeting was a significant political event. At the town meetings most adult males had their say, although the meetings served primarily to ratify decisions of the selectmen rather than to initiate policy.

Magistrates, as well as ministers, were called to be servants of the people. It was an exalted servitude, however, involving many responsibilities. Civil magistrates were expected to possess the qualities of wealth, piety, moderation, wisdom, and justice and to be as close to perfection as humankind's fallen nature would allow. These high expectations were coupled with a lofty view of the dignity of public office. Governmental authority was bestowed on individuals by means of a divine call (as evidenced by their election). Those who did not show proper respect to the Lord's agents were dealt with swiftly, such as Thomas Dexter who was fined, jailed, and disenfranchised in 1633 for commenting that Governor Winthrop was "but an atturney." Dexter was joined by others who paid dearly for insufficient deference, such as John Stone who ran afoul of magistrate Roger Ludlow by referring to him as "just ass" instead of "justice."[3] As the seventeenth century progressed, however, far less emphasis was placed on the majesty of public office, and the spiritual and moral dimensions of the ideal ruler were increasingly replaced by concern for "personal experience, common sense, and charter rights."[4] Yet the interplay of the spiritual and the temporal has been of continuing interest to historians long after it ceased to be a major issue in colonial New England.

Church-State Relations

How the Puritans viewed the respective spheres of authority of church and state has long been the subject of considerable controversy. Edmund S. Morgan observed that "nothing about the Puritans has been more widely misunderstood than their views of the relation-

2. Quoted in Timothy Breen, *The Character of the Good Ruler* (New Haven, 1970), p. 63.

3. Ibid., pp. 8, 66.

4. Ibid., p. 124.

ship between church and state."[5] The origins of this misunderstanding must be traced more to historians than to the Puritans themselves, who were rather clear about the whole matter.

Among the first generation of American Puritans, two individuals were especially significant in setting forth the orthodox Puritan position concerning church-state relations. John Winthrop, governor of the Massachusetts Bay Colony during most of the years from settlement in 1630 until his death in 1647, made several entries in his journal which deal with matters of church and state. John Cotton, New England's most acclaimed minister among the first generation of settlers, had much to say about church and state as well. In addition, we can glean information from the various actions taken by the General Court of the colony, the pronouncements of other clergy both individually and collectively in synods, and dissident voices such as Roger Williams who called into question the views on church and state espoused by the establishment.

The granting of the vote to church members, rather than being interpreted as a remarkable expansion of the franchise, has been interpreted by some historians as proof of the theocratic nature of New England. Winthrop's strategy should not be surprising in light of the colony's religious purpose, and the granting of voting rights to church members, he believed, would make at least the regenerate populace more submissive to leaders whom they themselves had chosen and at the same time keep power in responsible hands. While granting his government a wider popular base, Winthrop shared the widely accepted belief of his age that civil rulers received their authority directly from God.[6] Furthermore, Winthrop and other Puritan leaders in America were convinced that they were on a divine mission to the New World and that they must please God or perish.[7]

The closely knit relationship between church and state in Old England created major problems for a number of Puritans and indeed helped drive them on to America. With this in mind, the American Puritan leadership knew that church-state relations had to be developed rightly in the Promised Land. Governor Winthrop proceeded firmly but cautiously. In 1631 the infant church at Watertown selected as an elder Richard Brown, a man whom Winthrop described as holding to certain "Romish" beliefs and possessed of "a very violent spirit." The General Court, although a civil authority, addressed a letter of concern to the Watertown congregation inquiring if Brown were

5. Edmund S. Morgan, *Roger Williams: The Church and the State* (New York: 1967), p. 62.

6. Ibid., p. 80.

7. See Winthrop's "A Model of Christian Charity," in Paul Boller, Jr. and Ronald Story, eds., *A More Perfect Union* (Boston, 1984), pp. 12-15.

truly fit for his ecclesiastical office. There was such division in the congregation over Brown that both sides appealed to Governor Winthrop to settle the dispute. Winthrop and the deputy governor traveled to Watertown to mediate. In a characteristically wise and cautious move, Winthrop asked the congregation and pastor whether their mediation should be as magistrates or merely as members of a neighboring congregation. The decision was that they should not act as magistrates, but as fellow believers only.[8] Winthrop complied, yet he was convinced of the necessity that in all matters of authority the civil government should have undisputed supremacy.[9] The governor counted on the positive influence of the clergy who "have great power with the people, whereby through the good correspondency between the Magistrates and them, they are the more easily governed."[10] When the clergy became overly involved in political affairs, however, Winthrop spoke out. He criticized the ministry in Connecticut in a polite but firm way, saying that "though they were men of singular wisdom and godliness, yet, stepping out of their course, their actions wanted that blessing, which otherwise might have been expected."[11]

For the Puritans, church and state were both essential parts of God's economy for the human race. Church and state were partners, but they were not of the same essence. John Cotton expressed it well when he wrote, "God's institutions (such as the government of church and commonwealth be) may be close and compact, and coordinate to one another, and yet not confounded."[12] John Davenport likewise saw the church and civil government as "coordinate States, in the same place reaching forth help mutually each to [the] other, for the welfare of both, according to God."[13] In this arrangement, the civil magistrates were to function, according to Winthrop, as the "nursing fathers of the churches."[14] The codification of Massachusetts law in the 1641 *Body of Liberties* recognized the state's independence from the church and enumerated the freedoms the churches were to enjoy from the state while at the same time it allowed for general state supervision of church affairs. The hands of the magistrates were not tied when it came to the spiritual lives of their charges. According to John Cotton, it was "a carnall and worldly, and indeed, an ungodly imagination" which viewed the magistrates' jurisdiction as limited to the temporal

8. James K. Homer, ed., *Winthrop's Journal* (New York, 1946), 1:71.

9. Miller, *Orthodoxy in Massachusetts*, p. 212.

10. Quoted in ibid., p. 249.

11. Winthrop, *Journal*, 1:97.

12. Quoted in Charles M. Andrews, *The Colonial Period of American History* (New Haven, 1934) 1:450 n. 1.

13. Quoted in Miller, *Orthodoxy in Massachusetts*, p. 240.

14. Quoted in Andrews, *Colonial Period*, 1:448.

aspects of the people and would "exclude them from the care of their souls."[15] In *The Keys of the Kingdom of Heaven* Cotton declared that the church ought to be in subjection to the civil authorities in four areas that concern "civil peace":

The first area included "the things of this life," that is, the disposing of property, lives, liberties, customs, and worldly honors.

The second area was the establishment of pure religion in doctrine, worship, and government. Any reformation necessary to correct corruption should be within the purview of the civil government. Cotton further explained that

> It is true, the establishment of pure religion, and reformation of corruptions pertain also to the churches and synodical assemblies. But they go about it only with spiritual weapons, ministry of the word, and church censures upon such as are under church power. But magistrates address themselves thereto, partly by commanding, and stirring up the churches and ministers thereof to go about it in their spiritual way: partly also by civil punishments upon the willful opposers, and disturbers of the same.

The third area involved the exercise of public rituals of a spiritual nature, such as days of fasting, humiliation, and thanksgiving as well as the calling together of synods by the civil authorities.

Finally, the church must submit to the civil magistrates even if it results in suffering unjust persecution. The church must not offer physical resistance; it has not been granted the power of the sword. Cotton concluded that

> as the church is subject to the sword of the magistrate in things which concern the civil peace; so the magistrate (if Christian) is subject to the keys of the church, in matters which concern the peace of his conscience and the kingdom of heaven.[16]

Cotton warned against unlimited authority in either church or state, arguing that the corrupt nature of man would cause boundless power to "sometime or other run out to excess."[17] Final authority should rest not with the church, Cotton maintained, but with the

---

15. Cotton, *Bloudy Tenent*, p. 68.

16. Quoted in Larzer Ziff, ed., *John Cotton on the Churches of New England* (Cambridge, 1968), pp. 152–54, 156.

17. John Cotton, "Limitation of Government," in *The American Puritans*, ed. Perry Miller (New York, 1956, 1982), p. 86.

state, since "the head of the Church under Christ is the Civill Magistrate."[18]

The churches of New England frequently acknowledged their dependence on civil authority for the maintenance of a godly society. Discussions of the roles of church and state by a gathering of ministers in 1646 resulted in a statement which concluded with a description of the ideal relationship between the two institutions:

> The Churches desire, the Magistrate Commands; Churches act in a way of liberty, the Magistrate in a way of Authority. Moses and Aaron should goe together, and kiss one another in the Mount of God.[19]

Two years later a more formal synod produced the *Platform of Church Discipline*, better known as the Cambridge Platform of 1648. This document set forth the promise that

> Church government stands in no opposition to civil government of comonwelths, nor any intrencheth upon the authority of Civil Magistrates in their jurisdictions; but rather strengtheneth them, & furthereth the people in yielding more hearty & conscionable obedience unto them. . . . They may both stand together & flourish the one being helpfull unto the other, in their distinct & due administrations.

Magistrates are rightly concerned with matters pertaining to godliness, the platform maintained, and have a right, indeed an obligation, to punish heresy, idolatry, blasphemy, and anything else undermining "the worship and holy things of God." Significantly, the Cambridge Platform also observed that civil magistrates have no power over inward beliefs, but only over "acts of the outward man."[20] The clergy did find it advantageous, from time to time, to remind and encourage the civil authorities to exercise their powers. In 1635, for example, the General Court was encouraged to remember that they possessed legitimate power to enforce church attendance.[21]

The actions of the General Court of Massachusetts made it clear that while that body valued highly the churches and the ministry, and indeed frequently sought clerical advice on various matters, it was the civil government of the colony that held final authority. Clergy were called to meet with the civil magistrates of Massachusetts over sev-

---

18. Quoted in Miller, *Orthodoxy*, p. 259.

19. Quoted in Williston Walker, *The Creeds and Platforms of Congregationalism* (New York, 1893), p. 193.

20. Ibid., pp. 236–37.

21. Miller, *Orthodoxy in Massachusetts*, p. 254.

enty times between 1630 and 1649. In 1644, for example, a group of
clergy was called in to help reconcile the differences between the magistrates and the deputies concerning their respective powers. The
ministers gave careful and detailed written opinions which were appreciated by the civil authorities.[22] A number of ministers generally
attended the sessions of the General Court.[23] In addition, the annual
election sermons requested by the civil authorities permitted the
clergy to give pastoral advice, usually in general terms, concerning the
quality of leadership the colony should expect. It was never a con-
tested point, however, that ministers themselves should not provide
leadership in civil office.

In numerous ways, the government of the Massachusetts Bay
Colony made it clear that the churches were under their authority.
Concerned about the possible proliferation of unsound churches, the
General Court ruled in 1636 that all new churches must receive the
approbation of the court.[24] Early on, there was some disagreement between church and state concerning who should act first in dealing
with overt heresy. In 1639 a group of ministers presented a petition to
the General Court requesting that the civil government withhold
judgment against a church member for any offense until the church
dealt first with the matter. This was not acceptable to the General
Court. Governor Winthrop turned the matter around to arrive at a policy that a civil magistrate should not be responsible to his church for
actions arising from his magisterial office.[25] The General Court formalized this in a 1641 declaration that "no church censure shall de-
grade or depose any man from any Civill dignitie, office, or Authoritie
he shall have in the Commonwealth."[26] In 1644 the town of
Gloucester elected a representative to the General Court who ran
afoul of his church shortly after his election. The townsmen, taking
their cue from the church, sent a new representative to Boston only to
have the General Court send him home and insist that the original
representative be sent.[27]

Church-state separation and interactions were manifested in other
ways as well. Marriages were authorized only by civil authorities, and
while on occasion a minister might be present to offer a few words of
spiritual advice, he could not perform the ceremony. On occasion the
state stepped on the toes of the church, but rarely backed down. The
General Court in 1639 ordered a reduction in the number of weekday

22. Winthrop, *Journal*, 2:211.
23. David D. Hall, *The Faithful Shepherd* (Chapel Hill, N.C., 1972), p. 130.
24. Miller, *Orthodoxy*, p. 252.
25. Morgan, *Roger Williams*, pp. 72–73.
26. Shurtleff, *Records of Massachusetts Bay* 1:246, 271.
27. Morgan, *Roger Williams*, pp. 70–71.

lectures given by the clergy. It seemed that spiritual nourishment was interfering with physical nourishment and the government wanted to see more time spent in farming.[28] The civil government also had no hesitation in requesting that clergy come together in synods to discuss matters of common concern. In late 1636 the General Court called the elders of the churches of Boston to discuss "differences among the churches in point of opinion" during the antinomian controversy.[29] In 1646 the magistrates passed an order calling for a ministerial synod to draw up a confession of faith and plan of church discipline. Although there was some ministerial protest against meddling in ecclesiastical affairs, there was a general feeling of relief that the synod would carry more weight with the authority of the state behind it.[30]

The clergy by and large were eager to encourage the government to do its part in the promotion of godliness and ministerial privileges. Turning again to the Cambridge Platform, the churches admonished the state that

> It is the duty of the magistrate to take care of matters of religion. . . . The end of the magistrate's office is not only the quiet and peaceable life of the subject in matters of righteousness and honesty, but also in matters of godliness, yea, of all godliness. Moses, Joshua, David, Solomon, Asa, Jehoshaphat, Hezekiah, Josiah are much commended by the Holy Ghost for putting forth their authority in matters of religion. On the contrary, such kings as have been failing this way are frequently taxed and reproved by the Lord.[31]

Not all of New England's clergy were in agreement with the ways in which the church and state interfaced, but dissidents were a small minority. Roger Williams is the most famous voice of opposition, perhaps because what he advocated sounds so modern and reasonable. Yet he was a genuine radical in his day and found himself banished from Massachusetts because he demanded the total separation of the state not only from the church but also from God.[32]

Central and Local Authority

While church and state comprised realms of authority that were more complementary than competitive, the state itself had two dis-

---

28. Hall, *Faithful Shepherd*, p. 125.

29. Winthrop, *Journal*, 1:203–4.

30. Hall, *Faithful Shepherd*, pp. 127–28.

31. Quoted in Thomas Jefferson Wertenbaker, *The Puritan Oligarchy* (New York, 1947), p. 71.

32. Morgan, *Roger Williams*, p. 85.

tinct levels of authority—centralism and localism. This was not planned deliberately, as it was hoped that the colonists of Massachusetts would settle in one central community. This emphasis on unity and physical proximity fit well with the communal ideal and would have assisted in overall control of the colony. Expansion and dispersion into the wilderness took place, however, and had significant implications for authority and for the theory of a unified, organic society. The abundance of empty land and disagreement concerning the most desirable site for the Puritan "city on a hill" resulted in the founding of several towns almost at the outset. The wide powers of the central government posed no insoluble problems for these individual communities as long as ideals and basic purposes between the two levels of government coincided.

Localism proved to be a strong force in Puritan New England, in large part because local authority in both ecclesiastical and civil realms had been threatened and curtailed in England. When Charles I came to the throne in 1625, the young king designed a stronger central authority for the Crown at the expense of local authority in England's congregations, towns, and counties. What looked to the king like rightful responsibilities appeared to others as radical and disruptive policies. It is no coincidence that the great Puritan migrations to the New World occurred during his reign, as Puritan settlers sought to escape what they perceived to be an absolute ruler's imposition of unhealthy religious and social changes.[33]

The communal ideal of unity and the desire for as much local autonomy as possible thus proved paradoxical and resulted in strong towns, strong congregations, and a strong central government. What made it possible for this unlikely combination of authority to work so well was the shared commitment of most seventeenth-century New Englanders to the Christian faith and to the belief that order, peace, and unity were the highest political ideals. When these values were no longer so universally shared, political and religious dissent and conflict increased markedly in New England.

33. For a sound interpretation of this situation, see Breen, "Persistent Localism," 32:3–28.

11

The Cycle of Family Life

The Puritans were very much in awe of the institutions created by God. The church and civil government were two such institutions which, as we have observed, the Puritan faithful held in high esteem. Another God-ordained institution for the benefit of humankind was the family, and Puritan attitudes toward family life demonstrate the great importance of this basic institution in the history of early New England. Actually, the family was the most vital institution of all, for the Puritan household was a religious institution, a government, and a living analogy of Christ's love for his church all wrapped up into one. Furthermore, the family was the original human institution, dating back to the garden of Eden. When it came to explaining God's relationship to humankind, the Bible frequently used the human family as an analogy. The Puritan clergy placed much emphasis on interpersonal relationships; the saints thought of themselves as members of the family of God; and a good deal of Puritan theology was pictured in domestic terms.

Marriage

There can be no question but that the Puritans esteemed marriage very highly. In numerous sermons the biblical analogy of espousal and marriage was used to depict Christ's relationship to the believers comprising his church.[1] The clergy used other metaphors, but marriage, the most intimate relationship between mortals, was in Puritan

1. E.g., see Shepard, *Parable of Ten Virgins*, pp. 10, 67; Allin, *Spouse of Christ*, in Burgess, ed., *Dedham Pulpit*, p. 7.

eyes the closest comparison to the union between Christ and his true followers.[2] The Puritans were not only promarriage, they were anticelibacy. The wedded state was an expected part of life, and those not conforming to this expectation were generally viewed with some suspicion and often lived with a family rather than alone.

Although the Puritans held marriage in very high regard, their views of marriage and sexual union within marriage differed radically from the medieval Catholic tradition. For one thing, the Puritans did not see the marriage bond as indissoluble; as in the Anglican tradition divorce was a possibility in the cases of infidelity or desertion. Even prolonged impotence might be acceptable grounds for divorce. Marriage was not given sacramental status by the Puritans, and neither was procreation viewed as its principal purpose. The Puritans have an undeserved reputation for prudishness in sexual matters within marriage. The Reformation reintroduced the idea that marriage was not only tolerable, it was honorable, and sex within marriage was a good gift of God, a wonderfully pleasant expression of love and commitment and not merely a necessary evil for the purpose of producing offspring. The Puritans expressed these views quite openly, even by modern standards, and celebrated sexual love as a necessary part of a genuine marriage.

While our perceptions of Puritan sexual views have been shaped by Victorian attitudes, the Puritans themselves have been misunderstood in this area. What has probably given the Puritans the unfounded reputation of being sexually repressed is not that they found sex undesirable, or the human body unattractive, but that they valued sexual union in marriage so highly that they saw it as a very private, nearly sacred affair and did everything within their power to protect it. They found sexual promiscuity and perversion horrifying because they regarded sex as such a good and valuable gift of God; therefore, their laws reflected a protective attitude toward their biblical view of sex. Indeed, numerous passages of Scripture were cited frequently in sermons and writings of the Puritan clergy (a group which had no praise for celibacy) to give encouragement to healthy sexuality within marriage.[3]

The steps leading up to a Puritan marriage included a period of courtship which at times might involve the curious custom of "bundling"—being together in bed, fully dressed and under the covers for a little privacy within the sanctity and watchful eye of the home. Courting Puritan couples may or may not have fallen in love; that was

2. Morgan, *Puritan Family*, p. 162.

3. For an excellent analysis of Puritan attitudes toward marriage and sex, see Ryken, *Worldly Saints*, chap. 3.

not a prerequisite to "espousal" or "contracting" (engagement). Love was a vital part of Puritan marriage, but love was expected to grow during the espousal period and to continue growing in the marriage. Parental consent was generally required for a marriage, but in cases of parental denial an appeal was possible. The engagement was serious business, the breaking of which could result in a lawsuit.[4] Despite the religious nature of marriage, the wedding was a civil affair rather than an ecclesiastical one. Prior to the rather bleak and very simple wedding, performed by a civil magistrate (ministers did not perform weddings in Massachusetts until 1686) and lacking "worldly" wedding rings, the impending union was to be announced at three public meetings, a written notice was to appear on the meetinghouse door for fourteen days, and a report of the wedding was to be made to the town clerk within a month of the event.[5] A good part of the rationale for all of this publicity was to avoid the secret marriages and bigamy that were practiced all too often in seventeenth-century England.

Several studies have refuted the idea that colonial New Englanders married early. While statistics vary from community to community and generation to generation, the average first-time bride was about twenty-one years of age and the average first-time groom was about twenty-four years of age. Few teenage males married, and it was very unusual for a woman under the age of seventeen to marry.[6] Further demographic studies indicate that perhaps one woman in six died from complications of childbirth. Remarriage was common, and often followed swiftly after the passing of one's spouse. John Winthrop himself outlived two wives and obtained a third by the age of thirty. After the death of a spouse, relationships with one's in-laws were carefully maintained, even after remarriage, resulting in tangled webs of family relationships.[7] Despite these close family ties, the nuclear family was the rule in most households; rarely did extended families live under the same roof. Leaving father and mother and cleaving to one's spouse was held up as the biblical model for building a home.

A major concern to married Puritans was that they should love their mates, but not so much that their devotion to God would be hindered. God alone was worthy of humankind's highest love and

4. John Demos, *A Little Commonwealth: Family Life in Plymouth Colony* (London, 1970), pp. 154–55, 157.

5. Ibid., pp. 31–32.

6. See Robert Higgs and H. Louis Stettler, III, "Colonial New England Demography: A Sampling Approach," *William and Mary Quarterly* 27 (Apr. 1970) pp. 282–94. It should be noted that the data in this study focuses on the years 1720–1760, but it is likely that conditions were similar prior to 1700 as well.

7. See John Winthrop's experience in this regard in Morgan, *Puritan Dilemma*, p. 23.

adoration and to supplant the Creator with a mere creature was to fall into idolatry. To have a wife was to possess a good thing, but devout Puritan husbands were to "look at them not for their own ends, but to bee better fitted for Gods service, and bring them nearer to God."[8] Mortality was an ever-present reminder of the folly of placing too much affection on the transitory things of this world, including one's spouse. Thomas Shepard, whose wife nearly died in childbirth, learned that he had begun "to grow secretly proud and full of sensuality delighting my soule in my deare wife more then in my god whom I had promised better unto."[9] The marriage relationship ended at death, for in heaven there would be no marriage and all the Lord's saints would be equally beloved to one another. There were other Puritan couples, however, who needed to work at loving one another sufficiently. Such couples were urged not to set their expectations for their mates too high in a fallen world, but rather to exercise patience and discipline in making love grow and their marriages work.

Within the family and in society at large, it was a man's world. He was lord and master of the household, with power to represent his family in legal matters, and power to discipline those within his domain, including apprentices and servants. The husband was expected to exercise spiritual leadership and control, and was also charged with adequate support of his family. A Puritan husband was required to love and comfort his wife, and was restrained by law from beating her. By contrast, in most of the other American colonies outside of New England disciplinary wife-beating was acceptable within limits.

Children

While the primary purpose of marriage was viewed as companionship (as opposed to the medieval Catholic tradition that viewed procreation as the basic purpose), the birth of children was an expected and vital part of Puritan marriage. Children were clearly a gift of the Lord, but a gift that carried with it tremendous responsibility. It was also a gift that was bestowed frequently; families were generally large, with seven live births per family the average for New England during the years 1720–1760.[10] It was also common for births to be spaced out over a period of up to twenty years, producing siblings who varied widely in age. In seventeenth-century Plymouth children were usually

8. Quoted in Morgan, *Puritan Family*, p. 48.
9. Quoted in ibid., p. 49.
10. Higgs and Stettler, "Colonial New England Demography," pp. 286–87.

spaced at least two years apart.[11] One can safely conclude from this that birth control in one form or another was most likely practiced.

Parents had a divinely appointed task to train up their offspring in the fear of the Lord, with a child's most basic task being to follow the biblical injunction to honor father and mother. The frequency with which the raising of children was mentioned in Puritan sermons indicates the high priority the clergy placed on this facet of family life, as well as the difficulty of doing the job properly. It was expected that Puritan children would receive appropriate religious training in the home from spiritually zealous parents. "Let your children be most frequently catechized," declared Cotton Mather, "and let your Admonitions teach them, how they should think, how pray, and how live, before the Lord."[12] Parents were urged by the clergy to be good models because "Children are apt to follow their Example, especially in that which is evil."[13] Increase Mather recognized the importance of families to the health of the Commonwealth and in 1679 bemoaned what he perceived as their decline: "Families are the Nurceryes for Church and Commonwealth, ruine Families, and ruine all. Order them well and the publick State will fare the better; the great wound and misery of New-England is that Families are out of order."[14]

Since families were the "nurseries of the church," parents were exhorted to do everything possible to see that their children not only conformed outwardly to biblical norms but underwent conversion experiences as well. Although Increase Mather held the belief that God generally gave elect children to elect parents, it was an article of Puritan faith that all children were depraved from birth and lost in sin apart from faith in Christ.[15] God had no grandchildren; each generation was required to have a conversion experience and could not find salvation in the experience of their parents. Richard Mather, however, apparently believed that parents could be effective in guiding a child's spiritual destiny. He urged his congregation to "have pity" on their young children, "and do your best to teach them, and pray for them, weep for them, and wrestle with God for them, who knows but that the prayers and teares of a faithful Mother may be the salvation of the childs soule."[16] Nathaniel Gookin declared that "ye little ones of

11. Demos, *Little Commonwealth*, p. 69.

12. Cotton Mather, *Addresses*, p. 119.

13. Increase Mather, *Call from Heaven*, p. 21.

14. Ibid., p. 91.

15. See Cotton Mather, *Family Well-Ordered*, p. 19; Increase Mather, *Call from Heaven*, p. 3.

16. Richard Mather, *Farewell Exhortation*, p. 13.

Zion" were "earnestly to be prayed for by all that desire the welfare of Zion."[17]

Increase Mather asked, "Was it not with respect unto posterity, that our Fathers came into this wilderness? that they might train up a generation for Christ: Bless God that ever you had such Fathers." "The children of godly parents," Mather stated, "are under peculiar advantages and encouragements to seek the Lord." The duty of godly parents to pray for their children was one such encouragement.[18] A "daily Reading of the Word" was another.[19]

Godly households protected the community from disorder and upheavals, and through the reformation of family life it was believed that "God may be pleased to spare the whole land."[20] A key element of healthy family life was the proper disciplining of children, which included the parents' responsibility to provide a good example; in short, Puritan parents were to "bring up our children for god." Parents were told that they had "a stricter obligation now [with children] than before, in that you will not only break the Law yourselves, but provoke others [your children] to do so too." Tips for the correct raising of children were frequently included in Puritan sermons. Nathaniel Gookin urged his congregation to avoid the following with respect to child discipline:

correcting or reproving . . . when they do not deserve it

being misguided by affections in chastening of them

inordinate passion in reproving or correcting, do not strike in a passion

[disciplining] meerly for your own profit not minding their good

Gookin exhorted his congregation on another occasion that when children are disobedient, parents "must admonish them . . . so far as they are capable of it; only with meekness. Wee must also encourage them in their seeking after God."[21] Cotton Mather, who had much to say about many topics, offered parents his advice on child discipline:

---

17. Nathaniel Gookin, sermon of Mar. 3, 1686, *Substance of Sermons*, Huntington Library MS, p. 11.

18. Increase Mather, *Call from Heaven*, pp. 31, 2, 17–18.

19. Cotton Mather, *Service of the Tabernacle*, p. 26.

20. Cotton, *Covenant of Grace*, pp. 10–11.

21. Gookin, sermons of May and June, 1687, *Sermon Notes, 1687*, Harvard University MS, pp. 48, 114; sermon of Mar. 10, 1686, *Substance of Sermons*, Huntington Library MS, p. 15.

Ornately embroidered English bed hangings (1680–1720). Such hangings provide decorative touches as well as privacy, which was often at a premium. (Wadsworth Atheneum, Hartford. The Elizabeth B. Miles Collection)

A woman's leather shoe, owned by the second wife of Massachusetts governor John Leverett (ca. 1650). (Gift of the Honorable Leverett Saltonstall; photo, courtesy, Museum of Fine Arts, Boston)

Fringed leather gloves, worn by Massachusetts Bay Colony governor John Leverett (ca. 1645) (Courtesy of the Essex Institute, Salem, Mass.)

Striking English glassware such as this clear wine glass was used in late seventeenth-century Massachusetts. (Photograph by N. L. Stebbins, courtesy of the Society for the Preservation of New England Antiquities)

Early New Englanders appreciated style, as seen in this gilded silver cup with cover. (Wadsworth Atheneum, Hartford. The Elizabeth B. Miles Collection)

A silver sugar box made in Boston. Eating small lumps of sugar was often a part of courtship ritual. (Courtesy, The Henry Francis du Pont Winterthur Museum)

The Mason children (Boston, 1670). Children were often dressed and treated as miniature adults. (The Museum of San Fransisco, gift of Mr. and Mrs. John D. Rockefeller, III)

Gravestone art was full of symbolism through which Puritans sought to remember their dead and teach lessons about life and death. A winged Father Time has stayed the hand of the skeletal grim reaper until the appointed hour. The candle on the globe, symbolic of life on earth, will be snuffed out under the watchful eye of a God-figure sun. The leafy vine bordering the headstone signifies eternal life. (Boston Parks and Recreation Commission, on loan to Museum of Fine Arts, Boston. Courtesy, Museum of Fine Arts, Boston)

A hornbook used to teach Puritan children rudiments of writing and religious concepts. (The Folger Shakespeare Library)

In Adam's Fall,
We sinned all.

Thy Life to mend,
This Book attend.

The Cat doth play,
And after slay.

A Dog will bite
A Thief at night.

An Eagle's Flight
Is out of Sight.

The idle fool
Is whipt at School.

Learning the alphabet, Puritan style, from *The New England Primer.* (Courtesy, American Antiquarian Society)

New England Puritans valued time—and good pocket watches. This one, made before 1675 of silver and brass, was brought to America from London. (The Colonial Williamsburg Foundation)

Puritan interest in making theology a part of daily life is evident in this skillet on whose handle is inscribed wages of sin is death. (Museum of Fine Arts, Boston, Mass.)

Reprove not Furiously. . . . Remember, Nothing will be so well done in a passion, but what may be done better out of it. . . . do not Rage with a tongue set on fire of hell.

Reprove Reasonably. Let there be just Cause for it.

Reprove Scripturally. . . . A Reproof with a Scripture comes with a more than ordinary Majesty and Authority.

In another sermon aptly titled *A Family Well-Ordered*, Cotton Mather gave further advice to parents:

keep up so much Authority, that your Word may be a Law unto them. Nevertheless, let not your Authority be strained with such Harshness, and Fierceness, as may discourage your Children. To treat our children like Slaves, and with such Rigour, that they shall always Tremble and Abhor to come into our presence, this will be very unlike to our Heavenly Father. Our authority should be so Tempered with Kindness, and Meekness, and Loving Tenderness, that our Children may Fear us with Delight, and see that we Love them. . . .[22]

Some clergy perceived a declension on the part of New England's children in the last two decades or so of the seventeenth century. Increase Mather sadly observed in 1679 that "there is a doleful degeneracy appearing in the face of this generation [of youth], and no man can say, but that the body of the present generation will perish both temporally and eternally. . . ."[23] Cotton Mather, in a message entitled *Help for Distressed Parents*, set forth Old Testament examples of domestic difficulty and stated that ungodly children also constituted a common affliction in New England. Part of the problem, he maintained, was that parents were often too fond of their children. He admonished parents that "while your children are under your Government, so Govern them, that they may not have their way."[24]

Children were periodically urged from the pulpit to behave well. They were accused of engaging in "youthful pleasures," and according to Nathaniel Gookin they would regret such a waste of time "at an hour of death, and at ye day of Judgement." Parental dereliction of duty in child rearing, heinous as that was, was "not sufficient ground for the child to omitt his duty."[25] Cotton Mather urged the children of New England to benefit from parental guidance:

22. Cotton Mather, *Service of the Tabernacle*, pp. 49, 52; *Family Well-Ordered*, p. 22.

23. Increase Mather, *Call from Heaven*, p. 19.

24. Cotton Mather, *Help for Distressed Parents* (Boston, 1695), pp. 19–20, 28.

25. Gookin, sermons of June and Oct., 1687, *Sermon Notes, 1687*, Harvard University MS, pp. 91–92, 115.

You enjoy Parental Instruction . . . O refuse it not! Does not thy Father, or thy Master, or thy Mother, charge thee to remember God? Did they never charge thee to read the Word, and seek the Face of God, and to make Conscience of thy Wayes? Then, My Son, hear the Instruction of thy Father, and forsake not the Law of thy Mother.[26]

The consequences of a child's recalcitrance were severe in the clergy's opinion. Since it was "ye childrens duty to submitt unto their parents,"[27] and such a duty had its foundation in the Word, children who "rebel against their Parents" were engaging in "wickedness" which was "excessively great." Such children were warned that they "do usually dye before their time . . . what sayeth the Scripture?" "The tears of a godly Father, if his Children forsake the Lord," warned Increase Mather, "will make the flames of Eternal Fire burn the more fiercely upon their Souls forever."[28] Cotton Mather warned that "the heavy Curse of God will fall upon those children that make light of their parents."[29]

The Puritans seemed to have a certain ambivalence toward infants. John Robinson, minister to the Pilgrims before they left Holland, called them "a blessing great, but dangerous." The Puritans held that infants were born in sin, yet their innate depravity did not preclude their salvation if they died at an early age; in fact it was often expressed, perhaps as a form of consolation to bereaved parents, that it was better to, in the words of Cotton Mather, "have him dy in his Infancy, than live in cursed and lothsome Wickedness." Puritan parents loved their children and at the same time feared for their souls. The rod was an effective device for bringing about desired external behavior, but what Puritan parents really desired was an internalized submission and obedience to their authority. The breaking of the child's "self-will" was viewed as an essential step in developing mature character.

High expectations were placed on Puritan children. Childhood was certainly a less meaningful stage of human development than it is today, and the concept of "adolescence" was unheard of. Until the age of six, boys and girls were dressed in gowns and petticoats; following this the boys were dressed like little men. Girls wore feminine, restrictive clothing. The fact that children were dressed like miniature adults after the age of six should not lead us to the conclusion that children

---

26. Cotton Mather, *Early Piety*, p. 84.

27. Gookin, sermon of May, 1687, *Sermon Notes, 1687*, Harvard University MS, p. 51.

28. Increase Mather, *Excess in Wickedness*, pp. 14–15; *Call From Heaven*, p. 48.

29. Cotton Mather, *Family Well-Ordered*, p. 41.

were always treated like miniature adults. While standards were often high for children, their weaknesses were noted and religious conversions in young children were rarely treated as genuine.[30] The later years of childhood were often characterized as full of pride, worldliness, and rebellion, as children struggled to seek their own identity.[31]

The Puritans followed the English pattern of often placing their children in another home. This was not because of inadequate love for their offspring; just the reverse was true, for, as Edmund S. Morgan has pointed out, "Puritan parents did not trust themselves with their own children . . . they were afraid of spoiling them by too great affection."[32] On occasion the state demanded that children be placed in a more suitable home environment.

The law did not ordinarily require that parents apprentice out their children, but doing so did have some positive effects. Children were often uprooted to other homes as they were beginning to assert their independence and become resistant to parental authority. Finding themselves in a new environment where someone else was in charge of discipline enabled them to relate to their own parents with more ease and friendliness. Also, the new master would be less likely to overlook adolescent misdeeds out of personal affection, as a parent might be tempted to do. Parents were by no means excused from their obligations or affections at this juncture, however. Older children often returned home and, even if they did not, it was the parents' duty to sort out prospective marriage partners and give a parental blessing. The final decision in such matters was generally left to the children, but the range of choices was generally set forth by the parents. In fact, not to receive permission of a potential mate's parents even for courtship could result in imposition of a civil penalty.[33]

Family Religious Practices

Domestic religious instruction and practices were considered an indispensable part of Puritan family life and an aid to the effectiveness of the church. The church alone could not do the job of imparting the faith; the home was a vital partner in this crucial endeavor. The churches frequently encouraged and reminded their congregations to perform family religious duties. Every morning and evening the devout Puritan patriarch would lead his family in devotions which con-

30. David E. Stannard, *The Puritan Way of Death* (New York, 1977), p. 49.
31. Philip Greven, *The Protestant Temperament* (Ithaca, N.Y., 1977), pp. 45–46, 28, 31–32, 55.
32. Morgan, *Puritan Family*, p. 77.
33. See ibid., pp. 77–79.

sisted of Scripture reading, prayer, and quite likely the singing of psalms. Other family members, including the children, would not only participate in but also lead these family exercises.

Churches at times made public commitments concerning the carrying out of family religious duties. In 1680, Increase Mather's church in Boston made a covenant:

> We promise (by the help of Christ) that we will endeavor to walk before God in our houses, with a perfect heart; and that we will uphold the worship of God therein continually, according as he in his word doth require, both in respect of Prayer, and reading the Scriptures, that so the word of Christ may dwell richly in us; And that we will do what in us lyeth, to bring up our children for Christ, that they may become such, as they that have the Lords name put upon them by a solemn dedication to God in Christ, ought to be; and that therefore we will (so far as there shall be need of it) Catechize them, and exhort and charge them to fear and serve the Lord, and endeavour to set an holy Example before them, and be much in prayer for their Conversion and Salvation.[34]

Privacy and Conflict

Contemporary American society values personal privacy to a degree unimagined by the colonists of Puritan New England. Within the context of the family, privacy was nearly nonexistent and perhaps not even a meaningful concept. Many New England homes of the seventeenth century were a story and a half, consisting of one main room, sometimes with one end partitioned off for storage or sleeping space. Often an overhead loft, also used for sleeping and storage, was incorporated into the home. The typical seventeenth-century house was small and generally dark, with low ceilings and few windows. This appears to be the way many Puritans wanted it, as their view of nature was often more antagonistic than friendly. Their homes were fortresses to keep nature out. In these dark and cramped quarters, the drama of family life was played out. Since the family was the basic unit of society, the practice was that "basic disruptions and discontinuities must be avoided at all costs."[35] Families had little choice other than to get along together, since prolonged conflict in such a limited environment not only went against Puritan values, but would also be most unpleasant.

Historian John Demos has theorized, accurately I believe, concerning the nature of interpersonal hostility in Puritan New England.

34. Quoted in ibid., p. 140.
35. Demos, *Little Commonwealth*, pp. 29–31, 50.

Since families were expected, indeed forced by physical circumstances and the law, to get along together, aggression and hostility often manifested themselves in forms other than family bickering. While aggressive and hostile behavior was not acceptable in Puritan New England, such behavior was less unacceptable when directed at those outside the family. Demos has determined that psychological displacement was often practiced. Anger, hostility, and aggression that may have been triggered by circumstances in the family were often directed toward others, resulting in "chronic hostility among neighbors."[36] Even the Salem witchcraft episodes (see chapter 13) can be understood perhaps more clearly in light of the psychological displacement of hostility and frustration experienced by adolescent Puritan girls. Unable to confront their own mothers with their hostility, these girls, when given a little encouragement, turned their aggression on women (and a few men) of their mothers' generation and accused them of witchcraft.[37]

The Puritans and Death

Puritan families faced the inevitable process of dying more frequently than most modern Americans. Death was an enemy, yet also part of the natural order of things to be expected because of man's fallen, sinful nature. For the Puritan saint, death was viewed as both a punishment and a reward. Preoccupation with death was rampant, indeed thinking about death was encouraged and expected, even among Puritan children. Cotton Mather wrote that

> A prudent man will Dy Daily; and this one Thing in our doing too: Tis to live Daily under the power of such Impressions, as we shall have upon us, when we come to Dy. . . . Every Time the Clock Strikes, it may Strike upon our Hearts, to think, thus I am one Hour nearer to my last! But, O mark what I say; That Hour is probably Nearer to None than to such as Least Think of it.[38]

The Puritan ambivalence toward death is seen in the fact that "the Puritans were gripped individually and collectively by an intense and unremitting fear of death, while *simultaneously* clinging to the traditional Christian rhetoric of viewing death as a release and relief for the earth-bound soul."[39]

36. Ibid., p. 50.
37. See John Demos, "Underlying Themes in the Witchcraft of Seventeenth-Century New England," *American Historical Review* 75 (1970): 1311–26.
38. Quoted in Stannard, *Puritan Death*, p. 78.
39. Ibid., p. 79.

The ages and rates at which New England Puritans died varied throughout the seventeenth century and from community to community. A detailed study of Andover, Massachusetts, shows a remarkably low death rate in the 1650s and 1660s with the chances of children surviving to adulthood significantly greater than in similar Old World villages. Those of the first generation who did survive to adulthood in Andover could expect to live beyond the age of seventy.[40] In another study of seventeenth-century Dedham, Massachusetts, it has been found that the fundamental conditions of life, including the death rate, were considerably better than in Europe, due primarily to better diet, better housing, and lack of demographic crises.[41] On the other hand, the death rate in more crowded, cosmopolitan Boston was much higher and did not compare favorably with the situation in rural England. It can be safely assumed that 10 to 30 percent of infants did not survive to their first birthdays. Realistically, "a young couple embarking on a marriage did so with the knowledge and expectation that in all probability two or three of the children they might have would die before the age of ten."[42] David Stannard theorizes that the Puritans' practice of apprenticing out their children at a young age may have been an "intuitive response" to the possible death of a child and may have afforded "a means of insulating themselves to some extent against the shock that the death of a child might bring."[43]

Considerable importance and interest were focused on the deathbed scene of the soon-to-be departed Puritan. Deathbed accounts, including last words, were frequent diary entries which were thought to be instructive as one prepared for one's own death. While a peaceful death and last words of comfort were the ideal, even many of God's choice servants fell short of this in reality. It seemed that God exposed some to agony of spirit just before death, "plunging them on their death-beds in deep temptations, and casting their souls down to hell, to rebound the higher to heaven."[44] Indeed, deathbed anxiety among even devout Puritans appears to have been very common. Cotton Mather departed with the thought, "And is this dying! This all! is this what I feared when I prayed against a hard death! Is it no more than this! O I can bear this! I can bear it, I can bear it!" and his last word was reportedly "Grace!"[45] But, as Cotton Mather related,

40. See Philip Greven, *Four Generations: Population, Land, and Family in Colonial Andover, Massachusetts* (Ithaca, N.Y., 1970), chap. 2.
41. See Lockridge, *A New England Town*, chap. 4.
42. Stannard, *Puritan Death*, pp. 54–56.
43. Ibid., p. 58.
44. Quoted in Bercovitch, *Puritan Origins of the American Self*, p. 32.
45. Kenneth Silverman, *The Life and Times of Cotton Mather* (New York, 1984), pp. 421–22.

his equally devout father, Increase Mather, experienced a different response:

> he sometimes let fall expressions of some Fear lest he might after all be Deceived in his Hope of the Future Blessedness. His Holy Ministry having very much insisted on that Point, that no care could be too much to prevent our being Deceived in that Important Matter; tis no wonder, that as the Dark Vapours which assaulted and fettered his Intellectual Powers, broke in upon him, his Head should run much upon the Horror of being Deceived at the last. . . . yet it were a very Supposeable thing, and not at all to be wondered at, if the Serpent be let loose to vex a Servant of GOD in the Heel of his Life; and if the Powers of Darkness, knowing the Time to be short, fall with Great Wrath on the Great Opposers of their Kingdom, and make a very Dark Time for them just before the Break of the Eternal Day upon them. And how justly might it awaken the rest of us to Work out our own Salvation with Fear and Trembling, when we see such a man as Dr. Mather, concerned with so much Fear and Trembling, lest he should be Deceived at the Last? . . . The best Judges of Things have agreed in this Judgment; that going to Heaven in the way of Repentence, is much safer and surer than going in the way of Extasy.[46]

It seemed as though the best of Puritans were preoccupied with thoughts of falling short, in spite of a theology that discounted good works as a means of attaining saving grace.

Puritan Funerals

The first generation of New England Puritans practiced the simplest of death rituals. A procession of mourners would go to the burial ground without a funeral sermon or even a Scripture reading. Excessive mourning was considered inappropriate. The death of the founding governor, John Winthrop, in 1649 was the occasion for a change in funeral policy. Embalming of the corpse, which was generally not done for common folk in England at the time, was apparently a regular practice in New England, at least after the 1640s. The stark simplicity of early Puritan funerals was reversed by the end of the seventeenth century as funerals became major social occasions. Pairs of gloves were sent by the family to those invited to the funeral, an expense which could become considerable. The tolling of the meeting-house bell summoned mourners to the funeral procession, and they appeared wearing their funeral gloves, mourning ribbons, and other

---

46. Quoted in Stannard, *Puritan Death,* pp. 79–80.

symbols of grief. The coffin would either be carried to the burial ground by the mourners, or placed in a horse-drawn hearse, if one were available. Often small pieces of paper containing poems written by mourners for the occasion would be placed on the coffin. Back at the meetinghouse following the interment, the family of the deceased would provide food and gold rings for the mourners. These rings were designed with carvings of skeletons, coffins, and other death symbols. Funeral sermons which eulogized the departed, and prayer, once avoided at the actual time of burial, became common by the end of the seventeenth century. The expenses of the funeral, including coffins made of fine wood, could often eat up a good portion of the estate of the deceased. By 1724, the Massachusetts government began to legislate against this kind of extravagance as inappropriate in God's vineyard.[47]

---

47. For a detailed examination of death and burial practices in Puritan New England, see Stannard, *Puritan Death*, chap. 5.

12

Education, Cultural Life, and Recreation

T he Puritans' reverence for the Bible as the Word of God and their desire to live life as an integrated whole around the precepts of that Word help us to understand the ways in which their worldview was worked out in their lives. Their understanding of the Scriptures and their attempts to live according to that understanding influenced the importance they placed on education, the directions in which they expressed themselves culturally, and the conceptual limits which they imposed upon themselves in their use of leisure time.

Education

The Puritans regarded education as essential—not as an end in itself, but as a means of religious knowledge which could lead to the salvation of one's soul. The quest for learning was made possible in part because of the Puritans' refusal to compartmentalize life into things secular and sacred. From their perspective, all of life and learning was worth exploring; true knowledge possessed unity and meaning since it was a creation of God. Topping the list of Puritan educational concerns was the teaching of reading. The ability of individuals to read the Bible was much to be desired for the salvation of souls as well as the betterment of the entire community. "The matter of our learning," declared John Eliot, "is chiefly the Scriptures, that is the book above all books. . . ." Eliot went on to state that

The next book to that is the book of God's creatures, the works of God, where all the liberal Arts are to be found and learned. And the next books are the books, labors, and works of learned men, and especially of holy men, who lay open the treasures of wisdom and knowledge, which are laid up in Jesus Christ, laid out, displayed, and revealed in the Scriptures, and explained to our capacities in the Books of holy and learned men.[1]

From a Puritan perspective, man's chief enemy was ignorance, especially an ignorance of the written Word of God. The Roman Catholic Church was especially condemned in this regard for deliberately keeping the masses in darkness concerning the content of the Scriptures. "Ignorance," claimed Cotton Mather, "is the Mother (not of Devotion but) of HERESY."[2]

While the family had traditionally borne the chief burden of educating the younger generation in the ways of civilization, the Puritans were not satisfied with anything less than a formalized program to assure adequate learning. In 1642 the General Court of the Massachusetts Bay Company passed an act requiring the selectmen of each town to periodically review the educational attainments of the town's children, with particular attention to "their ability to read and understand the principles of religion and the capital laws of the country."[3] Should parents be found wanting in the carrying out of their instructional duties, they could be fined and have their children taken from the home and apprenticed in a suitable learning environment. Home training included mastery of the hornbook which contained the alphabet, lists of vowel and consonant combinations, and the Lord's Prayer. Following this, the child progressed to a primer and catechism, the most popular of which was *Milke for Babes* (ca. 1646) by John Cotton. In 1690 the *New England Primer* made its debut; this volume combined the teaching of reading skills with religious instruction and served colonial America well for nearly a century.

Educational practice was further formalized in early Massachusetts with the passage of a law in 1647 that required every town of fifty households to hire a teacher and every town of one hundred households to establish a grammar school. This law became known in later years as the "Old Deluder Satan Act" since it began with a preamble denouncing "that old deluder, Satan" who sought "to keep men from

1. Eliot, *Harmony of the Gospels*, p. 32.
2. Quoted in Morgan, *Puritan Family*, p. 89.
3. Quoted in Pauline Holmes, *A Tercentenary History of the Boston Public Latin School, 1635–1935* (Cambridge, 1935), p. 3.

the knowledge of the Scriptures."[4] While not all Puritan towns kept the law, most did so. In a society which boasted a much higher percentage of university-trained men than perhaps any other society in the world, there was widespread support for the idea that education should be taken seriously.

Grammar schools, the next step for youngsters who had done well in their basic home studies, were often taught by university graduates who were not interested in long-term teaching careers, but who were waiting for a suitable pastorate to come along. Where such training was available, boys enrolled about the age of seven or eight years and undertook a course of study that was designed to prepare them for a college curriculum. The serious study of Latin and rote memorization were characteristic of these early American grammar schools. Those who were not fortunate enough to attend such a school (including the vast majority of New England girls in the seventeenth century) completed their education at home, or in a so-called "dame school," a domestic classroom run by an educated woman. Reading and writing skills were reinforced in the home, with the result that early New England enjoyed the highest literacy rate in the world at that time.

Those boys who did well in grammar school might, after seven to eight years of study (or less in unusual cases), become candidates for New England's only seventeenth-century school of higher learning, Harvard College. Founded at Cambridge, Massachusetts, in 1636, Harvard provided a curriculum based largely on the program of studies at Emmanuel College, Cambridge, a school which many first-generation New England leaders had attended. The establishment of Harvard was a valiant attempt to maintain the best of the heritage and Christian civilization the Puritans brought with them from England. The college enrolled about fifty students by 1650 and had such a good reputation that even a few Puritan families in England sent their sons to study in the less corrupt American environment.[5] Designed as a training ground for the future New England ministry, Harvard was actually more than that. While theology permeated the curriculum, so did the liberal arts, and in the seventeenth century less than half of Harvard's graduates entered the ministry.[6]

The earliest recorded curriculum at Harvard (1642) included the original languages of the Old and New Testaments: Hebrew, "Chaldee" (a misnomer for Aramaic), Greek, and Syriac, and "there can be no doubt that they were included mainly, if not wholly, to en-

---

4. Quoted in Louis B. Wright, *The Cultural Life of the American Colonies* (New York, 1962), p. 103.

5. Ibid., p. 117.

6. Samuel E. Morison, *Harvard College in the Seventeenth Century* (Cambridge, Mass., 1936), p. 562.

able the student to read the Word of God in those languages."[7]
Throughout the seventeenth century at Harvard, religious exercises
and the study of the Bible formed the core of the curriculum. Other
subjects aided the student in the interpretation of the Bible for himself
or in the exposition and defense of the Word to others. The studies
and exercises, according to Harvard historian Arthur O. Norton, fall
into six groups:

> 1) The practice of piety. 2) The study and analysis of the Bible. 3) The
> principles of Divinity and Christianity. 4) The mastery of the lan-
> guages necessary to read the Bible in its original tongues . . . 5)
> Auxiliary studies—the arts and philosophies; history, and politics—
> necessary to correct interpretation of the Bible by the student. 6)
> Studies and exercises necessary to effective exposition and defense of
> one's interpretation—rhetoric, declamations, disputations, repetition
> of sermons, commonplaces.[8]

In order that students not lose sight of the proper Puritan priorities
while at Harvard, every scholar was "plainly instructed, and earnestly
pressed to consider well, the maine end of his life and studies is, to
know God and Jesus Christ which is eternall life, John. 17.3. and
therefore to lay Christ in the bottome, as the only foundation of all
sound knowledge and Learning."[9] Those desiring to pursue additional
study beyond the bachelor's degree and to be fully qualified for the
pulpit ministry could, if diligent, obtain the master of arts degree.

The New England Puritans' success in educational endeavors is due
in part to the concentration of settlers into towns, the high cultural
attainment of the founding generation, and the urgency they felt in
their mission to keep Christian civilization alive and well in a wilderness environment. Their educational practices were both value-laden
and utilitarian. Three overlapping concerns are evident: piety
(principles of religion), morality (law), and utility (vocational calling
and intellectual usefulness).[10] The Puritans were ahead of their time
when it came to valuing education. "In the context of the age," notes

7. Arthur O. Norton, "Harvard Text-Books and Reference Books of the
Seventeenth Century," Publications of the Colonial Society of Massachusetts,
Transactions 1930–1933, 28:364.

8. Ibid., pp. 367–68. A commonplace was a systematic discussion of divinity in
the form of a short sermon.

9. Quoted from Harvard College's Lawes About Holy Dutyes Scholasticall
Exercises and Helps of Learning (1655), in ibid., p. 369.

10. See Paul F. Scotchmer, "The Aims of American Education: A Review from
Colonial Times to the Present," Christian Scholar's Review 13/2 (1984): 99–119.

Bernard Bailyn, "the stress placed by the Puritans on formal schooling is astonishing."[11]

Literature

Puritan culture manifested itself in many ways, among the most notable being a significant literary output. The American colonies in general, and Puritan New England in particular, produced an enormous quantity of writing in the first century of settlement. The first printing press in the American colonies was established at Cambridge in 1638. Even before the establishment of an American press, the importance of literature to the Puritans can be seen by the fact that many of them brought numerous books from England. This is significant since freight was expensive, space was limited, and only possessions deemed essential were brought to the New World. Every family possessed a Bible, and usually several other volumes as well. Many family libraries contained works largely of utilitarian value for survival in the wilderness; volumes on medicine, law, farming, military science, and theology (which the Puritans saw more as utilitarian than theoretical) were common. A rather good one-volume encyclopedia also was popular in early New England. Known as *The French Academy*, this work was essentially an outline of all human knowledge with an emphasis on the natural sciences, complete with moralizing lessons, of course. Renaissance influence can be seen in the Puritans' interest in the classical writers of ancient Greece and Rome. Such authors were not off limits to Puritan readers because of the Calvinist doctrine of common grace, that is, the belief that God endows all humankind with the ability to experience truth, goodness, and beauty regardless of spiritual commitment. Even though they were pagans, "some among the heathen have been notable moralists, such as Cato, Seneca, Aristides, etc." and Increase Mather could in good conscience recommend that good Puritans might "find a friend in Plato, a friend in Socrates and . . . in Aristotle."[12]

When it came to their own literary efforts, the Puritans produced large quantities of sermons and other religious treatises, historical works (generally infused with theological meaning), biographies, autobiographies (in diary form), and some poetry. We have already examined the nature of Puritan sermons (see chapter 7). New England's first published historical work was Edward Johnson's *Wonder-Working*

11. Bernard Bailyn, *Education in the Forming of American Society* (New York, 1972), p. 27.

12. Quoted in Ryken, *Worldly Saints*, pp. 168–69. A good survey of colonial "books, libraries, and learning" is to be found in chap. 6 of Wright, *Cultural Life of the American Colonies*.

Providence of Sion's Savior in New England (1654). It is a chronicle of the triumph of God's people in spite of tribulation, and contrasts with the far less flamboyant account of Governor John Winthrop in his journal, later published as *The History of New England from 1630 to 1649*. An extremely wordy historical narrative, containing a hodgepodge of historical and biographical accounts as well as much personal opinion, was Cotton Mather's massive *Magnalia Christi Americana*. In this work Mather bemoans the loss of New England's original religious fervor; nevertheless God continues to faithfully work on behalf of his true people.

The most popular poetic work in early New England was Michael Wiggelsworth's *Day of Doom* (1662). It is a vivid portrayal of the last judgment—the redemption of the saved and the damnation of the lost according to God's eternal plan—that was memorized by many a terrified colonial youngster. Anne Bradstreet, while more gentle and metaphysical, was still preoccupied with moral instruction in her verse. Bradstreet's first volume of poems was published in London in 1650 as *The Tenth Muse Lately Sprung Up in America* and was followed several years later by a second posthumous volume. A third Puritan poet, notable in the twentieth century but not the seventeenth, was the English-born pastor, Edward Taylor. Taylor stands alone among Puritan poets for the richness of his imagery and the mystical yet sensuous flavor of his deeply theological poetic expression. Never intended for publication, his verses lay undetected in the bowels of the Yale library until 1937.

Music, Visual Arts, and Drama

In Puritan New England, music played a limited role in public worship, but not because the Puritans objected to music as such. Their objection to music and art in church was both a reaction against Catholic tradition and a desire to make the preaching of the Word the focus of the worship service. Music and instruments that were not acceptable in church were often found in the homes of devout Puritans. The Puritans did permit the singing of psalms in public worship, but without instrumental accompaniment. Organs, professional musicians, and songs in Latin had no place in Puritan worship. Outside of church, a wide range of vocal music was enjoyed by early New Englanders provided that the words were not "bawdy" or "lascivious."[13] The Puritans were fond of violins, trumpets, drums, lutes, flutes, Jew's harps, and organs.

---

13. Quoted in Wright, *Cultural Life of the American Colonies*, p. 191.

While it is true that the Puritans rejected most religious art as "popery" and an impediment to true faith, they had no aversion to nonreligious art. Neither did they object to rather macabre symbolic carvings on their tombstones. Decorative arts were highly developed in New England, but not much can be said for the limited portraits that were painted in the seventeenth century by individuals who clearly relied on other work for a livelihood. Of course, it must be remembered that a new society in a remote wilderness is an unlikely place to find patrons of the arts, especially of art forms with little or no utilitarian value.

Plays were common in seventeenth-century London, although many English Puritans regarded them as "immoral, indecent, and ungodly."[14] A distaste for drama was carried to New England, where actors and stage plays were unwelcome throughout the seventeenth century. Puritans viewed the theater more as a waste of time than as an inherent evil. Acting was not perceived to be a legitimate vocational calling, and anyone so engaged was held in low esteem, indeed not tolerated. Judge Samuel Sewall of Boston had been upset about a proposed magic show in his town in 1687 (which was cancelled) and several years later he was even more concerned about a proposed stage play, of which he stated, "as much as in me lies, I do forbid it."[15] New England was not alone in frowning on dramatic performances; colonial New York and Pennsylvania likewise shored up their moral defenses by prohibiting such frivolity and immorality.

Scientific Achievements

Puritan interest in scientific inquiry was not hindered by theological opposition. While it was not of the utmost importance (the principal business in life being the salvation of one's soul), it was a valid pursuit since the natural world was God's creation. Scientific study had both utilitarian and spiritual value. It kept people alive even as it fed the souls of those willing to glean spiritual insights from it. As long as the Almighty's hand was seen, and facts were not accumulated as an end in themselves, the study of science was profitable. All of creation, and hence all scientific study, bore witness to the existence of the Creator. "Every creature in Heaven and Earth is a loud preacher of this truth," declared Thomas Shepard.[16] Actually, the Puritans were more open to new scientific discoveries than many other groups

14. Ibid., p. 177.
15. Quoted in ibid., p. 179.
16. Quoted in Perry Miller and Thomas H. Johnson, *The Puritans* (New York, 1938), 2:730.

within Christendom. Beginning in the 1670s, astronomy was taught at Harvard, as well as in almanacs, based on Galileo's theories rather than the traditional Ptolemaic view. The very fact that science and mathematics had a role at all (even if a small one) in the curriculum of Harvard College was of significance in making early New England a place where systematic scientific study was encouraged.

American Puritans who were influential in the advance of science include Charles Morton, who arrived from England late in the seventeenth century and brought with him his natural science textbook, *Compendium Physicae* , which was soon adopted by Harvard College. This book was the first in America to instill an "observing and curious attitude" toward natural science among students.[17] Governor Winthrop's son, John, Jr., was elected as a fellow of the newly founded Royal Society of London in 1663. Winthrop had wide-ranging scientific interests, although as with virtually all "scientists" of his day, his studies were those of a gentleman whose livelihood from other pursuits permitted him the luxury of study and experimentation. One of Winthrop's significant contributions was his donation of a good telescope to Harvard College in 1672. Metallurgy, chemistry, and medicine were among the specialties that gained Winthrop considerable recognition, as was his fine library which he made available to other inquiring minds. Cotton Mather was another Puritan whose interests were not confined to matters of theology—he, too, made substantial contributions to early American science and was also elected a fellow of the Royal Society early in the eighteenth century. Mather's finest hour, when it came to his scientific interests, was his advocacy and strong defense of the use of inoculation against the deadly smallpox virus that all too frequently terrorized New England. Working in conjunction with Dr. Zabdiel Boylston, Mather helped make acceptance of the smallpox vaccine a reality, although he received much verbal abuse in the process.

Recreational Pursuits

The modern concept of leisure time as legitimate for its own sake would have struck most Puritans as bizarre and out of harmony with the purpose of life, which was to glorify God. Certain recreational activities were allowable, but more often tolerated than advocated. While recreational pursuits on Sunday were banned altogether, activities such as bowling, fishing, swimming, walking, archery, and others were perfectly acceptable under the right circumstances. The heinousness of Sunday recreation is seen in the diary entry of sixteen-

17. Wright, *Cultural Life of the American Colonies*, p. 221.

year-old Nathaniel Mather, who wrote that of the "manifold sins" that caused him to go "astray from God" at a tender age, the most memorable one was "whittling on the Sabbath Day. . . . A great reproach of God!"[18]

Certain recreational activities were viewed as inappropriate under any circumstances—they were immoral, harmful, or encouraged idleness by simply wasting time. Falling into these categories were all games of chance (which included card playing), bear-baiting, cock fights, and, as we have seen, attendance at stage plays. Dancing was also viewed as morally dangerous and unseemly, and the Puritans were "greatly troubled" over it.[19]

As Leland Ryken has shown, the Puritans were excessively utilitarian in their ideas about recreation and failed to enjoy leisure-time activities for their own sakes. Recreation was useful and tolerated only because it better prepared one for increased labor and service. In short, the Puritans took play too seriously and succeeded in making "recreation an appendage to their work ethic. . . . They were unable to rise to a genuine theory of leisure and pastime."[20] The intensity of the Puritan worldview was not to be weakened by the idle and unprofitable use of time.

18. Quoted in Ryken, *Worldly Saints*, p. 192.
19. Wright, *Cultural Life of the American Colonies*, p. 190.
20. Ryken, *Worldly Saints*, p. 191.

13

Challenges to the Puritan Way

The Puritan experiment to create a new Zion in the wilderness of America was a noble yet difficult undertaking, fraught with potential pitfalls and paradoxes, some of which were perhaps inherent in the Puritan system itself. The Puritans sought perfection, yet knew it to be unobtainable in this life; they exercised diligence in all their affairs as service to God, only to experience material prosperity which tended to undermine their spiritual commitments; they knew spiritual life to be a highly personal matter, yet they legislated the outward forms of spirituality and were dismayed when it did not produce godliness. There were severe challenges from both without and within which, by the end of the seventeenth century, succeeded in undermining the exclusive control which the Puritan system had held over most of New England from the beginning of colonization.

While an era cannot be adequately explained only in terms of specific events or situations, there were a number of challenges to the Puritan way of the seventeenth century that helped to shape, and generally weaken, the form in which Puritan Christianity in America would evolve and manifest itself.

English Politics

The English government, particularly the Crown (by which is meant not only the king but all major members of the king's government), was both a friend and enemy to the Puritan experiment. The American Puritans walked a fine line between loyalty and loathing when it came to the Crown; they were in Massachusetts at the permission of the Crown, yet they had left England to avoid the Crown's ungodly policies. They fully expected England to be judged by God, partly for what the Crown had done or left undone in the realm of religion and morals. Puritans in America knew that the Crown had every legal right to dictate to them. Their very charter was granted to them by the king, and yet the Puritans believed that behind the king was a sovereign God who had provided their charter. It became imperative, therefore, that the Puritans protect and preserve the charter at almost any cost. The Puritan leadership was faced with the difficult task of running the colony according to their perceptions of the will of God without antagonizing the Crown too much. Tracts and treatises were frequently penned in New England and addressed to the mother country as rational apologies for what was taking place in the New World, sometimes in response to critical letters written by New Englanders themselves.[1] From the perspective of the English government, New England's laws and practices were generally tolerated as long as they were not repugnant to English law.

In one sense, eventual Puritan success in England meant tough times for Puritans in America. The New World Puritan adventure was to be "a city on a hill" for England and the rest of Christendom to behold. The Zion in the wilderness would be an example of what great things could be accomplished by a people committed to the will of God. But then, the longed-for and yet unbelievable happened— Puritans in England had their day. After the English Civil War erupted in 1642 New Englanders faced the realization that events in the homeland were overshadowing their efforts in America. The New Englanders may have been a city on a hill, but no longer was anyone looking in their direction.

Charles I and the English Parliament had been feuding for some time before hostilities became overt; in fact, the king chose to get along without the lawmakers between 1628 and 1639. Ruling by fiat rather than by legislative processes, Charles imposed not only unpopular taxes but also unpalatable religious policies on his Puritan subjects. Enforcement of Anglican worship in Scotland resulted in open rebellion in that kingdom, and Charles was compelled to call the Parliament back into session to deal with the crisis. Demanding reforms in exchange for taxes, the Parliament proved less cooperative than Charles had hoped, and he again sent them home. When the Scots made bold advances into England, the king called Parliament to-

---

1. For a classic example, see Cotton, *Bloudy Tenent,* a response to Roger Williams' criticisms in *The Bloudy Tenent of Persecution for Cause of Conscience.*

gether once again, in the autumn of 1640, for what was to become the "Long Parliament."

The relationship between king and Parliament deteriorated further, and when Charles made an attempt to seize certain parliamentary leaders, military confrontation resulted. Charles portrayed himself as the champion of the established order which was being threatened by radical Parliamentarians. Those favoring the king in this struggle—the Cavaliers—generally included the nobility and their clientele, as well as conforming Anglicans and Catholics. Puritans, merchants, lawyers, the lower classes, and the navy were more likely to side with the parliamentary forces collectively known as the Roundheads. Puritan values came to predominate in the military forces of the Roundheads, labeled the New Model Army, organized according to the specifications of the staunch Puritan Oliver Cromwell. The victorious New Model Army thrust Cromwell into a position of power and influence, which he used to see that Charles was tried and executed for treason in 1649.

Attempting to rule England without a king proved more difficult than Cromwell and his Puritan followers had imagined. Various forms of republican government met with minimal success, and Cromwell eventually maneuvered himself into the position of Protector, an office which degenerated into a dictatorship. Cromwell had destroyed the monarchy only to take to himself the role of king without the title. The new order, led by Puritan men and Puritan ideas, failed to capture the imagination of most Englishmen. Following Cromwell's death in 1658, his son Richard became Lord Protector, only to be rejected within two years in favor of a restored Stuart monarchy under Charles II. The Puritans had their day in England, but England was not impressed.

In New England, the English Civil War was greeted enthusiastically as an opportunity for thorough reformation of the homeland. Some New Englanders even went so far as to suggest that credit for the movement belonged to the Puritan saints of the New World. Prayers for the Roundheads and denunciations of the royalists were standard fare in New England's meetinghouses throughout the 1640s, and a few New Englanders returned to England to participate directly in revolutionary events there.[2] While an occasional New Englander may have favored the king during these years, there is little doubt that the vast majority of New England Puritans, including the leadership, favored the Parliamentarians.

When the Puritan regime in England failed to capture the imagination and support of the English people and the Stuart monarchy was restored, many New England Puritans felt a sense of failure and disil-

2. Bremer, *Puritan Experiment*, pp. 108–9.

lusionment. While the civil war period brought with it excitement and hope, the overall results were damaging to the Puritan way in New England . An immediate effect of the conflict was a drastic slow-down in immigration. Puritans once ready to leave England now had reason to stay and await a future that they hoped would be under their control. New England's Puritan colonies were economically dependent on a steady influx of newcomers and the sharp decline of new arrivals significantly depressed the economy of the region. New Englanders, relishing Winthrop's concept that they were a "city on a hill," felt a sense of frustration and desertion as they realized that events in England eclipsed anything that was happening in New England. Following the restoration of the monarchy, New England lagged behind the times, shunning ideas of toleration now in vogue in the motherland and becoming more repressive in the rooting out of dissenters. And finally, another blow from the viewpoint of New England orthodoxy was the fact that after the restoration the English monarchy was increasingly interested in the colonies and more assertive of royal authority.

In the 1670s, Charles II tightened the reigns on England's colonies through a new government committee, the Lords of Trade and Plantation. Massachusetts came under the close scrutiny of this committee, which sent Edward Randolph to investigate the state of affairs in this part of His Majesty's dominions. Determined to be noticed by doing the king's business well in Massachusetts, Randolph unearthed sufficient evidence of colonial disregard for English laws and welfare to lead to the revocation of the Massachusetts Bay Company charter in 1684. Breen and Foster contend that New England political life was henceforth transformed. The revocation of the charter, they assert, "all but destroyed any lingering sense among the colonists that they formed a special, divinely chosen community."[3] A new government was not actually in place until 1686, however. In that year, the Dominion of New England was created and headed by Governor Edmund Andros. This "dominion" was expanded to include English colonies from Maine to New Jersey by 1688 and gave the governor sweeping powers while requiring religious toleration, a blow to Puritan purists. Andros proved ineffective and unpopular, as did his king, James II, who succeeded his brother Charles II to the throne in 1685. James was a Catholic in a country whose mood was largely Protestant. Fearing a continuing Catholic dynasty when James fathered an heir, leading English Protestants invited James' son-in-law, William of Orange, to take the throne. William and his wife, Mary, received the throne when James fled to the Continent in 1688

3. Breen and Foster, "Puritans' Greatest Achievement," pp. 18–20.

in a swift and bloodless "Glorious Revolution." New Englanders, hopeful that the new monarchs would dissolve the "Dominion of New England," took matters into their own hands and sent Andros packing. Although Increase Mather lobbied long and hard in London for the restoration of the old Massachusetts Bay Company charter, he was successful only in obtaining a new charter in 1691 which was an improvement over the "Dominion," but less than had been hoped for. The government of the new charter was clearly in the hands of the king rather than the people, and the ability of the Puritan leadership to restrict the vote to those of Puritan persuasion was at an end.

Roger Williams and Separatism

Roger Williams came to Massachusetts in 1631. He was a recent Cambridge graduate still in his twenties, who had taken Anglican orders but who desired to minister in the purer ecclesiastical environment of America. The Boston church had an interest in Williams, but that congregation's refusal to repudiate its ties to the Church of England bothered him and he would not accept a call to teach there. The Salem church held more appeal for Williams, but the intervention of the Massachusetts General Court, concerned over Williams' separatist tendencies, persuaded the Salem congregation to withdraw their offer, whereupon Williams went to Plymouth. Finding no more purity in Plymouth, Williams returned to Salem and eventually did accept the call to pastor there in 1634. From Salem, Williams continued to espouse ideas that won him the disfavor of Governor Winthrop and other Massachusetts Bay officials.

Williams, ironically, was too much of a purist for the Puritan leadership and insisted that his Salem church break off relations with all of the other churches in the colony. Governor Winthrop feared the results of extreme separatism of the kind Williams proposed, recognizing that the logical conclusion of such a posture would be the end of an organized Puritan state. Williams also alienated himself from the authorities with his insistence that the original charter granted to Massachusetts by the king was invalid, since it did not recognize the rights of the Indian inhabitants. Williams furthermore scoffed at the outward covenant, questioned the validity of infant baptism, and denied that Puritan New England was particularly special in God's eyes. It was Williams' contention that for all practical purposes the Puritans of New England had separated themselves from the Church of England and they might as well openly acknowledge the fact. When Williams insisted that the civil magistrates had no authority in matters of religion and conscience, it was more than even some of his supporters could bear.

To a social group which placed harmony and conformity high on the list of desired traits, the outspoken Roger Williams was a genuine radical not to be tolerated. His ideas did indeed threaten the established Puritan order and his personal charm and integrity only made him the more dangerous in the eyes of the authorities. Williams was summoned on several occasions before the General Court to explain his views; finally in 1635 he was ordered to remove himself from Massachusetts by the following spring. Persisting in the spread of his views, Williams was ordered immediately deported to England, but Winthrop feared for Williams' life and gave him the opportunity to escape the Bay Colony on his own. In early 1636 Williams fled and with a few followers established the settlement of Providence southwest of Boston, on land which he had purchased from the Narragansett Indians.

Having shifted from his earlier position of extreme separatism, Williams now recognized the impossibility of purity in this world and opened wide the doors to his colony. In 1644 Williams was able to receive from the Parliament a patent uniting and recognizing Providence and a few other scattered settlements in the vicinity of Narragansett Bay, thus forming the basis for the colony of Rhode Island.

Anne Hutchinson and the Antinomian Controversy

Another challenge to the Puritan establishment of Massachusetts came in the person and opinions of Anne Hutchinson. This intelligent and outspoken Puritan woman left old Boston in Lincolnshire with her husband in 1634, following in the footsteps of their pastor, John Cotton, who had accepted the position of church teacher in the new Boston in America. Hutchinson began to hold weekly meetings in her home, offering summaries of the sermons for women in the community who had been unable to attend the previous Sunday's worship meetings. These home meetings grew beyond their original purpose yet caused no controversy until Hutchinson began to criticize Boston pastor John Wilson for his views on the importance of preparing the heart for salvation. She moved beyond criticism of Wilson to expose other clergy in the Bay Colony for what she considered a doctrine of works rather than grace as a means of salvation. Right conduct, Hutchinson believed, was not the basis of one's salvation, which was, rather, a mystical work of the Spirit of God. She concluded, in fact, that John Cotton and her brother-in-law, John Wheelwright, were the only pastors in Massachusetts not contaminated by false doctrine in this regard.

Several prominent individuals believed Anne Hutchinson to be correct in her views, including the young and arrogant Henry Vane, elected governor of the colony in 1636. Those opposed to her criticisms labeled her an "antinomian," an offensive appellation carrying highly negative connotations of anarchy. For a time, Hutchinson's views seemed to prevail in the Boston church and Pastor Wilson barely escaped censure. Division became so rife in the Boston congregation that Hutchinson and her followers would leave the meeting when Wilson rose to give his sermons. In the midst of the controversy Winthrop recaptured the governorship, thus assuring that Puritan orthodoxy would prevail. The clergy gathered in a synod in the summer of 1637 to prevent further erosion of their authority and doctrinal views, arriving at a long list of errors the antinomians had committed and concluding that private religious meetings should be discouraged.

The antinomian controversy resulted in banishment for John Wheelwright (who moved north to establish a settlement in what was to become New Hampshire). John Cotton, whose reputation was on the line in this affair, saw both merit and error in Hutchinson and her critics but chose to side with the orthodox establishment. As for Hutchinson herself, her articulate self-defense before her judges served to alienate them further, especially when she claimed to receive direct revelations from God. She was banished from Massachusetts in 1638 and took refuge in Rhode Island and later New York, where she and several members of her family were killed by Indians in 1643.

Perceptions of Declension

The loss of purity and the original fervor of the Puritan mission was lamented loudly and often, particularly by the clergy of the second and third generations in New England. Historians have generally agreed with the assessment of the Puritan ministry that spiritual deadness and loss of piety were significant factors in the second half of the seventeenth century, although not all historians have lamented the transformation. Use of the term "declension" to describe the New England experience implies a slide from a higher, pristine state to a less desirable, less morally acceptable state of affairs. However, several recent historians have challenged whether "declension" accurately describes Puritan New England, and have insisted on a revisionist interpretation that "the concept [of declension] conflicts with social and institutional realities. It totally misconstrues what was going on in Massachusetts churches in the seventeenth century."

According to this perspective, declension was "nothing more than the maturation of a sectarian movement."[4]

Whether declension was actual or not, the clergy certainly seemed to perceive its existence. Many New Englanders, it was lamented, "will not yield professed obedience unto ye Lord Jesus Christ, this was ye Errand into this willderness; man forgot this Errand."[5] John Cotton complained of a "drousiness of spirit" and a "slownesse and dullnessee" in religious duties and spiritual responsiveness as early as 1645.[6] Other complaints about the decline of religious zeal included failure to both fear and love God, not walking humbly with God, and lack of fervor in prayer.[7] The perception that many saints were "very cold and lifeless" toward God and his Word was cause for lament.[8] The sin of the "Neglect of support and Maintaining the Pure Worship of god, By the Professing People of God" was, in the eyes of James Allen, a "God-provoking and Land-Wasting Sin."[9] The churches of 1670 were compared with the churches of the previous generation by Samuel Danforth. The congregations "in their first glory" had since begun to "cool in their affection" and were now "as nothing." "How is the gold become dim! how is the most fine gold changed!" was his cry. "Doth not a careless, remiss, flat, dry, cold, dead frame of spirit grow in upon us secretly, strongly, prodigiously?" he asked. The key to this problem was, Danforth believed, "our Unbelief: We believe not the grace and Power of God in Christ."[10] Cotton Mather perceived a decline in church attendance, indicative of a "Horrible Defection from our First loves, and our First Wayes. . . ." It was his concern that "though our Inhabitants are more than they were many years ago, yet are not our Communicants rather fewer, in many Towns?" Mather was further disturbed by the number of churches without a full slate of functioning officers, but what was "worst of all" was the sin of

---

4. Robert G. Pope, "New England versus the New England Mind: The Myth of Declension," *Journal of Social History* (1969–1970): 99, 108. On the topic of declension, see also Morgan, *Visible Saints*, p. 137; Michael McGiffert, "Puritan Studies in the 1960s," *William and Mary Quarterly* 37 (Jan. 1970): 34–52; Perry Miller, "Declension in a Bible Commonwealth," *American Antiquarian Society*, Apr. 1941.

5. James Allen, sermon of May 1, 1690, *Sermon Notes, Apr. 24–Aug. 13, 1690*, Harvard University MS, p. 43.

6. Cotton, *Covenant of Grace*, p. 4.

7. Gookin, sermon [1687], *Sermon Notes, 1687*, Harvard University MS, p. 27.

8. Gookin, sermon of 1690, *Sermon Notes, Apr. 24–Aug. 13, 1690*, pp. 138, 144; see also a rousing condemnation of traditionalism and complacency in worship in Moodey, *Great Sin of Formality*.

9. Allen, *Neglect of Pure Worship*.

10. Danforth, *New England's Errand*, pp. 5, 12–14.

unbelief—"the lamentable want of Regeneration in the Rising Generation."[11]

In the style of the prophet Jeremiah, New England's prophets looked back to the supposed golden age of the first generation. The comparison with their present situation was not encouraging; "all sides are agreed that things are in a declining posture, that there is a great degeneracy . . . that there is a defection and declension," declared Urian Oakes.[12] Samuel Willard decried the degeneracy of the church and stated that New England, once God's cultivated vineyard, was beginning to look like a spiritual wilderness. It seemed to Willard as though "Degeneracy, Apostacie, and Covenant breaking" were the "hereditary disease of the visible Church."[13] Increase Mather could not resist lauding the founding generation and condemning their sinful descendants:

> Our Fathers have been Davids, that is to say, eminent Reformers. . . . there never was a Generation that did so perfectly shake off the dust of Babylon, both as to Ecclesiastical and civil Constitution, as the first Generation of Christians, that came into this Land for the Gospels sake. . . .
> The present Generation in New-England is lamentably degenerate. . . . the first Generation of Christians in New-England, is in a manner gone off the Stage, and there is another and more sinful Generation risen up in their stead. . . .
> This Generation is not like the first . . . yea, the present Generation as to the body of it, is an unconverted Generation.[14]

It is not surprising that declension would be perceived by the ministry as New England society, originally founded on religious ideals, became a more fully developed commercial, capitalistic, and diverse social order. Foster argues that declension rhetoric was part of the Puritan system—that "men were supposed to condemn themselves, and they sinned all the more if they did not. . . . As long as New Englanders continued to denounce themselves, as long as they were sure they had deserted their ideal, they were faithful to it." According to Foster, Puritanism was truly in decline when the people "*stopped bemoaning their worldliness and no longer felt a sense of guilt. . . .*"[15] With changes in society and an inherent breast-beating in the Puritan

11. Cotton Mather, *The Short History of New England* (Boston, 1694), pp. 5, 40; *Unum Necessarium*, introduction.

12. Oakes, *New England Pleaded with*, p. 24.

13. Willard, *Fig Trees Doom*, p. 18; *Covenant-Keeping*, pp. 84–85.

14. Increase Mather, *Call from Heaven*, pp. 56, 61.

15. Foster, *Their Solitary Way*, p. 125.

system, it is difficult to ascertain the degree to which a genuine "falling away" from Puritan ideals really took place. An analysis of declension is also hampered by the fact that it was an inner quality of life and faith that was so essential to Puritan Christianity, not merely outward conduct.

Metacom's War

Puritan attitudes toward the native American inhabitants of New England were often ambivalent at best, and as English settlement expanded, so did Indian discontent. The most devastating Indian war in New England's history erupted in June of 1675. Named after the leader of the Wampanoag Indians, Metacom's War (Metacom was known as King Philip to the English settlers) took a ghastly toll on both sides of the conflict until Metacom's death in August of 1676. Irritated by English encroachments and a growing dependence on English goods, and upset by the fact that some Indians were seeking assimilation into colonial English society, some Indian leaders sought to put a halt to further erosion of the Indian establishment. Metacom was counted among the malcontents who prepared for possible use of force in 1671 against the English. In that year, warlike preparations were noted by observers near the Indian village of Mount Hope, and Metacom was summoned before colonial authorities where he was questioned, fined, and required to disarm his men. In 1675 a Christian Indian who had been serving as an informer to the English was murdered. Three of Metacom's braves were accused, tried, convicted, and executed for the act.

The Wampanoags were outraged by these executions and attacked the border settlement of Swansea. Raids on other settlements followed and towns including Deerfield, Northfield, and Brookfield were burned and their inhabitants slain or captured. Frustrated by their inability to lure the Indians into a major and decisive battle, the New Englanders retaliated with hit-and-run raids on Indian settlements which antagonized the Wampanoags and neighboring tribes even more. By the spring of 1676 a ring of security for the English colonists encompassed only the territory within a seventeen-mile radius of Boston. Hundreds of Puritan males from sixteen to sixty took part in the conflict and over five hundred of them lost their lives. Metacom's wife and son were captured, and the chief himself fell victim to an Indian in the service of the English. Metacom's head was displayed on a pole in Plymouth for a time.

Some 6 percent of the New England population had perished by the time the war ended, the most staggering toll in proportion to the population of any subsequent war in American history. The losses from this conflict included nineteen towns destroyed or damaged, as well as the virtual eradication of Indian tribal life in southern New England. No sooner had these disasters passed than new tribulations befell the saints. Two major fires swept through Boston, and hundreds died of smallpox in the spring of 1688. To the clergy, God's judgment on his wayward people was evident.

Commercial Interests

Founded with religious motives foremost on the minds of the first-generation leadership, New England was, nonetheless, never opposed to prosperity as long as it was kept in proper perspective. However, a certain amount of tension was felt, even very early, between the will of God and the ways of men when it came to economic gain. Those involved in New England commercial life were both necessary and suspect; Governor Winthrop complained that it seemed to be "the common rule that most men walked by in all their commerce, to buy as cheap as they could, and to sell as dear."[16] The Puritan leadership thus found themselves dealing with a merchant class whose existence was both essential and at the same time threatening to the mission of the godly society they wanted so much to create. Pastor John Higginson of Salem reflected the fear that commercial success could subvert the mission of New England:

> [T]his is never to be forgotten, that New England is originally a Plantation of Religion, not a Plantation of Trade. . . . Let merchants and such as are increasing Cent per Cent remember this . . . that worldly gain was not the end and designe of the people of New England, but Religion.[17]

The merchant class also was suspect because of its close ties with the mother country. Merchants found it commercially advantageous to be entangled in English affairs, often having family ties with merchants in London. Puritanism, which probably functioned best in isolation, was not the sanctuary for the true faith desired by the faithful as long as New England merchants maintained so many connections with Old England. The merchants, according to Bernard Bailyn,

> were prime movers in a gradual, subtle, but fundamental transformation of New England society. . . . Most of them did not seek the de-

16. Quoted in Bernard Bailyn, *The New England Merchants in the Seventeenth Century* (Cambridge, Mass., 1955), p. 49.
17. John Higginson, *The Cause of God and His People in New England* (Boston, 1662), pp. 10–12.

struction of the Puritan society; but they could not evade the fact that in many ways commercial success grew in inverse proportion to the social strength of Puritanism.[18]

The Puritan leadership desired the benefits of a flourishing trade, but were wary of the cost—increasing numbers of strangers in their midst who did not share the righteous vision, and the growth of an upper class of merchants who, even if unintentionally, led New England away from its original calling as a model Christian community.

While first- and second-generation ministers tended to force a choice between piety and prosperity, a shift had taken place by the third generation. Ministers near the end of the seventeenth century tended instead to attempt a reconciliation between Christianity and good business. Reasons for this included the fact that by this time many of the clergy were connected by ties of marriage to the merchant class. Also, the new colonial charter of 1691 changed the basis for the franchise from church membership to ownership of property. The clergy now saw the advantage in cultivating the merchant class for the good of the church's political and economic future. Greater attention to the material world in sermons of the third-generation clergy could well indicate a diminished priority for the spiritual dimension of life.[19]

Loss of Consensus

The original plans for the Massachusetts Bay Colony called for an intense spirit of Christian love and consensus. The realization of this consensus never fully materialized even in the first generation, but there was a remarkable degree of social and political harmony throughout many Puritan communities for a number of years. Yet by the end of the seventeenth century there were signs that consensus was deteriorating. Villages such as Dedham were expanding and fragmenting, in some sense trying to preserve consensus and at the same time destroying it by isolating factions from one another.[20] The growth of outlying populations created new towns and parishes, often over the protests of the original villages. Worse yet for the proponents of communality and consensus was the fact that increasing numbers of families were moving beyond the reach of towns altogether.

In the political realm, town meetings became more vigorous and the deference once accorded to the selectmen was less pronounced. Ad

18. Bailyn, *New England Merchants*, p. 105.
19. Heyrman, "Model of Christian Charity," pp. 78–79, 95.
20. See Lockridge, *New England Town*, chap. 6.

hoc committees and new offices such as "treasurer" were created later in the seventeenth century by the town meetings, with their powers carved from the authority of the selectmen. Incumbent selectmen were more often ousted and there was an increase in the length and number of public meetings.[21] Further evidence of loss of Puritan consensus can be seen in the growing belief that "political power was a source of personal gain" and the fact that such a belief "influenced the motives of officials and people. . . . The temptation to manipulate government for personal ends touched men of all classes."[22] In their attempts to find satisfaction or advantage in their dealings with government, New Englanders increasingly took their causes to higher levels of government at the county and General Court level, rather than to the towns. This mirrored the growing centralization of colonial government with an increased share of tax revenues going to these higher levels.

The churches were concerned about dwindling membership, growing numbers of dissenters, and a perceived lessening of respect for the clergy. Growth of clerical professionalism did little to endear the ministry to the general population.

In various ways—some political, some social, some economic, some religious, and virtually all of them unintentional—the hoped-for spirit of Puritan consensus eroded to the point that New Englanders increasingly defined the common good in terms of narrow personal interests. Loss of consensus by the late seventeenth century reflected the loss of key elements that had once held the commonwealth together: a commonly accepted ideology, trust in the colonial leadership, and widespread economic prosperity.[23]

The Salem Witchcraft Hysteria

One hesitates to give further attention to the Salem witchcraft episode whose significance, in the popular mind, has already been blown out of proportion. However, the situation did provide a further challenge to the Puritan establishment and its overall effect was to weaken the credibility of the Puritan magistrates, worldview, and clergy.

Salem Village was a small community near Salem, Massachusetts, where, in 1692, the behavior of several young girls caused great concern. The daughter and niece of the local minister, the Reverend

21. Ibid., p. 120.

22. Richard L. Bushman, *From Puritan to Yankee* (New York, 1970), pp. 139, 142.

23. Breen and Foster, "Puritans' Greatest Achievement," p. 20.

Samuel Parris, along with several of their friends, became ill and distraught after having spent sessions with a female slave from the West Indies in the Parris household. The girls also accused two other women of contributing to their affliction. Witchcraft was suspected, and the girls and women were interrogated, resulting in the slave woman's confession. During the interrogation of the other women, the girls fell victim to seizures, leaving little doubt in the minds of the magistrates that the powers of hell were at work. Further accusations were soon flying fast and thick, and the situation appeared to be out of control with overzealous judges adding fuel to the fire.

Massachusetts had just received a new governor under the new charter when this situation erupted. Governor William Phipps promptly established a special court in which to examine and try those accused of witchcraft. To their credit, some of the clergy urged caution in the proceedings, but were perhaps too muted in their protests lest they fall from Phipps's favor. The most devastating procedure was the admission of "spectral" evidence into the trials; those who claimed to be tormented by the vision of a person were given as much credence as if the accused person or persons had been physically present. Alibis were of no value; an accused witch's "spectre" could haunt an innocent victim while the "witch" lay asleep in bed or had tea with friends. With the tardy advice of the clergy the governor finally halted the trials, but not until well over a hundred people had been accused and nineteen persons had been hanged as witches.

It was soon realized that hysteria had resulted in the miscarriage of justice, but the damage had already been done. The government and the ministry had their reputations tarnished, unfairly in some cases. The reality of the supernatural, while not repudiated, was less likely to be unhesitatingly accepted as interpreted by the clergy.

While the facts of the case are fairly straightforward, interpretations vary. Perhaps the most reasonable explanation is a psychological one: fear resulted in hysteria. It has further been theorized that Salem's adolescent female accusers were displacing their hostility toward their own mothers onto other women (and an occasional man) in the community in a fashion that was more socially acceptable than denouncing one's own parents.[24]

It would be unfair to the Puritans not to put the witchcraft episode in perspective. There was nothing uniquely Puritan about belief in witchcraft. Intelligent people throughout seventeenth-century Europe believed in the existence of a spiritual dimension which included the practice of witchcraft. Persecution of accused witches was more

24. See Bremer, *Puritan Experiment*, p. 167; Demos, "Underlying Themes in New England Witchcraft," pp. 187–88.

prevalent in France and England than in Puritan New England. Even in America, belief in witchcraft was certainly not limited to New England. This is said not to excuse the heinous and disastrous events that transpired in Salem in 1692, but to demonstrate that no one group should be saddled with exclusive blame for a problem shared at the time by much of the human race.

Conclusion

The ideals that set Puritan New England apart were under assault even from the start of colonization. The ideal of a godly, communal, consensus-oriented community led by Christian magistrates and clergy, set as a city on a hill for all the world to see and emulate, was too lofty and too vulnerable to the ravages of human nature to ever come to fruition. The Puritans soon learned to expect the unexpected, and it is to their credit that New England civilization flourished by adapting to new situations. Politics, fanatics, heretics, breast-beaters, Indians, merchants, individualists, and even witches all contributed in one way or another to changes that challenged the Puritan way. Ultimately, and in a gradual fashion, adaptation to change reached the point where the original ideals were lost, and no longer lamented.

14

Conclusion
The Puritan Legacy

The serious Puritan represented an extreme of Christian devotion and piety uncharacteristic of most early Americans. Nevertheless, the Puritans' influence on American civilization has been stronger than their numbers would seem to warrant. Several factors help explain why this is so. First of all, timing was important. The early success of New England colonial ventures made the Puritans precedent-setters. Because of their lofty view of education, they were among the best read and most intellectual of all early Americans. Since many of their convictions had implications beyond spiritual concerns, it became possible to maintain Puritan perspectives in secularized form even after the faith had eroded. The Puritans were also quite mobile, and Puritan influence was to be found in most of the American colonies at one time or another. Spurred on by their strong religious convictions, the Puritans were not hesitant to speak and write articulately when they sensed that they were defending the true faith. The sweep of American history, modern American culture, and especially evangelical subculture can be more fully understood as we recognize the legacy we have received from our Puritan forebears.

The Puritans could be intensely pious people who took Christianity very, very seriously. Not every Englishman who set foot in New England in the seventeenth century was a true believer, or necessarily supportive of all aspects of what came to be known as "the New England Way." However, it is unlikely that ever a society was founded in America with greater zeal for the cause of Christ and greater devotion to the Bible as the Word of God than was the case with New England's Puritans. A good deal of what the Puritans believed was not unique to them but was shared by the larger Calvinistic Protestant world. However, these shared values were carried to America by English Puritans coming with their own set of cultural baggage, and refined with a special American flavor in the wilderness of the new Promised Land. The thrilling challenge of involvement in the creation of a new society and the sense that God was with them in a special way helped mold the Puritan perspective in New England's early years.

As dedicated as the Puritan leadership was to forming a "holy commonwealth" in New England, the realities of human nature soon played havoc with the dream. Secularization set in almost from the start, and while there were notable personal successes in pious living, the community at large missed the mark. The Puritans, like every generation of Christians, were inextricably caught up in interpreting the Christian faith in the light of the culture of their day. As with all human beings in all generations, they had their strengths and weaknesses. But in terms of an overall worldview that effectively integrated a knowledge of and response to God and biblical values into all areas of life, the Puritans of seventeenth-century New England were not to be outdone.

The reign of Puritanism was not to endure, however. Later generations of Americans began marching to a different drum beat—not because the Puritans were wrong, but because the Puritan pace was too intense and otherworldly. Within a few years of the founding of Boston, New Englanders were bemoaning the declension in their midst. By the time of the American Revolution, Puritanism survived in a secularized form, largely separated from its religious roots, as exemplified by the wise, frugal, diligent, creative, intellectual, but thoroughly worldly life of Benjamin Franklin, a secularized Puritan par excellence. To be sure, there were faithful, orthodox, Bible-believing Christians in America's Revolutionary age, but they were no longer Puritans. The all-encompassing Puritan worldview and intensity were things of the past.

What have endured are certain Puritan influences, some of which have affected American society in general, others which have been felt primarily in more conservative Protestant circles. Much of the Puritan legacy is valuable; some of it is unfortunate. Complicating our understanding of the Puritan legacy is the fact that the Puritans have been blamed for a wide assortment of ills, such as excessive prudishness in sexual matters, which are more accurately traced to the Victorian era.

While recognizing that this concluding section of the book is more interpretive and subjective than most other sections, I believe that there are at least fifteen areas where the Puritan worldview of the seventeenth century has had a lasting impact on the American character, and especially on evangelical Protestantism.*

Education

The first public schools in America were established by the Puritans of New England. Education was highly prized for two basic reasons: it enabled each person to read the Bible, the written Word of God, and it helped one to better understand God's world. The Puritans' view of knowledge was holistic and noncompartmentalized; the current cliche "all truth is God's truth" was unnecessary for them because no other alternative ever crossed their minds. Within six years of the founding of Boston, Harvard College was established in nearby Cambridge as a training ground for the colony's future ministry. Harvard was in many respects a prototype of the Christian liberal arts colleges of our own day. While it was assumed that many, if not most, graduates would pursue careers in the ministry, the Harvard curriculum included a healthy dose of liberal arts in addition to theology and biblical languages. Integration of faith and learning was not discussed, but it flowed naturally out of the Puritan worldview, at least for a couple of generations. When Harvard's orthodoxy began to waiver, Yale was established in 1701 as the conservative alternative. These early experiments in Christian higher education helped prepare the way for scores of later institutions designed with similar purposes.

Participation in Government

The Puritan colony of Massachusetts Bay was not a full-fledged democracy by modern standards, yet strides were taken to give more of a voice to the governed than was the case in most of the Western world at that time. The colony of Massachusetts Bay, like Virginia, was in principle a business venture, sponsored by a corporation with stockholders who hoped for a profit. Yet the overriding concern among the colony's leadership was that spiritual objectives would be met. Governor Winthrop was a wise man who discerned that if the settlers were given a significant voice in the new colony's affairs, they would have less grounds for dissatisfaction, and material and spiritual objectives would be better achieved. Therefore, the franchise was extended to adult male church members with minimum property qualifications. What has been difficult for some twentieth-century scholars to accept is the fact that the franchise was limited to church mem-

---

*The order in which these summary ideas are presented is not meant to imply a ranking of importance.

bers. It must be realized, however, that according to the colony's charter the vote did not have to be extended at all. By restricting the franchise to church members, Winthrop believed that the foundational religious purpose of the colony would be preserved. When it came to participation in local government, the New England town meeting was of sufficient interest to become legendary. A considerable degree of democracy did exist on this level, but it must also be remembered that deference was practiced, resulting in a small group of leaders being returned repeatedly to office. Democracy was alive and well enough in the Puritan scheme of things to provide a limited model for the fuller democratic expressions of the Revolutionary era and beyond.

Church Membership

The Puritans of New England revived the New Testament concept of the church as an essentially spiritual entity whose membership was limited to the regenerate. This was a radical departure from the medieval European tradition which held that church membership was the automatic result of living in Christendom—"Christ's kingdom"—regardless of personal profession. While church attendance was encouraged, indeed mandated, for all New Englanders, only God's elect made up the true church and possessed the benefits of church membership. By the second generation, however, the pull back to the old ways was too strong, especially as fewer of the rising generation were experiencing conversion than had been expected. The "halfway" membership policy instituted in many New England churches after the 1660s provided a type of associate membership for interested but as yet unconverted children of church members. Thus, the era of "pure" church membership was quite limited, but attention was drawn to the importance of a profession of faith as a part of the church membership process, a policy that is followed by most evangelical churches today.

Church Government

One of the most objectionable features of life in England that had encouraged Puritans to come to America was the harassment they received at the hands of the Anglican Church. The Puritans found the church hierarchy essentially unresponsive or hostile to their needs and desires, and felt that it was too easy for godless men to assume positions of power within the religious establishment. In coming to America, the Puritans never technically broke with the Church of England (as opposed to the Separatists of Plymouth Colony), but for all practical purposes the break was complete. With three thousand miles of ocean separating them from the nearest Anglican bishop, the Puritan congregations were able to design their polity and worship according to their own tastes. Congregationalism—lay authority over the affairs of each independent local church—became the established New England way. To a degree this polity mirrored the increased participation of the citizens in secular political affairs. The Puritan minister's authority was moral rather than legal, and his future depended on the whims of his congregation. The Puritan minister, while dependent on his congregation for his position, was free to select his own sermon topics instead of parroting material passed down to him under the English episcopal system.

Biblical Preaching and Bible Study

Another major contribution to contemporary evangelicalism was the Puritans' insistence on biblically based sermons and an emphasis on the personal, regular reading of the Scriptures. The Puritans in England and America had the highest regard for the Old and New Testaments as the divinely authored, authoritative, impeccable Word of God. Devout non-Puritan Anglicans acknowledged these same beliefs about the Bible, but would generally stop short of the Puritan obsession with justifying their every action and attitude from the pages of Holy Writ. Any Puritan pastor worth his salt was sure to bolster his pulpit pronouncements with ample scriptural evidence (even if sometimes interpreted in a rather parochial manner). Worshipers were encouraged and expected to heed only that in the sermon which had sufficient biblical support. The mere opinions of this or that good man were treated literally as dung if they were contradictory to, or even lacking in support from, a word from the Word.

The Puritans placed a high priority on the private reading of and meditation on the Bible. Even preadolescents spent considerable time reading the Scriptures, and many Puritans kept a journal at one time or another in which they traced their spiritual development and generally bemoaned the fact that their lives did not meet the standards set forth in God's Word. In their worship and private devotional lives, the Puritans demonstrated their dependence on, and reverence for, the Bible. They were clearly a people of the Book; it was preached and studied with zeal as the unquestioned touchstone of legitimacy for belief and practice in the lives of the Puritan faithful.

Separation of Church and State

The Puritans made substantial contributions to the theory and practice of church-state relations. Here again is an area of Puritan activity that has often been misunderstood by later historians. Because church and state in Puritan New England shared the same basic commitment to uphold a godly society, it has been assumed by some that church and state were inextricably intertwined. In actuality, the American Puritans took great pains to divide authority between the civil and ecclesiastical realms with less overlap than would have been found anywhere else in the Western world at the time, at least until Roger Williams began his radical settlement at Providence. The roles of magistrates and ministers were carefully defined, and any power the clergy held over civil rulers was limited to advice-giving and moral persuasion. If one institution had power over the other, it was the state which was supreme, not the church. It is true that church and state were not as separated in seventeenth-century New England as they are in America today. Yet the basic concept that church and state are different entities, with different responsibilities and spheres of authority, was a major contribution to American life which has been refined further over the years. If one counts the ideas of the dissenting Puritan Roger Williams, church-state separation was developed very nearly to the level of today.

The Ministry

One Puritan contribution which reflects the importance of education in general was the emphasis placed upon a professionally trained ministry. It was unthinkable for a man without substantial university training, and usually at least a bachelor's degree (and often a master's degree), to aspire to a seventeenth-century New England pulpit. The clergy were seen as spiritual and intellectual leaders whose task was to give meaning to all aspects of life from a theological perspective. Thus they were expected to be conversant with many disciplines and ideas and to be capable of bringing the Bible to bear on virtually any subject. Since God was the author of truth, no area of knowledge was off limits. God and his people could not be well served by ignorance, and so the finest available academic and professional training was sought by those preparing for the ministry. While some fundamentalists have gloried in their lack of secular learning, the Christian community in general has wisely followed the Puritan example of seeking a well-educated ministry.

Sunday Activities

The Puritans of New England kept Sunday as a sabbath day in the Old Testament tradition. They believed that this was a day set apart for worship and meditation and little else. The average Puritan spent several hours in worship services each Sunday. The city of Boston, which was connected to the mainland by a narrow land bridge, was literally sealed off from the rest of the world at sundown on Saturday and the free movement of people and goods in and out of that town did not resume until sundown on Sunday. One did no shopping or manual labor on the Lord's Day, and Sunday leisure activities were likewise prohibited.

This general attitude toward Sunday activities has endured until quite recently in some parts of New England, and has carried over into other parts of the country as well. The evangelical community today varies widely in its approach to Sunday activities, but the Puritan view that the first day of the week is the Lord's Day—a high and holy day—continues to exert an influence in some quarters.

Personal Conduct

Related to their attitude toward the Lord's Day is the Puritans' attitude toward personal conduct in general. The Puritans were very conscious of three things: sin, authority, and a sense of communal obligation. This proved to be a deadly combination when it came to the monitoring of personal conduct, for in a real sense each Puritan was his brother's keeper. There was far less freedom to act out of personal conviction than out of group pressure in an environment where the authorities were convinced that the success of their "holy experiment" depended on the outward conformity of all members of society. There was little if any room for a reasoned discussion of the rules governing Puritan society. Part of this was due to the high view of authority held by the Puritans, especially since the authorities supposedly based their conclusions on the Word of God. Another contributing factor to a legalistic attitude was a lack of clarity concerning the role of "good works" in the Christian life. While few Puritans believed that good works could save one's soul, there was considerable controversy on what role good works might have in "preparation for salvation," or in the validation of one's election to salvation. The struggle has not ended.

Works.

The Puritan Work Ethic

The Puritans were devout followers of the Protestant work ethic which stressed the sanctity of all valid callings. God could be served well through one's vocation, and every calling was to be diligently pursued for the glory of God. One did not work merely for the sake of accumulating wealth, although if wealth resulted, few objected. Being busy in one's vocation was somehow inherently right to the Puritans, who strove to make every minute count. One's calling became a form of Christian service when it was believed that each person's calling was divinely ordained (this belief also made a vocational change less likely). Puritans were made to feel guilty when they were wasting time—time was one of God's greatest gifts to mankind, and its misuse was counted as sin. To the Puritan mind, one's time was used well in caring for one's family, worshiping, learning spiritual lessons, and being diligent in one's vocation. Idleness was roundly condemned, and little concept of the value of leisure activities existed. Activities such as card-playing and theater attendance were dismissed as sinful not because of anything inherently wrong in these activities, but rather because they were perceived as a waste of time. While one can argue effectively that the Puritan work ethic is losing its grip on America, it has by no means disappeared.

Thriftiness

The Puritans maintained a biblical view that all of life was a stewardship entrusted to individuals by God. This meant that one must be careful in the use of one's time and resources. The combination of diligence and thrift helped create wealth, which was seen as more of a by-product of a well-ordered life than an end in itself. Wealth was a blessing but also posed a special challenge since the love of money was fraught with spiritual danger. Yet it was a risk that many were willing to take. There was a fine line that the devout Puritan had to walk between saving and hoarding, diligence and avarice.

Attitude Toward the Indians

Relations between the Puritans of seventeenth-century New England and the Indian inhabitants of the land were especially significant since an attitude was established which served as a precedent for later colonists and pioneers. Seeing themselves as a "New Israel" in the wilderness, called to the work of saving Christianity from the corruptions of England and the rest of the world, the Puritans professed a desire to preach the gospel to the heathen. But their actions demonstrated that they carried their view of themselves as a New Israel to the point of viewing native Americans who were unresponsive to the gospel as "Canaanites" in the Promised Land. Most Puritans had little use for the Indians and saw them as pagan interlopers in the way of

God's program in the New World. Certainly few Puritans would consider social or marital intermingling. There were notable exceptions to this low view of the Indians demonstrated by such men as John Eliot and later David Brainerd who poured out their lives in Indian evangelization efforts. Christianized Indians were certainly given better treatment than their pagan counterparts. But in general the Puritans established the pejorative view that native Americans were essentially undesirable because they were nonwhite, heathen, and a hindrance to white expansion and prosperity.

Attitude Toward Human Sexuality

If there is any area in which the Puritans of early America have been badly misunderstood, it is in the realm of their approach to human sexuality. The picture of the Puritans conjured up by present-day minds portrays them as prudish and sexually repressed to the point that one wonders how the population of New England was maintained. In reality, the Puritan attitude toward human sexuality was rather revolutionary and liberating, especially in comparison with the medieval Catholic tradition which celebrated celibacy and scarcely tolerated sex within marriage. The Puritans saw sexuality as a good gift from God, not as something verging on unholiness that God grudgingly tolerated. Sexual relations were to be engaged in by husband and wife not merely for purposes of procreation but enjoyment. In fact, the Puritans valued the sexual act within the marriage bond to the point that deliberate failure to meet a spouse's needs in this area could be grounds for both divorce and excommunication from the church. Sexual union between husband and wife was viewed as so meaningful and sacred that it was protected by restrictions against its misuse. The Puritans put strict biblical parameters around sex because they valued it, not because they were embarrassed by it or opposed to it. Of course, in an "anything goes" age, the Puritans with their crackdown on adultery, fornication, and homosexuality come off looking like prudes. But we really owe a debt of gratitude to the Puritans for breaking with the medieval Catholic tradition and presenting us with a healthy view of this dimension of life.

Anti-Catholic Sentiment

Colonial America was overwhelmingly Protestant. It was possible to be a Catholic and survive, but one's chances were probably slimmest in Puritan New England. The Puritans were absolutely convinced that Roman Catholics were heretics of the worst order who could not possibly have any part in the kingdom of God. Puritan interpreters of the Apocalypse almost invariably equated the Roman Church with the "great whore" and saw the pope as the Antichrist. There was no room for Puritan-Catholic dialogue in a land where Foxe's *Book of Martyrs* could be found in nearly every home. The American Puritans despised Roman Catholicism so vehemently that Christmas and certain other religious holidays were not observed in New England because they were thought to be "popish." In some rural areas of New England, Christmas was not observed until after the Civil War.

It must be pointed out that the Puritans were not the only anti-Catholics in early America, but they were exceedingly vocal. Strong anti-Catholic prejudice became a major factor in American social history even well into the twentieth century. The nineteenth-century nativist movements and the Ku Klux Klan were dedicated to the maintenance of a Protestant America. Only one American president to date, John F. Kennedy, has been a Roman Catholic and even as late as 1960 his Catholicism was a major campaign issue. Only in recent years have many evangelical Protestants acknowledged the possibility of true Christian fellowship with Roman Catholics.

A Sense of American Identity and Mission

The Puritans came to the shores of America in the seventeenth century convinced that they were on a divine mission, and that they were in covenant with God to carry it out to his satisfaction. They were his chosen people in a new age—a New Israel whom the Lord had called out of the corruptions of the Old World into the Promised Land of the New World. There was a sense of destiny in the minds of at least the first generation or two of settlers in God's vineyard of New England. They were convinced that God had great things for them to accomplish, and that he would enable them to do mighty deeds as long as they did not waiver in their faithfulness.

Later generations of Americans have shared the Puritan belief that America is a very special land, a shining "city on a hill," a beacon of righteousness to the world, the closest thing to the kingdom of God on earth. The nineteenth-century expansionist impulse in this nation wrapped the desire for increased territory in the religious rhetoric of "manifest destiny"—it was clearly God's will that the American way of life and faith be spread across the continent, even if it meant seizing half of Mexico. Historically, American foreign policy has been largely set forth in moral terms. In some circles today it is still axiomatic that the United States of America can do no wrong, for we are the people of God.

Concluding Observations

The Puritan spirit yet within us calls us to lives of devotion and diligence. The American nation in general and the evangelical Protestant subculture in particular continue to abide in the shadow of the intensely God-centered people of early New England. Yet it must be remembered that, according to their own criteria, the Puritans of New England failed. As enduring as some Puritan values have been, the foundation of the system was eroded all too soon by the acquisitive instincts of later generations, by secularization of thought, by individualism, and by cultural and religious pluralism. These destroyers of the Puritan Way have themselves become great American values, replacing some of the most basic Puritan ideals.

We must also note that the Puritans were culture-bound in their religious outlook, as are any people. While the gospel of Christ transcends cultural boundaries, the perspectives of individual Christians generally do not. Even as we may laud the Puritans for their seriousness of purpose in striving to live in obedience to the Word of God, we must also expect to find errors of judgment, misplaced priorities and parochial, self-serving interpretations of Scripture. Not all of the contributions of this intensely devout culture were specifically Christian, yet if ever a society aspired to godliness, it was the American Puritans. But the Puritans failed, and they realized it. A recognition of failure was, in fact, one of their strengths. As long as they bemoaned their failures and strove for perfection, they were still holding fast to their ideal of a Christian society. When the Puritans stopped caring about their shortcomings, it was a sign that Puritanism as a system was finished. Yet, in various forms, the rich legacy of Puritan Christianity in America endures.

Appendix
*Biographical Overview
of New England Ministers Quoted*

William Adams was born in 1650, presumably in New England. He graduated from Harvard College in 1671 and later earned the M.A. degree from that institution. Adams was called to become John Allin's successor in the pulpit at Dedham, Massachusetts, in 1671, a position he held until his untimely death in 1685.

James Allen was born in 1632 and died in 1710. He apparently did not graduate from Harvard College as Sibley makes no mention of him. Very little biographical information is available other than the fact that he served as teacher of Boston's First Church from 1668 to 1710.

John Allin, first pastor of the Dedham congregation, was born in Norfolk, England in 1597 and received the B.A. and M.A. from Cambridge in 1615 and 1619, respectively. He settled in Dedham, Massachusetts, in 1637, a year after the town's founding, and accepted a call to the pastorate the following year, a position he held until his death in 1671.

Joseph Belcher , who was born in Milton, Massachusetts, in 1669, was raised by his grandparents as his parents were separated (a rather rare phenomenon in seventeenth-century Massachusetts). Belcher was a member of the Harvard class of 1690, and later completed the M.A. there as well. He was ordained at Dedham in 1693, preached there until 1721, and died in 1723.

William Brattle was born in 1662 and graduated from Harvard in 1680. Later he completed the M.A., also at Harvard. He was not or-

See Allen Johnson and Dumas Malone, eds., *Dictionary of American Biography* (New York, 1958); and John Langdon Sibley, *Biographical Sketches of Graduates of Harvard University, in Cambridge, Masachusetts* (Cambridge, Mass., 1873).

dained until 1669 at Cambridge, where he became Nathaniel Gookin's successor. His preaching career at the Cambridge church extended until a year before his death in 1717.

John Cotton was born in 1584 in Derbyshire, England. He took his bachelor's and master's degrees at Cambridge in 1603 and 1606, respectively, served as a fellow at Emmanuel College, Cambridge, for six years, and at age twenty-seven became vicar of St. Botolph's, Boston, Lincolnshire. A friend of John Winthrop, Cotton departed for New England in 1633. That same year he was chosen as teacher of the church in Boston, where he remained until his death in 1652. Cotton was probably the most well-known New England pastor during the first half of the seventeenth century, with a reputation in Old England as well. He was a strong apologist for New England Congregationalism and a church membership restricted to professing and "visible" saints. A number of his sermons and treatises were published during his lifetime.

John Danforth, the son of Reverend Samuel Danforth of Roxbury, Massachusetts, was born in that town in 1660. His maternal grandfather was Reverend John Wilson of Boston. Danforth graduated from Harvard in 1677 and later completed the M.A. there as well. He began a forty-eight-year ministry in the Dorchester church as the successor of Josiah Flynt in 1682 and died in 1730.

Samuel Danforth was born in Suffolk County, England, in 1626 and was brought by his father to New England in 1634. After his father's death he was cared for by Reverend Thomas Shepard of Cambridge. Danforth graduated from Harvard in 1643 and began as an assistant to Reverend John Eliot at Roxbury in 1650. In 1651 he married the daughter of Boston's pastor, John Wilson, and fathered twelve children, the first four of whom died in early childhood. Samuel Danforth's works include a published treatise on comets as divine signs.

John Davenport was English-born in 1597 to the mayor of Coventry. He attended Oxford but withdrew for financial reasons and returned a few years later, in 1625, to complete the bachelor of divinity degree. By 1629 he had acquired Puritan leanings, influenced largely by John Cotton and Thomas Hooker. Davenport contributed fifty pounds to the Massachusetts Bay Company and was also helpful in the procurement of that company's charter from the Crown. In 1633 he left England for Holland where he encountered opposition over his narrow view of baptism; consequently he emigrated to Boston in 1637. He served in New Haven's pulpit for thirty years and came to Boston's First Church in 1668 after the death of John Wilson. Davenport's opposition to the Half-Way Covenant, his advancing age, and the less than honorable circumstances surrounding his release from the New Haven church created dissension among his Boston flock to the point that several families withdrew and formed Third Church in Boston. Davenport died in 1670.

John Eliot was born in Hertfordshire, England, in 1604. He earned a B.A. at Cambridge in 1622 whereupon he taught in a grammar school. He soon came under the influence of Reverend Thomas Hooker and sailed for New England in 1631. He preached for a time in Boston during the absence of John Wilson and then accepted a call from the Roxbury church in 1632 where he remained until his death in 1690. During much of his tenure at Roxbury Eliot was engaged in Indian evangelism and in the development of fourteen semiautonomous Christian Indian communities in Massachusetts. Metacom's War (King Philp's War) of 1675–1676 created strong anti-Indian sentiments among many New Englanders and basically ruined Eliot's years of effort.

Josiah Flynt, a nephew of Harvard's President Hoar, was born in New England in 1645. In 1664 he graduated from Harvard and then assisted in his father's Braintree, Massachusetts pulpit until the elder Flynt died in 1668. Some of the younger Flynt's Braintree sermons resulted in charges of heresy, but Flynt was examined and exonerated by an investigative body. He began a pastorate at Dorchester in 1671, where he succeeded Richard Mather. He died in 1680.

Nathaniel Gookin was born in 1656 in Cambridge, Massachusetts. He earned the B.A. and M.A. at Harvard in 1675 and 1678, respectively. From 1678 to 1682 he preached at Sherborn, Massachusetts, and from 1682 until his death a decade later he pastored the Cambridge church. Rejecting political involvement urged on him by some, he spent the turbulent 1680s quietly "feeding his flock" from the Scriptures.

John Higginson came into the world in 1616 at Leicestershire, England, and moved to New England at the age of thirteen. He is an exception to the rule of ministerial education and ordination; while he pastored successfully in Connecticut and Salem, Massachusetts, he apparently had no university training nor was he ever formally ordained. Recognized in his maturity as one of New England's leading clergymen, his own daughter was among the accused in the Salem witch trials. Higginson died in 1708.

Thomas Hooker was English-born in 1586 and fled to Holland in 1630 for his nonconformist Puritan preaching. In 1633, Hooker sailed for Massachusetts where he pastored at Cambridge, but he soon had a dispute with John Cotton and expressed discontent with the strict theological control he experienced in the Bay Colony. He and many of his congregation left and founded Hartford in 1636, where he pastored until his death. Hooker was one of the authors of the Fundamental Orders (1639) which served as a basis of colonial government for Connecticut.

Cotton Mather, son of Increase Mather and grandson of Richard Mather, was born in Boston in 1662. He graduated from Harvard in 1678. In 1681 he began serving as his father's assistant in Boston's Second Church, a position which became official and permanent in 1685. A man of many interests and abilities, Cotton Mather was influential in scientific, political, and literary endeavors in addition to his theological and pastoral interests. Many of his sermons and treatises were published during his lifetime; he not only wrote prolifically, he also fathered thirteen children. Cotton Mather died in 1728.

Increase Mather, the youngest son of Richard Mather, was born in Dorchester, Massachusetts, in 1639. In 1656 he graduated from Harvard College and journeyed to Dublin to visit his brother who was pastoring there. While in Ireland Mather took his M.A. at Trinity College, then went to England where he was offered, and declined, several Anglican pulpits. He returned to New England in 1661 and became teacher of Boston's Second Church in 1664, a position he held until his death in 1723. Mather disagreed with his father and openly opposed the Half-Way Covenant, but later reversed this stance. Increase Mather was the moving force behind the 1679 synod, known as the "Reforming Synod," which sought to inquire into the reasons for God's recent heavy judgments (Indian uprisings, smallpox outbreaks, major fires, and a general perceived declension) and to promote reformation. After the Massachusetts charter was revoked, Mather was sent to London as an agent of the colony for four years, returning in 1692. For a time, Mather served as president of Harvard College.

Richard Mather, father of Increase Mather and grandfather of Cotton Mather, was born in Lowton, Lancashire, in 1596. He received some higher education at Oxford, but apparently did not earn a degree. He was suspended from preaching by the Anglican Church in 1633 for nonconformity, and in 1635 he arrived in Boston. In 1636 he accepted the call of the Dorchester church where he served until his death in 1669. Mather was a strong supporter of New England's Congregational system, and he championed the cause of the Half-Way Covenant.

Jonathan Mitchel was born in 1624 in Halifax, England. He arrived in New England at the age of eleven and graduated from Harvard College in 1647. Mitchel was offered the Hartford pulpit as the successor to Thomas Hooker, but he declined and instead succeeded Thomas Shepard at Cambridge, where he remained until his death in 1668. Mitchel was very influential in shaping the Half-Way Covenant during the synod of 1662 at Boston.

Joshua Moodey, English-born in 1633, arrived in New England when one year old. He was a member of the Harvard graduating class of 1653 and afterwards pastored at Portsmouth, New Hampshire, for several years. He declined an offer to take the presidency of Harvard in 1684. That same year saw increased royal control and the revocation of the Massachusetts charter, and Moodey was incarcerated for thirteen weeks by royal authorities for his refusal to administer the Lord's Supper according to the rites of the Church of England, thus becoming the first New England divine to be so persecuted. Also in 1684 he became assistant pastor at Boston's First Church, a position he maintained until his death in 1697.

John Norton , born in 1606 in Hertfordshire, England, received the B.A. (1624) and M.A. (1627) at Cambridge. In 1635 he arrived in Separatist Plymouth, where he was invited to remain, but he chose instead to accept a call as teacher of the Ipswich church. In the 1640s Norton played a significant role in the synod which drew up the Cambridge Platform. Norton was John Cotton's hand-picked successor at Boston, but he was not installed until 1656, four years after Cotton's death, due to Ipswich's reluctance to release him. An avowed enemy of Quakerism, Norton advocated the use of the death penalty for the rooting out of heresy. In 1662 he traveled to England on behalf of the colony, but was able to wring few concessions from the new English government. He died in 1663.

Urian Oakes was born in England, probably in 1631, and migrated to New England with his parents while still a child. He graduated from Harvard in 1649 and returned to England to teach and preach until he was silenced by the authorities in 1662. He was issued a call by the Cambridge church to succeed the late Jonathan Mitchel, but Oakes did not arrive back in New England for three years, during which time the Cambridge congregation kept open its invitation. He began pastoring there in 1671 and in 1675 Oakes was named fourth president of Harvard College. He held both posts, pastor and president, to the time of his death in 1681.

John Oxenbridge was born in 1609 in Northamptonshire, England. He received degrees from both Cambridge and Oxford, and began preaching at the age of twenty-one. Oxenbridge held a pastorate at Beverly, then taught at Eaton College, and left for America in 1662. His first stop was the Dutch colony of Surinam in South America where he remained for five years. After two additional years in

Barbados, he arrived in New England in 1669. He followed John Davenport as pastor of Boston's First Church in 1670 and died in 1674.

Samuel Sewall was born in England in 1652 and taken to Massachusetts as a child. He graduated from Harvard in 1671 and took a pastorate, but gave up the ministry to manage a printing press and later to assume public office. He served in the Massachusetts General Court, and later served as one of the judges presiding over the Salem witch trials. In 1697 he publicly acknowledged errors in those proceedings, and accepted the blame for them.

Thomas Shepard was born in Towcester, England, in 1605 and took a B.A. in 1624 and an M.A. in 1627 at Cambridge. Silenced for nonconformity in 1630, he left England and arrived in Boston in 1635. That year he was chosen as pastor of the church at Newtown (later renamed Cambridge), where he remained until his death in 1649. Shepard was noted as a great foe of antinomianism and a great defender of Congregationalism.

Thomas Thacher was born in Salisbury, England, in 1620. He made his own way to Boston at the age of fifteen. There he had the good fortune to be taken in by Charles Chancey, later president of Harvard, who tutored him. Even without a formal college education, Thacher was deemed theologically competent and was ordained as pastor of the Weymouth church in 1644. In 1669 he became pastor of Boston's newly formed Third Church. He died in 1678.

Samuel Willard was born in Concord, Massachusetts, in 1640 and graduated with the Harvard class of 1659. He began preaching at Groton in 1663 but the town was destroyed by Indians and temporarily abandoned during Metacom's War in 1676. Willard was called to Boston's Third Church in 1678 as a colleague of Thomas Thacher, who died shortly thereafter. Governor Andros seized Willard's church building for Anglican worship in the 1680s over Willard's strong objections [the Third Church congregation was permitted to hold services each Sunday after the Anglican services were finished]. Willard served as vice-president of Harvard College, was an opponent of the Salem witch trials, and died in 1707.

Roger Williams, born around 1603 in England, graduated from Cambridge in 1627 and took Anglican orders. He embraced Puritanism and went to New England in 1631. After a time in Plymouth, he became minister of the Salem church. Some aspects of his religious beliefs and political views were viewed as radical and dangerous by the colony's authorities, particularly his extreme separatism and his denial of the validity of the Massachusetts charter. Williams also carried the idea of separation of church and state further than most thinkers of his era. The General Court banished him in 1635 and he traveled south to establish Providence on land purchased from the Indians of that region.

John Wilson, born in Windsor, England, in 1591, was a Cambridge graduate, (B.A. 1610; M.A. 1613). He became a Puritan under the influence of William Ames and lectured at Sudbury, with numerous suspensions for nonconformity, until 1630 when he emigrated to Boston. He was pastor of the Boston church for a year, then returned for his wife in England. Back in Boston, Wilson shared the pulpit with John Cotton until Cotton's death in 1662. Wilson died five years later.

Select Bibliography

Adair, John. *Founding Fathers—The Puritans in England and America.* Grand Rapids, 1986.

Bailyn, Bernard. *The New England Merchants in the Seventeenth Century.* Cambridge, Mass., 1955.

Beales, Ross W. "The Half-Way Covenant and Religious Scrupulosity: The First Church of Dorchester, Massachusetts, as a Test Case," *William and Mary Quarterly* 31 (July 1974): 465–80.

Bercovitch, Sacvan. *The Puritan Origins of the American Self.* New Haven, 1975.

Bozeman, Thedore Dwight. "The Puritans' 'Errand into the Wilderness' Reconsidered." *New England Quarterly* 59 (June 1986): 231–51.

Breen, Timothy H. "The Non-Existent Controversy: Puritan and Anglican Attitudes on Work and Wealth." *Church History* 35 (1966): 273–87.

____. *The Character of the Good Ruler.* New York, 1974.

____. "Persistent Localism: English Social Change and the Shaping of New England Institutions." *William and Mary Quarterly* 32 (Jan. 1975): 3–28.

____. *Puritans and Adventurers.* New York, 1980.

Breen, Timothy H., and Stephen Foster. "Moving to the New World: The Character of Early Massachusetts Immigration." *William and Mary Quarterly* 30 (Apr. 1973): 189–222.

____. "The Puritans' Greatest Achievement: A Study of Social Cohesion in Seventeenth-Century Massachusetts." *Journal of American History* 60/1 (June 1973): 5–22.

Bremer, Francis J. *The Puritan Experiment.* New York, 1976.

Bridenbaugh, Carl. *Cities in the Wilderness.* New York, 1955.

____. *Vexed and Troubled Englishmen: 1590–1642.* New York, 1968.

Bushman, Richard L. *From Puritan to Yankee.* New York, 1970.

Colinson, Patrick. *The Elizabethan Puritan Movement.* Los Angeles, 1967.

Coolidge, John S. *The Pauline Renaissance in England.* Oxford, 1970.

Demos, John. *A Little Commonwealth: Family Life in Plymouth Colony.* New York, 1970.

____. "Underlying Themes in the Witchcraft of Seventeenth-Century New England." *American Historical Review* 75 (1970): 1311–26.

Dickens, A. G. *The English Reformation.* New York, 1964.

Edwards, David. *Christian England.* Grand Rapids, 1984.

Elliott, Emory. *Power and the Pulpit in Puritan New England.* Princeton, 1975.

Fiering, Norman S. "Will and Intellect in the New England Mind." *William and Mary Quarterly* 29 (Oct. 1972): 515–58.

Foster, Stephen. *Their Solitary Way: The Puritan Social Ethic in the First Century of Settlement in New England.* New Haven, 1971.

Greven, Philip. *Four Generations: Population, Land, and Family in Colonial Andover, Massachusetts.* Ithaca, N.Y., 1970.

____. *The Protestant Temperament.* New York, 1977.

Gura, Philip F. *A Glimpse of Sion's Glory—Puritan Radicalism in New England, 1620–1660.* Middletown, Conn., 1984.

Hall, David D., ed. *The Antinomian Controversy, 1636–1638.* Middletown, Conn., 1968.

____. *The Faithful Shepherd: A History of the New England Ministry in the Seventeenth Century.* Chapel Hill, N.C., 1972.

____. "Toward a History of Popular Religion in Early New England." *William and Mary Quarterly* 41 (Jan. 1984): 49–55.

Hambrick-Stowe, Charles E. *The Practice of Piety.* Chapel Hill, N.C., 1982.

Hill, Christopher. *The English Revolution 1640.* 3d ed. London, 1955.

____. *Society and Puritanism in Pre-Revolutionary England.* 2d ed. New York, 1967.

Holifield, E. Brooks. *The Covenant Sealed: The Development of Puritan Sacramental Theology in Old and New England, 1570–1720.* New Haven, 1974.

Holland, DeWitte, ed. *Preaching in American History.* Nashville, 1969.

Kenyon, J. P. *Stuart England.* New York, 1978.

Knappen, M. M. *Tudor Puritanism.* Chicago, 1939.

Labaree, Benjamin. *Colonial Massachusetts, A History.* Millwood, N.Y., 1979.

Levy, Babette May. *Preaching in the First Half Century of New England History.* New York, 1945.

Lockridge, Kenneth A. *A New England Town, The First Hundred Years.* New York, 1970.

Maclear, J. F. "New England and the Fifth Monarchy: The Quest for the Millennium in Early American Puritanism." *William and Mary Quarterly* 32 (Apr. 1975): 223–60.

Marsden, George M. "Perry Miller's Rehabilitation of the Puritans: A Critique." *Church History* 39 (Mar. 1970): 91–105.

Mather, Cotton. *Magnalia Christi Americana.* Hartford, 1853.

McGee, J. Sears. *The Godly Man in Stuart England.* New Haven, 1976.

McGrath, Patrick. *Papists and Puritans under Elizabeth I.* London, 1967.

Middlekauf, Robert. "Piety and Intellect in Puritanism." *William and Mary Quarterly* 22 (July 1965): 457–70.

____. *The Mathers: Three Generations of Puritan Intellectuals, 1596–1728.* New York, 1971.

Miller, Perry. *Orthodoxy in Massachusetts.* Cambridge, Mass., 1933.

____. *The New England Mind: The Seventeenth Century.* New York, 1939.

____. *Errand into the Wilderness.* Cambridge, Mass., 1956.

Miller, Perry, and Thomas H. Johnson. *The Puritans.* 2 vols. New York, 1938.

Morgan, Edmund S. *The Puritan Dilemma: The Story of John Winthrop.* Boston, 1958.

____. *Visible Saints: The History of a Puritan Idea.* Ithaca, N.Y., 1963.

____. *The Puritan Family.* New York, 1966.

____. *Roger Williams: The Church and the State.* New York, 1967.

Morison, Samuel E. *Builders of the Bay Colony.* Boston, 1930.

____. *The Founding of Harvard College.* Cambridge, Mass., 1935.

____. *Harvard College in the Seventeenth Century.* Cambridge, Mass., 1936.

Notestein, Wallace. *The English People on the Eve of Colonization.* New York, 1962.

Pettit, Norman. "Hooker's Doctrine of Assurance: A Critical Phase in New England Spiritual Thought." *New England Quarterly* 47 (Dec. 1974): 518–34.

Pope, Robert G. *The Half-Way Covenant.* Princeton, 1969.

____. "New England versus the New England Mind: The Myth of Declension." *Journal of Social History* (1969–70): 95–108.

Porter, H. C., ed. *Puritanism in Tudor England*. London, 1971.

Powell, Sumner Chilton. *Puritan Village*. Middletown, Conn., 1963.

Powicke, Maurice. *The Reformation in England*. London, 1941.

Rosenthal, Bernard. "Puritan Conscience and New England Slavery." *New England Quarterly* 46 (Mar. 1973): 62–81.

Russell, Conrad. *The Crisis of Parliaments—English History 1509–1660*. London, 1971.

Rutman, Darrett B. *American Puritanism*. Philadelphia, 1970.

____. *Winthrop's Boston*. Chapel Hill, N.C., 1965.

Ryken, Leland. *Wordly Saints*. Grand Rapids, 1986.

Scarisbrick, J. J. *Henry VIII*. Berkeley, 1968.

Schucking, Levin L. *The Puritan Family: A Social Study from the Literary Sources*. New York, 1970.

Scobey, David M. "Revising the Errand: New England's Ways and the Puritan Sense of the Past." *William and Mary Quarterly* 41 (Jan. 1984): 3–31.

Seidman, Aaron B. "Church and State in the Early Years of the Massachusetts Bay Colony." *New England Quarterly* 18 (June 1945): 211–33.

Silverman, Kenneth. *The Life and Times of Cotton Mather*. New York, 1984.

Stannard, David E. *The Puritan Way of Death*. New York, 1977.

Thomas, G. E. "Puritans, Indians, and the Concept of Race." *New England Quarterly* 48 (Mar. 1975): 3–27.

Turnbull, Ralph G. *A History of Preaching*. Vol. 3. Grand Rapids, 1974.

Twombly, Robert C., and Robert H. Moore. "Black Puritan: The Negro in Seventeenth-Century Massachusetts." *William and Mary Quarterly* 24 (Apr. 1967): 224–42.

Vaughan, Alden T. *New England Frontier: Puritans and Indians, 1620–1675*. Boston, 1965.

Walker, Williston. *The Creeds and Platforms of Congregationalism*. New York, 1893.

Walzer, Michael. *The Revolution of the Saints: A Study of the Origins of Radical Politics*. New York, 1968.

Wright, Louis B. *The Cultural Life of the American Colonies*. New York, 1962.

Young, J. William, Jr. "Congregational Clericalism: New England Ordinations before the Great Awakening." *William and Mary Quarterly* 31 (July 1974): 481–90.

Ziff, Larzer. "The Social Bond of Church Covenant." *American Quarterly* 10/4 (1958): 454–62.

____. *Puritanism in America.* New York, 1973.

Zuckerman, Michael. *Peaceable Kingdoms—New England Towns in the Eighteenth Century.* New York, 1970.

Index